LOVING SEX

THE BOOK OF JOY AND PASSION

Laura Berman, PhD

contents

introduction: *love and sex*

The intertwining of love and sex is one of the most beautiful things two people can share. Of course you can have love without sex, and you can have sex—even good sex—without love. But it's only when the two meet that sparks really fly, and you and your partner can discover your full potential for intimacy and pleasure.

The problem is that loving sex doesn't happen by itself—whatever you may see in the movies. The media tell us that sex is simple, that romance is everywhere, and that happy couples reach orgasm each and every time. Of course, reality is much less perfect. Loving sex needs time, it needs effort, and it needs a commitment from both of you to explore each other's desires and prioritize each other's pleasure. Loving sex is mindful sex.

Many people believe that, over time, the spark of excitement in a relationship inevitably dims. It's true that there is a biological imperative for a natural downturn in your sex life. When we first meet a potential partner, our brains are flooded with chemicals that excite and thrill us. We can't stop thinking about this new person. This intense physical and emotional reaction is our bodies' way of making sure that we feel a connection—and, thus, that we consummate the relationship to produce offspring. It might not sound very romantic on paper, but our sexual urge is as instinctive our urges to breathe, sleep, and eat.

Once you have been with your partner for some time, these biological cues slowly dissipate. Our brains simply can't run on that level of obsession forever, nor can we maintain a balanced life with such a one-track focus. And, of course, as our lives progress, we have many other demands on our time—we become so busy with work, kids, chores, and a million other commitments that we barely have time to sit down and talk, let alone be romantic!

On top of this, the longer you and your partner stay together, the more time and energy it takes to make your sexual experiences explosive. In a long-term relationship, you have likely had sex with your partner thousands of times. This brings stability and intimacy, but it also means that you can become stuck in a rut—or, worse, that you take your partner for granted.

These are all common issues that couples face, which is why you must take a comprehensive approach to spicing up your sex life. The flush of first love can indeed fade, but that doesn't mean you can't spark it back to life whenever you want. One of the marvelous things about sexuality is that every experience can feel new and unique. A new lover represents uncharted territory, new lands to discover, and new wonders at which to marvel. And your long-term partner can be infinitely full of surprises, able to thrill you each and every time that you are together.

The process of learning and growing is never complete, no matter how long you have been together. Sexuality is fluid and ever-changing, and our desires and needs are different at each stage of our lives. It's important to reevaluate your sexual relationship as you grow together, making the necessary changes to keep your bond strong.

The result is that you can not only recapture this intense attraction, but you can also experience it in a more meaningful context. In place of puppy love, you will establish a deep, meaningful, and spiritual bond with your partner that will support you, challenge you, and sustain you throughout your lives. All it takes is a little bit of know-how and a commitment to improving and enjoying your sexual experiences.

Thankfully, by reading this book you have already taken the first and most important step to invigorating your love life: being proactive in creating your own sexual pleasure. You need to know how to make sex more spontaneous; how to create romance even on a boring weekday night; how to juggle kids, careers, and a home; how to create a healthy lifestyle and have positive body-image; how to treat issues such as menopause and low libido—and, of course, how to have amazing sex! This book addresses all of these important issues, and takes an intimate look at the tools and toys, positions and practices that human beings have dreamt up to add spice to their love lives. Consider this your new go-to guide for all things bedroom-related, a place to find answers to all those questions you wouldn't dare ask aloud.

Ready to begin? Grab your partner and start reading!

Laura Berman

loving sex is...

physical

The heart and soul of sex is the physical heat it creates between two bodies. Sometimes playful, sometimes passionate, sometimes pure and sweet, this skin-to-skin connection renews your bond and strengthens chemistry. In a long-term relationship, remembering the unique physical traits you love about your partner—her breasts or bottom, his abs or arms—can help your connection to feel special, sexy, and new all over again.

the beauty of the body

Even in a society that often seems to value beauty above all else, it can feel a bit shallow to place physical appearance on a pedestal. After all, isn't it what's on the inside that counts? Of course. And yet we cannot deny our natural attraction to the people we find sexy. Whether it's built on a bright smile, beautiful eyes, or toned legs, physical attraction plays a special, irreplaceable role in nearly every sexual relationship.

enjoying the body We seek beauty everywhere in life, but especially when it comes to our mates. It's okay to enjoy and explore that side of our sexuality, especially because, in a healthy relationship, it's just one important piece of the much larger puzzle of chemistry and attraction. Admiring your partner's body strengthens the intimacy that is the unique glue of a romantic partnership.

One of the best ways to connect the beauty of the body with great sex is to express desire openly. Nothing builds passion like showing someone that you want them. In a committed relationship, it's easy to take this for granted, but it's crucial to say these things out loud and make your appreciation of your partner's physical beauty known. And the more you voice this appreciation and validation, the more your partner will respond in kind. The tips below are a good place to start.

worship the body It's easy to become blindly accustomed to your partner's body. When we see and touch each other every day, we forget to appreciate the little things, like how soft her skin is, or how his neck smells. Yet although these things are small, they are infinitely special. In order to sustain an amazing sex life, couples must worship each other's bodies and find new ways to treasure these physical gifts. Go back to noticing how strong his body feels in the middle of the night, or how good it feels to have her wrapped around you while making love.

compliment at least once a day Keep at least one compliment a day focused on your partner's appearance. It might initially be a struggle to find a new compliment every day, especially if you are not used to focusing on the positive in your partner. Sadly, it is a lot easier for most of us to reflect on the negative ("Why is he wearing that shirt again?" or "Why does she wear so much eye makeup?"). It's always the beginning of the end of passion if we fall into that trap and stay there. Compliments, in contrast, create positive energy that resets our way of thinking and helps make appreciation a habit rather than a deliberate exercise. (For more on the art and power of appreciation, see page 47.)

give honest feedback Nevertheless, it's also important to give honest feedback about your partner's appearance. This might sound daunting, but the truth is that it is much kinder to be truthful than to allow the sexual flame to dampen. Being dishonest does a disservice to the relationship and weakens your bond. This is not the path to great sex. So, begin by establishing a rule that all feelings are shared, even if that indeed means admitting that her dress is not flattering. There's no need to state directly that it makes her backside look large. Instead, try saying, "Actually, that dress doesn't do justice to your figure. How about that black one you wore last month? I can't stop thinking about you in that!" Remember, it is always possible to be both honest and kind if you approach the conversation lovingly.

It is equally important to learn to accept negative feedback. Our natural reaction might be to feel hurt, but keep in mind that your partner simply wants to benefit your relationship. It's okay to feel upset; however, if you wait a few minutes, you might begin to feel thankful that your partner is open enough to be honest about his feelings.

commit to *being sexy*

Sexuality stems from feeling desirable, attractive, fit, and healthy. Devouring a giant bowl of macaroni and cheese, or lounging around the house in an old pair of sweats every night, does not a sexy person make. And—let's be honest—our partners don't feel as attracted to us when appearance isn't a priority. This goes for both men and women. Sometimes maintaining a body that is ready to be worshiped takes work—but it is always worth it. (For more tips on improving physical and sexual health, see page 32.)

One of the joys of lovemaking is reveling in the beautiful, unique details of your partner's body. Show your appreciation through slow, sensual, lust-filled touch.

the biology of *arousal*

Desire. Arousal. Plateau. Orgasm. Resolution. We feel what's happening during sex, but many of us don't know the mechanics of our sexual response. Understanding how arousal works can help our sex lives become more creative, satisfying, and passionate beyond measure.

desire We know how powerful feelings of physical attraction can be, but where do these feelings come from and what is their role in our lives? Desire occurs when we see something that sexually excites us. Perhaps it's a tall stranger on the bus, or a woman with an exceptionally curvaceous figure. Maybe it's a specific perfume that triggers a sensual memory. For both men and women, desire is inspired by a mixture of our emotions, our history, and our personal preferences.

Desire is the inception of our sexual energy. It may inspire arousal or, as often happens, arousal may inspire desire. The term arousal can also refer to awakening, such as being roused from sleep, and the same is true for sexual arousal: your sexual potential might be sound asleep, only to be awakened by an attractive man or woman passing by. The arousal/desire process might end there. Or, if circumstances allow and it's deemed appropriate once passed through your moral and emotional filters, you might act on that desire and continue the arousal process through the other stages of sexual response.

arousal In the midst of sexual arousal, we are receptive and present, in tune with our senses, and open to pleasure and connection. During this stage, we undergo numerous physical changes. Our heart rate quickens, cheeks flush, and pupils dilate. (In ancient times, women used to attempt to mimic this effect by putting drops of belladonna in their eyes—not recommended, as belladonna is toxic! The point, however, is that signs of arousal can be attractive to your partner.) Also during the arousal stage, a woman's nipples perk up and circulation to the genitals increases. If the arousal continues, a man's penis will become erect, and women will experience genital changes as well. The clitoris will swell, as will the labia, and the vaginal opening will enlarge slightly in preparation for intercourse.

arousal and hormones Part of the beauty of sexual response is that your entire body responds to arousal like an orchestra, with each instrument chiming in at its appointed time. All of these changes, no matter how minor, play a role in your sexual response and sexual pleasure, and they occur thanks to your hormones. Your hormones control everything from your appetite to your sleep habits, your mood, and your sexual experiences. The two hormones that primarily impact your sex drive are well-known: testosterone and estrogen.

testosterone Testosterone is mostly produced by the sex organs, although it can also occur in the adrenal glands. In men, testosterone is primarily produced in the testes; in women, the ovaries are largely responsible for this job. Testosterone helps to produce body and facial hair, stimulates the growth of sex organs, and helps with muscle and bone growth. It also plays a significant role in determining genital and nipple sensation, as well as general sexual desire. On average, the male body produces 10 times more testosterone than the female body, but it is still a crucial hormone for women.

estrogen Again, both men and women have this hormone, although women have vastly larger amounts. The majority of estrogen in the female body is produced by the ovaries; in men, estrogen is produced in the testes. This hormone regulates the female menstrual cycle and also helps prepare her body for pregnancy. Low levels of estrogen (which occur most notably during perimenopause and menopause) can have a wide range of side effects including vaginal dryness, hot flashes, irritability, and reduced sexual response.

plateau This is the stage where arousal is high and orgasm is imminent. During the plateau stage, we enjoy the rush of passion at our partner's touch, but haven't yet reached the stage of orgasmic bliss. If you want sex to last longer, this is the place where you should slow down and try to maintain your arousal level while delaying orgasm. If you want to master the art of multiple orgasms, this is the stage where you should try to linger after orgasm.

orgasm Orgasm is the intimate climax of our sexual experience. We all experience it differently, but by definition an orgasm is a contraction in the genitals that causes feelings of pleasure and release. Sometimes the contraction is intense and sometimes it is only a whisper. (For more on orgasm, see pages 94–95.)

resolution During the resolution stage, we experience feelings of calm, peace, emotional euphoria, and even fatigue. Sometimes an orgasm can be as powerful as a sleeping pill, but whenever possible, use this time to bond with your partner and create deep intimacy. (For ideas on how to do this, see pages 260–261.)

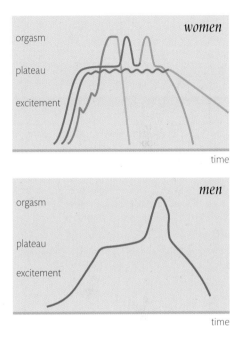

the *sexual response* cycle

The pattern of arousal and sexual response works differently in men and women. Knowing how sexual excitement works will help you understand your partner's sexual responses.

women The ability to experience multiple climaxes is unique to women. Sometimes women linger in the plateau phase and are able to enjoy a double or multiple orgasm, as seen in the pink line above. Sometimes there is a quicker climb toward a single orgasm, as in the green line; and at other times, women experience a lengthy plateau period that does not end in climax (the blue line).

men The cycle for men is more straightforward, with a steady climb toward plateau and a sharp peak at climax, followed by resolution.

the power of *pheromones*

Other hormones that can affect sexual response are ecto-hormones, more traditionally known as pheromones. Pheromones are chemical messengers that send silent signals to our brains and bodies, and they can have a huge impact on sexual response. In animals and insects, pheromones help to attract mates, offer protection, and are also used to communicate danger, arousal, and other important messages.

sensing arousal Although the jury is still out as to whether pheromones can have such a strong impact on humans, some research does suggest that men and women can sense each other's arousal. In a study performed at Rice University in Houston, men were asked to place pads under their armpits, once while they performed normal activities, and again while they were aroused by pornography. Women were then asked to smell these samples, and scans of their brain activity found that they responded most notably to the pads from the aroused men. This suggests that women can actually sense a man's arousal, even if only subconsciously.

The same is true for men. In a recent study published in the journal *Psychological Science*, men were asked to smell the shirts of numerous women, some of whom were ovulating and some who were not. Saliva tests were then performed in order to compare the men's testosterone levels. Men who smelled the shirts of ovulating women had testosterone levels that were 37 percent higher than men who smelled the shirts of women who were not ovulating. This suggests not only that men can pick up on these cues, but that their own bodies actually react in a way that prepares them for sexual activity. Could it be that nature is silently working behind the sexual scenes, helping us to attract mates and prolong the species?

nerve "O" Perhaps nature is at work in our sensory responses—however, research in this field is still new. In fact, just recently researchers discovered an olfactory nerve that they believe is the route through which pheromones are processed. Nerve "O," as it is called, slipped under the radar for many years because it is so tiny. However, when the nerve was discovered in a whale, scientists began looking for it in humans as well. And they believe they've found it.

The key importance of nerve "O" is that smells are received in the nasal cavity as usual, but the nerve fibers from the nose actually bypass the olfactory cortex where smells are consciously processed, and go directly to the sexual regions of the brain. Hence, we know that nerve "O" does not contribute to our conscious sense of smell, but helps us identify sexual cues from our potential partners unconsciously.

What sexual cues do our scents give off? For one thing, we are more likely to be attracted to people who have a differing immune system from ours. Family members often share similar chemicals, so our attraction to differing chemical makeup suggests that unconscious olfactory sexual cues evolved to protect close family members from procreating together. On the other hand, pregnant women seem to be drawn more often to the scent of people with a similar chemical makeup. Scientists believe that during this vulnerable time, women are more apt to seek out family members than potential sexual mates.

pheromones in relationships
Research has also shown that the unconscious cues processed in nerve "O" can make or break a relationship. Couples who have high levels of immune chemicals in common are more likely to encounter fertility issues, miscarriage, and infidelity. So, science suggests that the more dissimilar your chemical makeup from your partner's, the better chance you will have of successfully procreating and staying together.

Only time will tell what role nerve "O" plays in future sex research, but all of these interesting studies illuminate a simple principle: There is so much more to attraction than meets the eye. You might think that you chose your mate because of his great build and blue eyes, or because of her sexy legs and cute laugh, but it could be that your brain was just picking up silent cues that your future lover was secreting. This is actually good news, because it means that even when physical beauty fades, your sexual attraction doesn't have to!

Pheromones are what makes attraction so very personal. They may also safeguard your attraction to one another over time.

the contraception trick
So how can you create the scent that will keep you and your partner in the land of happily ever after? Unfortunately, you can't. Perfumes and colognes can't fool nerve "O"—the scents that humans and animals are attracted to are intangible and instinctive.

However, if you are taking a hormonal contraceptive, you might be bucking an evolutionary tide. Women who are on the pill are more likely to be attracted to men with a similar chemical makeup—most likely because their bodies are fooling them into believing they are pregnant, and so, much like actual pregnant women, their nerve "O" leads them to kin instead of mates. This means that if you were on the pill when you met your partner, you might experience a diminishing attraction when you cease taking it.

erogenous zones

Our complex feelings of sexual desire demand exploration—so it's a good thing our entire bodies are covered with erogenous zones. The peak male and female arousal spots are extremely sensitive and create feelings of pleasure when touched, stroked, caressed, and kissed. In short, they are what make every one of us crave foreplay.

mouth, neck, and ears The mouth is one especially intimate erogenous zone—in fact, the lips have more nerve endings than any other part of the body. This is one reason that kissing is such a turn-on: it takes full advantage of this sensitive spot, and invites us to play with the mouth's sweet sensuality.

In addition to caressing the lips and sometimes tongue, we often find it arousing to stroke, lick, or nibble our partner's ears and neck—all areas that are filled with rich nerve endings. To explore them fully, move from kissing to nibbling or stroking the neck. Or, in the middle of lovemaking, try gently biting or sucking on your partner's earlobe.

scalp The scalp is also primed for pleasurable sensation, ready to be rubbed and caressed so that tingles of pleasure cascade down the body. Heighten arousal and desire by sensually shampooing your partner in the bath, or simply let your fingers run through your partner's hair

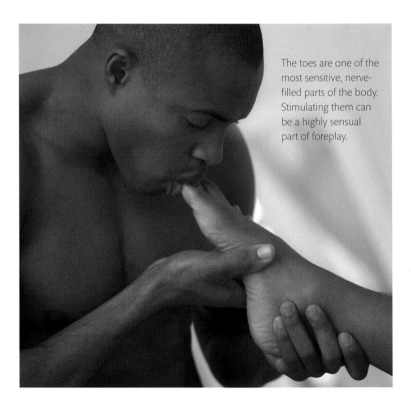

The toes are one of the most sensitive, nerve-filled parts of the body. Stimulating them can be a highly sensual part of foreplay.

while you are relaxing on the couch watching television. Use your fingernails for a gentler sensation, or knead more firmly to really release tension. What's nice about this erogenous zone is that it seems so innocent: hair-play can occur in an overtly public setting, but still feel intimate and even a bit naughty, preparing you for any number of sexual escapades to follow.

feet and hands A foot or hand massage is soothing and sensual. In fact, after the mouth and genitals, the fingertips are the second most sensitive part of the human body. Gently massage and pull on the fingers, releasing and relaxing the joints. When giving a foot massage, use a firm touch and knead your fingers up and down from the soles to the tops of the feet, paying special attention to the arches and toes. The feet are often very sensitive, so ask your partner how firm your touch should be as you begin your massage. For extra sensuality, finish by sucking on each toe individually, building desire by increasing the pressure of your mouth as you move.

arms The arms are an excellent place to begin foreplay: massage the full length of this erogenous zone as you watch television or talk about your day. Use your hands to stroke the muscles in his arms, starting from the tops of his shoulders and moving down to his fingertips, alternating your pressure between firm kneading and light scratching. Then, work your way back to the tops of his shoulders and apply deep pressure, alternating with short, sweet kisses. You can finish by lightly brushing your fingertips along his skin: the contrast in pressure will send shivers down his spine.

thighs and knees The thighs and knees are two especially sensitive spots—and their proximity to the genitals makes them one of the sexiest areas for foreplay. There are so many ways you can seduce: Use your fingers to trace a trail along the backs of her thighs and knees, moving up to her buttocks and then down again. Breathe gently on his inner thighs, as you kiss and caress this hidden sweet spot. Trail your fingers in between her thighs (circling but not touching the labia), and gently stroke or tickle the backs of her knees. The key to maximizing pleasure in this area is to listen to your partner's body and watch his or her response to see what touch is most electrifying.

do this when . . . you want to subtly seduce

Many women find it sensual and relaxing to have their hair gently tugged. Men can maximize this erogenous zone while making love (or even while simply kissing) by running four or five fingers up under her hair, taking hold of a handful close to the scalp, and gently pulling. After each pull, move to a new area on the scalp and repeat. She'll be melting by the time you are finished.

erogenous zones
for men

For most men there are two types of foreplay: having their penis touched and waiting to have their penis touched. This does not mean that his erogenous zones aren't sensitive and important, but it does mean that women shouldn't wait too long before getting to the genitals, even while kissing or stroking other erogenous zones as well. This is different than what women want—slow, escalating stimulation of a range of erogenous zones before touching the nipples and clitoris. The good news is that both partners can stimulate each other in these different ways at once. She can go right for his penis, while he spends time on a number of other erogenous zones first.

back We think of the back as a place we carry stress, but often forget that it's also a peak erogenous zone. Stimulating and massaging this area can be an incredible turn-on. To start, consider your positioning: lying down offers complete relaxation, but sitting gives you greater access to other arousal spots. Once you're situated, try one or all of these simple strokes: trace your fingers gently along her back to awaken the nerve endings, then massage with greater intensity. Let your fingers glide across her back, then reach around to stimulate her breasts (awakening both of these erogenous zones at once may intensify her arousal). Use long, firm strokes, and play with her desire by kissing her neck or ear intermittently.

stomach The stomach—especially the lower stomach—is another popular erogenous zone. Like the thighs, its proximity to the genitals means that it is sensitive to stimulation (in fact, some women find the lower stomach to be a greater source of arousal than the genitals). It is also a spot that lends itself to generating a long, slow burn of arousal: stroke it lightly early in the evening, while you are cuddling on the couch, and you'll plant the seeds of desire.

This is an area that calls for gentle touch. Stroke your fingers lightly over your partner's stomach, working your way from top to bottom. You can trace circles, lines, even letters to help vary the speed and rhythm of your touch. Don't forget the sides of the stomach, which can be stimulated with a slightly firmer stroke. And of course, just above the stomach, the breasts can be a hotbed of arousal for both men and women (for more on stimulating the breasts, see page 22).

buttocks Knead, rub, scratch, kiss, caress: there are so many ways you can stimulate the buttocks. This area is highly sensitive in both men and women, although, as with most erogenous zones, the type of touch we enjoy varies greatly. Experiment by rubbing this area lightly, perhaps when your partner is still clothed. Make your touch firm but gentle—your goal is to arouse, not tickle. Watch for your partner's reaction: does she arch her back and move closer? does his body stiffen? If it brings pleasure, try this again when you're between the sheets, at which point things get more interesting: massaging the buttocks leads naturally to anal play (for more on this, see pages 228–229).

Many of us also enjoy stimulation that feels a little more naughty. In the heat of the moment, try slapping this erogenous zone (if your partner agrees) for the perfect blend of pleasure and pain. Or, if you're feeling really adventurous, you can lick, suck, or bite.

Biting can be just as arousing as licking, kissing, or stroking. Try this on areas that are slightly less sensitive, like the shoulders or upper back.

trace her curves *softly and slowly*

stroke her inner thighs,
then let your fingers wander

caressing the body Instead of fondling the same few parts every time you make love, view your partner's body like a map filled with pleasure points—to bring her to unbearable levels of arousal, all you need to do is connect the dots. Lightly stroke her stomach and sides, massage her inner thighs, kiss her neck and the backs of her knees, building desire with every touch.

slip off his waistband *to kiss his stomach*

breasts and nipples

Big, small, perky, or cone-shaped, breasts are always beautiful. For many women (and men), they also happen to be highly erotic and rich in nerve endings. Some women can even reach orgasm simply by having their breasts stroked and massaged.

stimulating the breasts It's a well-known fact that light massage, stroking, or caressing of the breasts arouses most women, but remember: stimulating the breasts does not have to involve the hands alone. The *Kama Sutra* notes that biting or even scratching the breasts can be erotic. Try doing this (gently at first), or try licking, kissing, or sucking on the breasts. Varying sensation increases the surprise factor and turns foreplay into a sensually creative act.

The nipples are also highly sensitive when stimulated. Some women enjoy having their nipples touched, licked, and kissed, while others find that this area is too sensitive (or even painful) when aroused. It depends on personal preference, so it is important to communicate as you explore this erogenous zone together. A woman's nipples often become erect when she becomes sexually aroused, which is a good visual cue for her partner to follow.

Men can also enjoy chest or nipple stimulation. Experiment with this erogenous zone by kissing his chest or running your fingernails gently up and down his torso. Sucking or lightly nibbling on his nipples can also be quite pleasurable, but remember that this is a very sensitive area. For both men and women, the important thing to know when it comes to this part of the body is to be careful and to listen to your partner's body language.

breast stimulation during sex There are many other ways to enjoy the breasts, especially during intercourse. Men often like to have their partners on top in order to enjoy the view of their favorite female parts, but he can also reach around and stimulate this erogenous zone in other positions, such as man-from-behind.

If you crave more stimulation in this area, you can draw his attention by wearing a revealing shirt, a sheer bra, or even nothing at all. Or try fondling yourself in his view—many men find watching their partner touch herself highly erotic, and it's also a good way to highlight any spots where you want more touch.

timing your touch Although most men tend to head right to the breasts (and genitals) when stimulating their partner, it's important to remember that women need to build up to breast and nipple stimulation. Erogenous zones like these need to have time to become aroused before intense stimulation begins; otherwise, it can be too jarring. Spend plenty of time on the other, less sensitive erogenous zones, such as the neck, thighs, or lower stomach before heading to the breasts and nipples. Play with these areas and tease them at first: try touching the area around the breasts first, before moving slowly inward. Stroke the breasts lightly, then move to another area of the body, returning to the breasts after a few minutes. Do this multiple times to increase her desire and excitement. Gradually work your way to the nipple, keeping your touch gentle, and then increase your intensity and pace. She will be yearning for your touch by the end.

Rub lightly around the breasts at first, noticing as her nipples become erect with desire. Then, make your touch more firm, moving in toward the areolae.

the male *genitalia*

The genitals are a virtual playground of pleasure. Exploring and discovering these areas as a couple is exceptionally erotic, particularly since everyone responds differently to touches and caresses. With men more than with women, genital touch is truly the key to sexual satisfaction.

penis and scrotum The external male genitalia are comprised of the penis (made of spongy tissue) and the scrotum (containing the testicles). When blood circulation to the penis increases due to arousal, it becomes erect. The tip of the penis, known as the glans penis, is one of the most sensitive areas, particularly near the frenulum, which is just below the glans on the underside of the penis. Lightly licking or sucking on these areas is highly pleasurable.

If a man is uncircumcised, his glans will be covered by foreskin, a small fold of skin that is also known as the prepuce. When he becomes erect, the foreskin usually retracts and the glans is exposed. If you have never been with a partner who is uncircumcised, there are no major differences involved in pleasuring your partner, although some uncircumcised men believe that they experience more sensation.

The testicles are encased in a sack of skin known as the scrotum, which forms the other half of a man's external genitalia. These vary in size, shape, and color. The testicles are a crucial part of the male reproductive system, since they store the male sex glands and sperm. From puberty onward, men begin producing sperm—and even a man in his nineties is technically capable of impregnating someone! The scrotum is rich in nerve endings, and many men enjoy having this area stroked or gently pulled during oral or manual stimulation.

vas deferens, urethra, perineum, and anus When a man is aroused and nearing climax, his sperm is carried from his testicles to the vas deferens. The vas deferens connects the testicles to the urethra, which is the opening through which sperm and urine leave the body. Men can release up to 500 million sperm per ejaculation, although this number can be affected by age, hormones, or an unhealthy lifestyle.

The perineum is located between a man's genitals and his anus. It's a small area filled with nerve endings that pack a big arousal punch. You can bring waves of pleasure by stimulating this area with your fingers or tongue. However, remember that, because this area is so sensitive, it's best to use a light touch at first, experimenting with a firmer, deeper pressure if your partner responds with pleasure.

The anus is another area that has plenty of orgasmic potential for men and women. In fact, according to recent data from The Kinsey Institute, 10 percent of men and 9 percent of women have engaged in anal sex in the last year. If you're hesitant to have this area stimulated, it's always fine to avoid it. However, keep in mind that everyone has this pleasure center and that it is natural to enjoy being touched there. To truly maximize sexual pleasure, I recommend that you explore this region, taking it slow if you need to.

Men can thank their prostate gland for the pleasure of anal sex. Located about two inches inside the anus, on the belly-button side, the prostate gland is a small, walnutlike bump. Apply light stimulation or deep pressure with a finger, or, if you're feeling adventurous, use a sex toy to stimulate this area.

increasing sperm count
Many factors can lower sperm count, including a body temperature that is too high (this can be from recurrent hot tub or sauna use, or even from resting a laptop computer on your lap). To increase sperm count, first see a specialist to determine if there are any medical concerns. In many cases, the first step is to lose excess weight and eat a healthy diet that includes adequate levels of zinc. Low zinc levels can impact testosterone and decrease sperm production, so it's important to eat plenty of zinc-rich foods, such as eggs, seafood, yogurt, beef, and turkey.

how do I measure up?
Men are often plagued with anxiety over the size of their penis. From the locker rooms of their childhood through adulthood, most men wonder whether they are big enough. The truth is that the average penis is about six inches (15cm) long when erect. Of course, this is only an average, and variation of a few inches in either direction is completely normal. Regardless of the size of his penis, any man can satisfy his partner with creativity and a commitment to foreplay. Only the first third of the vagina is rich in nerve endings, so size isn't quite the issue men fear it is. Foreplay and skillful oral or manual stimulation trump size any day.

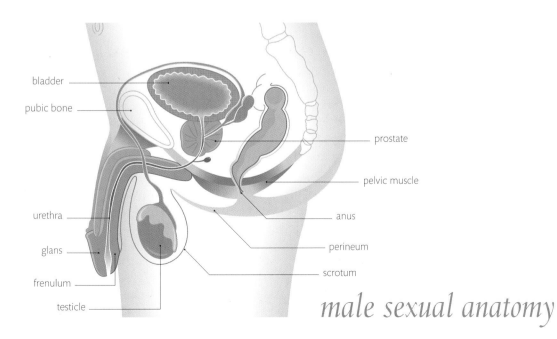

bladder

pubic bone

prostate

pelvic muscle

urethra

anus

glans

perineum

frenulum

scrotum

testicle

male sexual anatomy

the female *genitalia*

It has been said that the male body is straightforward and utilitarian, while the female body is mysterious and circuitous. This certainly seems true when comparing genitalia, where the biggest difference, of course, is that the male sex organs are largely external and the female sex organs, internal. This means that finding and stimulating a woman's genitals can be a little more difficult, although no less pleasurable.

loving your genitals Although the beauty of female genitalia has been studied and replicated in everything from ancient Egyptian artifacts to the paintings of Georgia O'Keefe, many women feel ashamed of their private parts. If you struggle to accept your genitals, remember that healthy genital self-image is crucial to achieving sexual pleasure. Women who don't know how their bodies work don't know how to bring themselves to orgasm, and thus are simply unable to achieve the sex life they want. Luckily, understanding the female genitalia is relatively simple. All you need is a good hand mirror, some privacy, and the illustration on this page.

mons pubis and labia The mons pubis is the small mass of flesh that sits above the genitals on top of the pubic bone. Generally it is covered with hair, although today this depends on a woman's personal grooming preferences (see page 28 for more on female genital grooming). Combined with the labia majora and the labia minora, this is what people typically think of when they hear the word vagina, although in reality this is not the vagina at all.

The labia majora are the "lips" of the vagina, the fleshy cushion that protects your inner labia. Labia majora generally aren't perfectly symmetrical, and many women find that one lip is slightly longer than the other. This is healthy and completely normal; in fact, labia come in all different shapes, sizes, and colors, from purple to pink to dark brown to variations thereof.

Next come the labia minora, or the inner folds of skin that surround the vaginal opening, with the clitoris at the top. The inner labia also come in numerous colors, ranging from bright pink to deep purple. When you are aroused, the labia minora secrete sebum, which lubricates the vagina and prepares you for intercourse.

the clitoris Perhaps the best-known part of the female anatomy is the clitoris. The clitoris is the only organ that exists purely for sexual pleasure, so it's no wonder that this small piece of tissue has made such a name for itself. However, the truth is that the clitoris is actually much larger than people have traditionally believed.

There are three parts to the clitoris, all of which work together to create sexual pleasure and orgasm. The clitoral crura are the internal "legs" of the clitoris. They reach almost to the pelvic bone, and are about 4–5 inches (10–12cm) in length. When a woman becomes aroused, the clitoral crura fill with blood. The crura are connected to the clitoral shaft, which is found down near the vagina. The clitoral head (the part that can be seen with the naked eye) is located near the top of the labia minora, between the labia majora. The head is under the frenulum or hood, and typically becomes exposed and larger with sexual arousal. It feels like a small bump, and, after the lips, has more nerve endings than any other part of a woman's body. Stimulation of this area can bring women to what is known as a clitoral orgasm, the most common type of orgasm (for more on orgasm, see page 96).

the G-spot Some people question whether the G-spot really exists, and this is mostly because it is difficult to find if you are new to the terrain. However, as many happy women can tell you, this pleasure center is very real!

The G-spot is located about two inches inside, on the front wall of the vagina, and women often say that it has the same spongy feel as the tip of the nose. Inserting a finger into the vagina and making a "come-hither" motion can help locate this spot, as can a specifically

the tissue *connection*

Despite the obvious differences, there is a surprising similarity between the male and female genitals: all of our sexual organs start from the same tissue as we develop in the womb. In fact, the clitoris consists of the same tissue as the glans of the penis, the inside of the shaft of the penis is from the same tissue that becomes the internal shaft of the clitoris, and the scrotum is built from the same embryonic tissue as the labia.

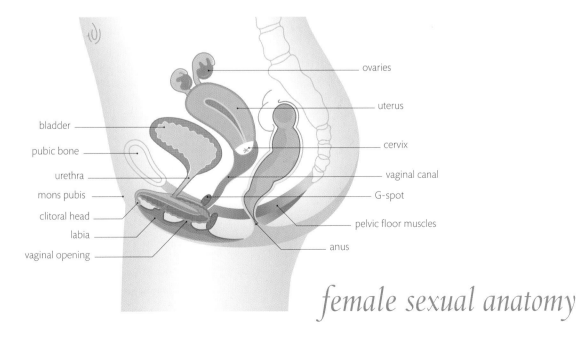

ovaries

uterus

bladder

cervix

pubic bone

urethra

vaginal canal

mons pubis

G-spot

clitoral head

labia

pelvic floor muscles

vaginal opening

anus

female sexual anatomy

your *perfect* vulva

It's important not to get hung up on whether or not your genitals look "perfect" or like the genitals you see in erotica. The truth is that no one's labia look like the pictures in erotic magazines and on websites, including those of the models themselves (thanks to Photoshop)! Most porn stars have been waxed and bleached within an inch of their lives, giving them that generic and even boring appearance we have to come to associate with female genitalia. However, in real life, female genitalia are as varied and unique as sex itself and, for your own sexual confidence and pleasure, it is crucial that you embrace your own genital appearance wholeheartedly.

designed G-spot toy. Initially, stimulating it might make you feel as though you have to urinate, since the G-spot is located close to the bladder, but with continued stimulation that feeling will pass. (For more on G-spot stimulation during sex, see pages 156–157.)

the vagina The vagina is the inner canal into which the penis is inserted during vaginal intercourse. The whole of the external female genitalia is actually called the vulva, not the vagina as it is commonly known. I always find it disturbing that we as a culture reduce this beautiful external system of pleasure into what is basically just the internal canal. Although it's only a name, I think it's also a symptom of a larger issue, a lack of comfort women feel with their own bodies and with celebrating their genitals and their pleasure. It's only when you know and use the correct terminology for your body, and understand it inside and out, that you can give and receive true sexual pleasure. So the name really is important. Differentiating between "vagina" and "vulva" shows that you understand and care about your body and about your sexuality.

The vagina is not only the canal through which life comes into the world, it is also host to plenty of pleasurable hot spots, such as the G-Spot and the A-spot. However, only the first third of the vagina is truly rich in nerve endings. Vaginal orgasms are still very powerful and pleasurable, but they differ from clitoral orgasms and can be harder to initiate, which is why learning how to stimulate this area is very important. (For more on vaginal and clitoral orgasm, see page 96.)

vaginal surgeries Precisely because there is no one "right" appearance for your genitals, labiaplasty and other genital reconstruction surgeries are usually unnecessary and can even be dangerous, resulting in damaged nerves and blood vessels, or a loss in the integrity of your vagina's shape. My research has shown that the number one reason women consider getting vaginal tightening surgery is because a partner has told them they were "too loose." My response to this is usually, "Are you sure he's not just too small?" I'm speaking only half in jest. A woman's Kegel muscles and transverse abdominals contribute to vaginal strength, as does any damage that's been done to the pelvic floor during childbirth or other injuries. However, long before surgery, vaginal tightening exercises and even a gynecological physical therapy visit should be considered (see pages 34–35 for more on Kegels and transverse abdominal strengthening). Surgery should only be a last resort in the most extreme cases.

Learning about your genitals can be quite a sexy education. If you've never seen your vulva up close, choose a private time and place to explore. Don some lacy lingerie, find a hand mirror, and discover this intimate piece of your identity as a woman—a piece that your partner loves.

hidden *hot spots*

The body is full of hidden erotic zones that can match the pleasure capabilities of the breasts and genitals. Discovering them is one of the true joys of sex. Couples who fully explore and understand these areas are on their way to becoming expert lovers.

perineum This small, nerve-rich area is located between the anus and the genitals in both men and women. Explore with your finger, your tongue, or a sex toy. The prostate in men and the perineal sponge in women (found underneath the perineum) are also highly sensitive. When these little areas are stimulated, the results can be quite pleasurable—even orgasmic.

A-spot Also known as the AFE spot, this female hot spot is a relatively new discovery. It is located between the G-spot and the cervix, at the very end of the vaginal canal on the anterior wall (for visual reference, see page 27). This is also known as the perineal sponge, which can be stimulated during anal sex. When aroused, this area can lead to intense orgasms, along with plenty of vaginal lubrication (in fact, the area was discovered by sex researcher Dr. Chua Chee Ann, who was looking for a way to treat women with painful vaginal dryness).

P-spot The P-spot is a male hot spot named for the prostate gland. It is a small bump located just inside the anus, which can lead to deep orgasms when stimulated. Be prepared for fireworks when playing with this erogenous zone—it's known as the male G-spot for a reason.

Devote an evening to discovering these private places without rushing through to lovemaking. This sort of intimate exploration is the ultimate turn-on.

U-spot Another female hot spot, the U-spot's name comes from its location just above and around the urethral opening. (As seen on page 27, the urethra is the tube that is connected to the bladder and releases urine.) Some women also release ejaculate from the urethral tube during orgasm. This is completely normal, and can be a thrilling sexual experience for both partners. Women also find stimulation to the area around the U-spot, called the peri-urethral region, very arousing due to the many nerve endings located there.

physical health *and sex*

Physical health and sexual health go hand-in-hand. When our health suffers or we are not comfortable in our bodies, it translates to less pleasurable sex and loss of libido. Put simply, no one wants to have sex when they aren't feeling their best. On the other hand, when we take care of our bodies, our sexual energy and abilities thrive.

nutrition Eating healthily is a key part of sexual health. This is partly because good eating habits help all of us look better and feel more confident, but it can also protect against a number of serious medical conditions, including diabetes, high cholesterol, obesity, and vascular disease. Thankfully, there are many simple ways to develop eating habits that contribute to better sexual health. Choose to implement these small changes as a couple, and reap the benefits in the bedroom.

don't live to eat, eat to live It's okay to enjoy the foods that you love, but moderation is always key. Sometimes all that's needed to satisfy a sweet tooth is a bit of dark chocolate. Listen to your body and follow its cues when you're deciding what to eat and how much. Stop eating when you are full, and only eat when you are hungry. And always take a few minutes to consider what food your body really needs, as opposed to eating mindlessly.

This doesn't mean that you should go on a diet. Diets are restrictive and painful to maintain, often leaving you weak and irritable. You can feel better about yourself by changing that way you eat, but you must make real lifestyle changes rather than relying on quick fixes such as crash diets or diet pills. Eating foods such as fruits, vegetables, lean protein, and whole grains can help bring about the natural benefits of more energy and improved self-esteem, and will also help redirect unhealthy cravings toward the food your body really needs.

make mealtime sensual Eating is a very sensual experience. It engages the senses, from touching the food to smelling the aromas to tasting the different flavors and spices.

Certain foods have more sex appeal than others. Anything that resembles genitalia is overtly sexy, whether it is a ripe banana, a crisp cucumber, or a moist, succulent fruit like an avocado. Foods that you eat with your fingers, such as strawberries, grapes, and cherries, are also sensual. Jalapeño peppers and other spicy foods can also be erotic because they increase your heart rate and send a warm flush over your body. Studies suggest that chocolate, too, can improve libido.

The food alone isn't all that brings sensuality to the dining experience. It's the act of preparing a meal with a lover that is sexy—cutting the vegetables, tasting the sauce for flavors, feeding each other, and simply spending time together. Make an event of it. Play some romantic music, build a fire, and enjoy a glass of wine. Or flip through a cookbook and choose a recipe blindly. Make a pact that you will cook whatever recipe it lands on, no exceptions allowed. Then hit the grocery store for the ingredients and get cooking! The goal is to make mealtime something special and sensual, rather than something that is rushed through thoughtlessly.

be good to yourself All of these lifestyle tips are meant to bring the focus back to being good to yourself, which also means taking the time for good grooming. Make time every day to feel happy and confident in your appearance, and this will in turn translate into increased sexual attraction, both from within and from your partner. When you make these efforts, you will find that your life feels more whole and balanced, and that you have more interest in and energy for sex.

the power of *touch*

Part of being good to yourself is setting aside time for relaxation. Massage is one of the best ways to renew your body and your mind—and if you involve your partner, it is also one of the best ways to bring peace to your relationship.

Massage can make for excellent, erotic foreplay, or it can simply be a way to reconnect and de-stress at the end of a long day. No matter how you use it, taking the time to connect through touch also means that you are taking the time to care for your body. (For more on massage technique, see pages 88–89.)

Touch is restorative, and a crucial part of our well-being. Take time every day to touch your partner's body, no matter how briefly. This physical connection will help you stay emotionally and spiritually connected, too.

building *sexual fitness*

Taking time to become sexually fit is all part of loving sex. Exercise improves self-esteem, circulation, quality of sleep, and sexual experience. Stronger muscles and improved circulation in particular equate to increased fitness in the bedroom, which in turn leads to better orgasms and more pleasurable sex sessions. Just as important, a sexually fit person is proud of her body and won't shy away from having sex with the lights on.

Kegel exercises Kegel exercises are an important part of a woman's sexual health. They help strengthen the pelvic floor and improve vaginal tone, which makes sex more pleasurable for both partners. Kegel exercises can also help create longer, stronger orgasms, and, for men, can increase orgasm control.

To strengthen this area, find your Kegel muscles by isolating the muscle used to stop and start your urine flow. Once found, work your way up to doing 100 quick contractions and 100 slow ones. You can perform this exercise anywhere, whether you are in traffic, watching a movie, or in a meeting.

transverse abdominals Strong abdominal muscles are also key to sexual fitness. Like your Kegel muscles, the transverse abdominals work to support your pelvic floor, and can enable deeper orgasms. To strengthen the transverse abs, try these simple exercises:
• **The plank** Begin on your hands and knees, extending your arms before you so that you are resting on your elbows with your palms flat on the floor. Then extend your legs behind you so that you are resting on your toes. Hold in your abs as tightly as you can, keeping your body straight and flat (don't stick your bottom in the air). Hold this pose for 30 seconds. Perform this pose once a day, and build up your endurance until you can reach 60 seconds or more. (If you aren't able to perform

Keep your weight balanced on your toes and elbows as you stretch your leg during the plank lift. This will ensure your core muscles receive the right exercise.

this position without struggling, begin with a simpler variation: Support yourself on your elbows, but rest on your knees instead of your toes. Hold pose as described above.)
• **Plank leg lifts** Begin in a plank position as above. Next, lift your right leg slightly in the air (about 8 inches off the floor) and hold for 30 seconds. Perform the same exercise with your left leg.
• **Plank crunches** Begin in a plank position as above. Bring your right leg into your body, reaching toward the left side of the body. Perform 15 of these, then swap to the left side.

loving exercise

We often exercise with our bodies in mind. We want to lose weight, flatten our tummies, or bulk up our muscles. Often, our inner monologue during a workout is nothing but self-loathing. All of this can be physically and emotionally draining, and it certainly isn't motivating. The best way to change this is to reset the way you think. Exercise isn't a punishment; it's a privilege. The very movement of your body, whether you are running, dancing, or biking, is a gift.

Exercise makes you stronger, less stressed, and able to dwell more fully in the present. Whatever your exercise of choice happens to be, make sure that it is something you love and appreciate. If you haven't found that exercise yet, keep looking. Your body, your sex drive, and your partner will thank you.

grooming together

It's a good idea to make grooming part of your new focus on sensuality. Be purposeful and present while you take care of your body. Instead of rushing through a shower every morning, light a few candles and take a relaxing bath before bed. Or share the grooming process together by washing each other's hair in the shower, or giving a light massage. If you are feeling daring, experiment with shaving each other's pubic hair, or take a smaller step and simply enjoy being naked with your partner. Don't rush to dress. Spending time together without clothes is fresh and sexy, and brings us back to the worship of the human body that is so critical to a happy, healthy sex life.

During the plank crunch, keep your abdominal muscles tight for maximum impact as you bring your leg in toward your body.

loving sex is...
emotional

Part of the pleasure of sex is its emotional power. Sex has the ability to bring us to the highest peaks of intimacy, establishing a bond that is unrivaled in any other human relationship. This intimacy is what keeps our relationships intact and interesting over a long period of time; it's what allows another person to truly become an extension of our own selves. Emotional, intimate sex is all about unity and spiritual depth—and it's incredibly restorative.

the evolution of sex

You might think that sex is the one constant that hasn't changed since the early days of civilization, but the truth is that it has undergone numerous changes, often as a result of the evolving ways that men and women relate to each other. While it has always been a driving force in the dynamics of male-female relationships, it has meant different things to different peoples at different times.

the tribal rule In the early days, men were the hunters and protectors of the tribe. They killed the bison, warded off wild animals, and generally used their brawn to keep their families and loved ones safe. Women found strength in numbers, remaining with other women in the tribe, and performing the crucial and life-sustaining tasks of gathering food, tending to the children, and forming social bonds.

These gender roles meant several things for the men and women of the tribe. First, men wanted to procreate and have a large, flourishing family. This meant that they craved sex with as many women as possible. However, they also wanted to be sure that their chosen mate was carrying their baby, so it was important to mate with someone who wasn't having sex with the whole tribe. After all, no man wanted to be left mistakenly caring for another man's child. Hence, men wanted to have numerous sex partners, but they didn't want their women to do the same. Thousands of years later, we still see these roles play out in much the same way. Men explore their sexual possibilities and boast about their conquests, while women fear appearing "loose" and thus often hide their sexual desires.

Of course, cavewomen also had sexual desires, but it didn't serve them to have sex with plenty of mates. Without birth control, sex in those days meant a child was a very real possibility. This was not only inconvenient; it was dangerous. Pregnancy and childbirth were not easily survived before the invention of hospitals and anesthesia, so women tried to limit their sexual partners in order to increase their chances of survival (and their baby's chances of survival). In addition, if a woman was impregnated by a mate who didn't have the status to support her and her child, then she would be alone, unprotected, and at risk. Hence, women were very careful in selecting mates, choosing men who were strong and assertive. This explains why women are still attracted to strong, alpha males, long after the days when brawn meant more than brain.

monogamy then and now Monogamy existed in those early days, although anthropologists believe that men and women were serially monogamous. Most couples likely had relationships that lasted about three years, or the same amount of time it took for their offspring to begin maturing. Once the child was old enough to walk on its own and the mother no longer had to nurse, she was better able to protect and feed herself and her child. When that milestone was reached, it is believed that many couples went their separate ways, each moving on to a new mate. This is why anthropologists such as Helen Fisher propose that it's in our DNA to have a "three-year-itch," rather than a seven-year one. Indeed, divorce statistics from around the world support this three-year time frame.

In modern reality, of course, long-term monogamy is possible, and making the decision to be monogamous forever can be one of the most beautiful journeys you will ever take. Having a partner that you can always rely on is a priceless gift. However, this doesn't mean that monogamy is easy. Life is full of temptations, and at times our very bodies work against us. It is perhaps due to our evolutionary past that a relationship that is several years old does not feel as exciting as one that is brand new. Luckily, there are steps you can take to safeguard your relationship and keep your fidelity happily intact.

sex today

Sex in the 21st century certainly has its roots in the attitudes of our ancestors, yet it is in many ways a very different phenomenon. To start, our modern generation is learning that sexual pleasure should work both ways, and that women should enjoy and desire sex just as much as men. As our sexual goals and mores have evolved, we have moved into a less judgmental climate. Today, by and large, sexuality is celebrated and valued. Our culture has moved forward, leaving us more comfortable acknowledging and appreciating the important role sex plays in nearly every fulfilling and lasting relationship.

Showing daily affection and passion is one of the best parts of monogamy—and it can help keep your relationship feeling fresh and new.

commit to
spicing things up

Try one new product, position, or experience at least once a month. Sex is either as boring or as exciting as you make it. It's easy to fall into a rut, especially if you have been with someone for years, but lazy sex isn't going to keep you or your partner interested. Get out of your comfort zone and try something new.

keep up your half of the sex bargain If you are in a monogamous relationship, then you must realize that you are your partner's only sexual outlet. If you shut him down every time he wants sex, or don't care to meet her sexual needs, then you're holding your partner sexually hostage. Not only will this often lead to the demise of a relationship, but it also means your partner will be more likely to stray. Cheating is always wrong, but you can't blame your partner for having sexual desires. Every couple must work to meet each other's desires within a healthy context. The best way to do this is to talk about what you want in the bedroom, and to respect your partner's needs. If you want different things, it's critical that you talk until you reach a conclusion that makes both of you happy. If you don't do this, your bedroom runs the risk of becoming a place filled with dissatisfaction and even resentment.

understand that temptation exists Sexual desires never go away, no matter how happy your marriage. It's okay to notice attractive people, and even to fantasize about them in the privacy of your own mind. It's only when you act on those desires that you have a problem.

use temptation as a relationship enhancer When you notice yourself wanting to flirt in any significant way, think about why. It's very likely that you are feeling the loss of something in your relationship. Take responsibility for your role in what's not working and talk to your partner. For instance, you may say, "I'm finding myself tempted to flirt with other people, and it's not because I'm interested in them, it's just that I miss flirting. So I want us to get back to flirting with each other—is that okay with you?"

make a contract with your partner Agree that neither of you will behave or speak to anyone of the opposite sex in a way you wouldn't in front of your partner. This way there will be no questions about what lines are okay to cross.

Are we bucking biology by being monogamous? Perhaps a little bit. After all, monogamy is a relatively modern institution and was invented after we began to live well past our reproductive years. Lifetime monogamy is not easy to achieve when the average life expectancy is close to 80 years. This doesn't mean it's not a worthy goal. It just requires communication and effort, along with a commitment to take care of each other physically and emotionally, and to nurture and grow a healthy sex life.

In a long-term relationship, part of maintaining a happy sex life is keeping an element of surprise. Show your partner you want him with the occasional act of overt seduction.

sex and *pleasure*

Evolutionary predispositions aside, why do we have sex? Is it because we crave the excitement of foreplay, the release of orgasm, and the pleasure of the post-coital glow? Or is it something deeper? For most of us, sex is about more than pure physical pleasure. In fact, the connection that sex fosters can be almost spiritual in nature.

spiritual sex Our sexuality is part of our soul. Tapping into our deepest sexual desires can be profoundly fulfilling. Whether you prefer sex that is fast and furious or slow and sensual, this physical union is a powerful way to connect with your lover *and* your most true self. Physical intimacy leads to emotional intimacy, so the more you connect with your partner sexually, the more bonded you will feel long after the sexual experience has ended.

the male perspective While we might all have a similar need for sex, it's still true that men and women rarely think about sex in precisely the same manner. This is because we are hard-wired and socialized to utilize sex differently. Men are instinctively goal-oriented. Their evolutionary history implores them to spread their seed far and wide, so sex for them is often relatively straightforward. It feels good. It involves orgasm. And it's through sex that men can connect most intensely to their mates.

In addition to this biological imperative, it is fairly universal for society to applaud male sexual experience and prowess. Men are typically capable of enjoying sex without the distractions of self-judgment, body image concerns, and insecurities that many women experience. This isn't to say that men don't bring baggage to the bedroom, but their suitcases tend to be easier to manage than the ones women carry.

the female perspective For women, sex is much more intimacy-focused and much less orgasm-focused. Women want sex in order to feel close to their partners. Orgasm is important and desirable, but women don't view it in quite the same goal-oriented manner as their partners. For them, the pleasure of connection is the most powerful part of sex.

Many women also have to negotiate a host of emotional roadblocks before they can freely enjoy sex, including early childhood lessons in which

Equal parts passion and intimacy, the more good sex you have, the more you will want, and the stronger your relationship will become.

they've been told (verbally or nonverbally) that "nice girls" don't enjoy sex, or that their bodies, desires, and genitals are shameful. Many of us were taught to be responsive in our sexuality, not directive. Overcoming these initial sexual lessons is difficult, particularly since we still live in a society in which men are encouraged to be sexual throughout their lives (think: Viagra) while women tend to be mocked for their sexual desires (think: the "cougar" phenomenon).

the sex and intimacy cycle One of the best ways to treat the emotional disconnect between how men and women view sex is to understand the cycle of sex and intimacy. As we've learned, for men, sex is usually a requirement in order for them to feel deeply intimate with their partner. Without this sexual connection, he will feel distant, and he won't feel motivated to give his partner the emotional feedback that she needs in order to feel sexually inspired.

This is an area in which many men and women tend to get stuck. Women feel unsatisfied and disconnected because their emotional needs are not being met, but instead of being honest about how they feel, they tend to pout or retreat from their partner. However, men aren't mind-readers, and they often have no clue as to why they are receiving the cold shoulder. Soon it reaches the point where neither partner is getting what they need, sexually or otherwise.

breaking away from the cycle Of course, all of this can be avoided if we simply talk to each other about how we are feeling. Try asking your partner the questions below, and sharing your own answers.
• What does sex mean to you in our relationship?
• How do you feel when we aren't having regular sex?
• In what ways do you think we could improve our emotional connection during sex (e.g., be more honest about our sexual desires, commit to having sex more regularly, etc.)?

Improving your emotional connection in the bedroom will provide benefits throughout your relationship. When you are open about your needs, you are able to celebrate sex not just as a physical pleasure, but also as an emotional one. You will have more fulfilling sex and be more present in your sexual experiences. Whatever your needs, the more you talk about sex, the more you will be able to enjoy it as the emotional and physical pleasure it is designed to be.

the dual *double* standard

Although somewhat more permissive, society's standards for men in the bedroom are no less defined then the standards for women. Men are expected to be experts in bed; to always be ready for sex; to have strictly platonic, unaffectionate relationships with other men; and to rarely show emotion. These rigid definitions of male gender expression create a limited view of sexuality and sexual exploration. They also create quite a lot of pressure.

Breaking down these barriers, as well as the emotional barriers that women face, means being honest about insecurities, open about friendships, and unconfined by old standards. When we let go of our old-fashioned ideas of sexual behavior, we are on the way to creating a new sexual environment in which sexuality for both genders is celebrated and respected.

the psychology *of attraction*

Our emotions dictate our sexual response and libido. In fact, much of our attraction to our mates is emotional, dating back to early memories and subconscious cues that lead us to pick a certain type of person. These strong feelings of attraction are the result of our lovemaps—subconscious patterns that we follow when picking a mate or when developing feelings of physical attraction.

the lovemap The lovemap theory was developed by sex researcher and psychologist Dr. John Money, who believed that there is a reason why some women always date bad boys and why some men are only attracted to blondes. It all goes back to our childhood and our first memories of attraction. These memories can be conscious, or buried so deeply in our psyches that we aren't aware that we are acting on them. Often these first memories of attraction aren't even sexually driven, but may have simply stemmed from an innocent attachment to a kind neighbor or an interesting teacher.

Our lovemaps not only play a role in our mate selection, they also impact our sexual desires long after we have chosen our partners. Your history can dictate the types of interaction you crave, both inside and outside the bedroom. For example, maybe you have a lovemap that stems back to the smart, witty teacher you had in grade school. Years later, you might still find intelligent and humorous conversation to be the sexiest form of foreplay, and you might feel disconnected if you don't get to interact with your partner on this level. Understanding your lovemap and these very personal needs will help you to plan ahead, so you can get the connection you crave.

the relationship map I have expanded on Money's lovemap theory to include "relationship maps." A relationship map shows how the models we grew up with impact our emotional interactions in a committed relationship. An unhealthy relationship map might be the result of witnessing negative interactions between key caretakers as a child, or of being the recipient of negative messages or treatment. For example, perhaps you don't know how to express difficult emotions without yelling, or maybe sharing your feelings makes you uncomfortable or embarrassed.

In contrast, a healthy relationship map helps you choose relationships that fulfill you and make you a stronger, happier individual. This can significantly impact your enjoyment in the bedroom. If you don't have a healthy emotional connection, your sexual ties will suffer as well. It will be difficult to communicate your desires and needs to one another in a way that makes sense, and you may even feel unsafe with your partner, or unable to be honest about your needs. This is why an authentic connection and a healthy relationship map are the foundation of every happy sex life.

Humor and playfulness are qualities that you might prioritize in potential partners, based on your own unique relationship map.

flirting and lust

Flirting and other expressions of desire are how we communicate feelings of lust and attraction to our partners or our potential partners. From the first glance across the room to the culmination of sexual pleasure, expressing these physical feelings of desire is an art form that everyone should master.

flirting for singles Successful flirting is all about timing. Know when to look, when to listen, and when to laugh and the object of your desire will reciprocate your interest in no time at all. A healthy dose of self-confidence is pretty sexy, too—along with just the right amount of mystery and visible interest.

make the first move Nothing expresses desire and confidence like making the first move, whether it is giving the attractive man at the bar your business card, or asking out the woman on the train that you have been eyeing for weeks.

listen more than you talk Simply paying someone the compliment of listening to what they have to say is flirtatious. It's a simple way to let your date know that you are interested in his thoughts and experiences.

be a master of body language Let your body do the talking before you even make it to the bedroom. Mimic your date's body language (known as "mirroring") to create instant feelings of closeness and attraction. Avoid crossing your arms or your legs, and balling up your fists, all of which are signs of discomfort and tension. Women, increase your sex appeal by flirtatiously touching your clavicle. This draws attention to one of the sexiest parts of your body—your breasts.

the eyes have it Eye contact is a critical part of human connection, so make your gaze work for you. Look at your "prey," then look away. Do so again and give a sweet smile. Remember, your thoughts will be reflected in your face and even in your eyes. So make sure that your thoughts are something along the lines of, "I can't wait to meet that sexy stranger," instead of "I bet I look like a loser right now."

be hard to get It sounds as though I'm contradicting my first tip, but note that I said, "be hard to get," not "play hard to get." Live a life that is full, interesting, and meaningful, independently of your partner or potential partner—whether that means getting active in your community or your church, working less so that you have more time to focus on your creative goals, or committing to staying healthy. Nothing is more desirable than a happy person—and the happier you are, the more positive, flirtatious vibes you will send out.

flirting for couples Many couples forget that flirting is just as important in a long-term relationship as it is when you are on the prowl. A good rule of thumb is to treat your partner as you did when you first met: as a sexy person that you want to impress and titillate, not like a platonic friend. It takes work and commitment, but once you make a habit of it, you may just find that you can't rein in your flirting.

woo your partner Once you are used to having sex with your partner, it may seem unnecessary to woo each other with sexy lingerie or extended foreplay. However, gestures like these are critical to maintaining passion. Be affectionate with your partner every day and take the time to set the mood like you did in the early days of dating. And make physical contact: wink at your partner across a crowded cocktail party or grab his bottom when no one is looking.

get creative The best flirting is personal. Let your partner see how well you know him by catering your flirtation to him. If he's into sports, surprise him with a date to see his favorite sports team, or encourage him to watch the game and don a sexy cheerleader outfit when it's over. Or, if she loves music, wow her by making her a surprise playlist or taking her to see a great local band.

take the time to look good Nothing is more flirtatious than putting time into looking sexy, yet for many of us this kind of effort falls flat in the face of our busy schedules. However, the truth is that neglecting your appearance means neglecting your self-esteem. This is especially true for women. Not only will your libido take a hit as a result, but your partner will wrongfully assume that you don't care to entice him any longer. Exchanging your sweats for some form-fitting jeans or your ponytail for a blow-dry every so often will go a very long way.

small gestures speak volumes You don't have to spend tons of time and money in order to blow your partner away. Small, meaningful gestures, performed often, can do more for your relationship than any expensive gift or tropical vacation. Consider simple things like filling up her gas tank without being asked, or remembering to buy her favorite cereal, or offering him a relaxing massage at the end of a stressful day without expecting one in return.

flirtatious gestures

Subtle physical gestures are some of the biggest turn-ons for both men and women, so don't forget to incorporate these into your date night. Tailor your flirtation to your partner's personality and needs (for example, physical advances work well with men; emotional ones with women). Women, smile into your partner's eyes, lick your lips, play with your hair, or cross and uncross your legs seductively. Men, remember to pull out your partner's chair, hold the door for her, and place your hand at the small of her back as you walk through the restaurant. Gestures like these will feel intimate and protective, and will bring her back to those early days when even these innocent touches would spark desire.

flirtatious foreplay The beauty of foreplay is
that it always feels new. The rush of adrenaline, the warmth
of arousal, the longed-for caress of lips and hands—it all
represents the very best part of lovemaking. In foreplay,
we find that thrill of connection, that mix of intimacy and
passion that revitalizes our relationships time and time again.

pull him toward you: *be rough, then gentle*

brush his nipple
with your lips

slip off her strap *to kiss her breast*

emotionally *intimate sex*

The best sex is the sex that you have with someone you love, trust, and feel completely comfortable with. Creating this safe emotional space takes a certain amount of work, especially if you are just beginning your sexual journey as a couple, but it is always worth it. An emotionally healthy sex life means that your relationship will grow, flourish, and become more and more sexy over time.

talking about your needs Early in your relationship, it's a good idea to talk about sexual boundaries and desires. For some people, this might mean sharing that you aren't comfortable having sex until you are in a committed relationship. For others it might mean sharing a sexy fantasy. Whatever the case, creating a climate of honesty and openness will help emotional intimacy flourish. In this environment, physical intimacy will improve almost effortlessly because you will know you are with a partner who respects you.

Emotional intimacy isn't just necessary in new relationships. No matter how long you have been with your partner, your connection is vulnerable if you stop sharing with one another. Whether it's a sexual secret (perhaps you have been faking orgasms) or a personal secret (maybe you feel dissatisfied with your life or even downright lonely), sharing these feelings is crucial in maintaining a satisfying sex life.

overcoming fear Sadly, many people avoid sharing these confessions because they don't believe their partner will accept them, or they are afraid of hurting their partner. However, these feelings of shame and fear can be stifling. Anytime you hold something back from your partner, no matter how insignificant it may seem, it becomes a wall between the two of you. Fortunately, there are ways to make the journey to emotional intimacy smoother. Consider the following tips:

pick a neutral time and place to talk People often keep things in, only to explode at the worst possible times, such as right before a family celebration. If you plan ahead and pick a time to talk, you can create emotional intimacy without undue stress or embarrassment.

talk as soon as possible The more you put it off, the bigger impact it will potentially have on your relationship. Never let an issue fester. When you share your fears openly, they will lose their power.

never accuse It's easy to get upset and accuse your partner of things like, "You never do anything romantic for me," or "You always make love to me in the same way," but this type of confrontation won't get you anywhere—except in the middle of a huge fight. Instead, express your needs with "I" phrases, such as "I want us to have a special date night," or "I need more variety in the bedroom."

keep your relationship private Although it's often tempting, it's never a good idea to discuss your relationship issues with friends and family. It's okay to want to vent, but by sharing these intimate details with other people, you cheapen your emotional intimacy and betray your partner's trust. If you have major issues that you need an outlet for, it might be a good idea to see a couples' therapist with your partner, or to see a therapist individually.

Although all relationships are prone to ups and downs, if you have a strong bond and an open, honest relationship that allows you to share your feelings, you can surmount any obstacle. Just as important, your emotional intimacy will stand the test of time. For more resources on how to get what you want out of your relationship, including how to fight well and how to address problems, see pages 264–265.

Cherish postcoital intimacy. Cuddle together in bed, share intimate secrets, and enjoy these moments to focus only on each other and strengthen your bond.

maintaining your *sexual bond*

Forging a strong emotional connection with your partner is important for many reasons, but perhaps first and foremost is the impact it can have on your physical relationship. As discussed earlier in this chapter, the sex and intimacy cycle often determines the strength of your bond. This is because men and women have different needs and expectations when it comes to matters of the heart—and matters of the bedroom.

remaining lovers It's important that your spouse is your close friend and partner, but just as important is making sure that your sexual connection remains intact. This means that you need to be able to view each other as sexual beings, not just as platonic helpmates. In fact, the word platonic should never be a part of your relationship vocabulary.

One way to do this is to make sure that you are not relying on your partner for all of your social interaction. It's easy to fall into the trap of making your partner your "everything," to the extent that you stop spending time with old friends and give up on old interests. Making your partner the center of your world might sound romantic, but the truth is that it puts a lot of unnecessary stress on your relationship, and also chips away at your sexual bond.

In order to prevent this from happening, spend time each week with friends that you had before you met your partner. Meet up with your girlfriends at the gym, or make a regular appointment for a round of golf with the guys. A few hours apart each week can give you the social connection you need. If a face-to-face meeting with friends isn't possible, then a long phone call can often suffice (for women, at least).

Along these same lines, it's important not to try to turn your partner into one of the girls or one of the guys. It might be tempting and convenient to drag your partner out to sushi and the latest vampire chick flick, but doing so will make him feel like a girlfriend rather than a lover, which will negatively impact both of you and your sexual relationship. The same goes for men; her attraction toward you will suffer if you're regularly indulging in bathroom humor or pigging out on wings and beer without wiping your mouth. To avoid this, make an agreement that she won't subject you to any more chick flicks, and you won't throw manners and charm to the wind.

sexy communication Communication often becomes too casual when you and your partner are comfortable with each other, but to keep your sex appeal intact it's important to pay attention to what you're really saying. Are you venting about your annoying coworker for the umpteenth time while your partner's eyes glaze over? Are you giving sordid details about your stomachache after lunch? Conversations like these matter in a way that they don't when you are talking to a group of friends. A valuable part of a romantic relationship is keeping a level of privacy and mystery between you and your partner.

your unique *sexuality*

Sexuality is unique and multifaceted, and no two people ever relate to sex in the same way. Our desires, fantasies, and needs are as different as we are. This is part of the appeal of sex, and it's why we seek to connect on this level with our lovers. In many ways, getting to know someone's sexual preferences means getting to know the deepest part of their self.

However, this can't happen unless we talk about our desires. Ultimately, our brains dictate a great deal of what happens in our bedrooms, which is why it's so important to be honest about our most intimate thoughts, especially with ourselves. Attraction and arousal might be predetermined in some ways, but we can help make our sex lives the healthiest and happiest they can possibly be, simply by opening up about our private needs and desires.

Express your desire for your partner through small gestures and surprise signs of affection.

Remember that privacy doesn't mean secrecy—it just means choosing to keep certain things to yourself. By talking less, you can actually communicate more, because you will focus on sharing what's truly important. This will also help to keep some mystery alive in your relationship, which is a key part of sexual attraction no matter how longstanding the relationship. You might be surprised at how a little bit of reticence can make your sexual bond spicier.

choosing *happiness*

A happier love life translates into a happier you. When you are happy with your relationship you will have better sex, you will feel more joyful, and you will be more fulfilled and present in every single one of your relationships. So, how do you accomplish this? The answer is straightforward, if not always simple: take the time to build a peaceful and meaningful bond with your partner.

prioritizing your life Creativity is the cornerstone of all great relationships. Routine sex is born of routine date nights, routine conversations, and routine kisses. If you feel like you have simply been going through the motions of your relationship lately, then it might help to know that you aren't alone. Nearly every couple gets stuck in a rut at some point. This is mostly because it's hard to find time to be creative and committed to a sexy, sensual relationship when there are so many other pressing things on your to-do list, such as doing laundry, mowing the lawn, and overseeing your kid's science project.

Fortunately, the solution to monotony is easy because, when it comes down to it, laundry and any other chore on your to-do list pales in importance to your relationship. First, convince yourself that this is true. Second, try to go through your day asking this question: "What will bring me and my partner the most happiness and comfort?" This question will help put things in perspective. Will spending your few hours of free time in a whirlwind of cleaning make you and your family happy? Or will you find more happiness by doing the most pressing chores and then stopping to spend quality time together? Is that email so important that it can't wait until tomorrow? Or can you shut down your laptop for a few hours to relax with your partner?

Even if you know the "right" answers to those questions, it's still not easy to pare down your to-do list to the essentials, especially if you are a perfectionist who finds peace in controlling everything around you. The key is to come to the point where you can recognize that it is impossible to control anything in the world except for your own state of mind. Even more important, you must recognize that this will suffer if you never relax or make time for your partner.

If it helps, try to commit to a timeline that will keep your need for control in check. For instance, you can decide to spend just two hours each week cleaning, or to cook a homemade dinner no more than four times a week. You can make a commitment to keep your weekends email-free, or make a no-computer rule after 8 p.m. Whatever rules you decide to put in place, find a balance that works for you and then rely on your partner and other people in your life to help accomplish necessary tasks, whether that's asking Grandma to babysit the kids so you can have the afternoon off, hiring a housekeeper to clean the house thoroughly once a month, or buying prepared foods for your next dinner rather than spending hours in the kitchen.

Once you have eliminated unnecessary stress from your day-to-day life, you will have more energy to focus on escaping routine and adding excitement to your relationship. For example, on your next date night, forget dinner and a movie and, instead, take a long drive to a park or a nature preserve for a sexy outdoor picnic.

make time every day
Date night is important, but the truth is, it's not enough. In order to build the happy relationship and the spicy sex life you want, you must commit time to each other every day, even if it's just 10 minutes. During this time, do things that have no purpose besides making you happy and helping you remain present in your relationship. This could mean staying up an hour later so that you can enjoy a hot bath together, or getting up early to start the day off with a little morning sex. Perhaps you can simplify your commute by arranging a carpool with other parents, or you can plan to use one vacation day a month just to play hooky with your partner and enjoy simple pleasures like going to brunch or seeing a matinee. Taking advantage of stolen moments like these will make all the difference in your connection.

Find new ways to spend time alone with your partner every day, whether that is a romantic dinner for two or a quickie before you get up in the morning.

living in the present
The most important thing to remember is that you shouldn't postpone happiness. When you do this, you are also postponing the full potential of your sex life and your relationship. No message is more important than this: Start making your life more sexy and fulfilling right now. Don't wait to take that romantic trip with your partner, or put off buying that sexy little dress until you lose weight. Put aside fears of being selfish and impulsive. Everyone in your life, including your children, will benefit from a more joyful and positive you. Try something new and the sense of renewal will spill over into the bedroom, making your relationship that much sexier.

dealing with *sexual anxiety*

Throughout this book, I talk about sex as a healthy, normal part of life. From reflecting on our ancestors and their sex lives to analyzing our current relationships and sexual views, sex is discussed as a pleasurable and intimate experience. However, it is also true that there are many of us who struggle to enjoy sex, who worry that our desires are strange or unhealthy, and who feel so ashamed or uncomfortable during the act of lovemaking that it becomes difficult to let go and experience orgasm.

common worries about sex If this sounds familiar, rest assured that you aren't alone. Every one of us has sexual anxiety in some form, particularly as it relates to our sexual desires. In fact, the main question that I get asked is "Am I normal?" People want to know if their fantasies are weird, or if their genitals are strange, or if they are the only ones who struggle with sexual performance.

We all want to feel accepted and good about ourselves, especially when it comes to sex, yet this can be very difficult to do, largely because many people don't feel comfortable talking about sex. If they did, they would know that everyone feels embarrassed, nervous, and even ashamed in the bedroom at times.

For many people, this shame comes from childhood lessons surrounding their bodies and sex. Perhaps you were told that sex is dirty or bad, or that people who have sex are sinful. These fears were probably very real to you as a child, and even though you might think that you have grown out of these beliefs, it is likely that they still haunt you subconsciously. If you feel uncomfortable with your body, particularly your genitals, or if you feel uncomfortable expressing your sexual desires and enjoying sexual pleasure, then some of these past experiences are probably preventing you from being able to let go and enjoy sex.

Confiding in your partner about any
sexual anxiety you feel is the first step
toward relieving your worries and moving
forward in a happy, healthy relationship.

talking about anxiety The good news is that
you can overcome these sexual concerns. First, it will
be helpful for you to talk to your partner about how
you have been feeling. Perhaps your partner has sensed
some of your discomfort, but doesn't know where it is
coming from. In fact, he or she might even think that you are
no longer happy in the relationship, which sets off a whole new
chain of sexual anxiety. As you can see, shame is a vicious cycle.

The best way to overcome this cycle is to be honest about your
feelings. Tell your partner when you feel intimidated or ashamed in
the bedroom. It is easiest if you take a straightforward approach, by
saying something such as: "Sometimes when we are having sex, I feel
really self-conscious and it makes it hard to enjoy myself," or "I judge
myself very harshly in the bedroom, and I often feel like I am doing
something wrong." Explain to your partner that these are your
insecurities and that you want to work to overcome them. Let him or
her know that the best way to support you is simply to be understanding
and to listen, because at the end of the day, no one else can make you
feel better about your sex life. Only you can. (One caveat: You can talk
about the idea that you feel insecure, but try to avoid going so far as to
point out your flaws, whether it's recent weight gain or any other
insecurity. When you identify these flaws, all you do is highlight them
to your partner, which means he or she will be more prone to start
noticing them as well.)

reflecting on sex You might also consider keeping a sexual
journal in which you can write down your sexual fears, your desires
for your sex life, and maybe even a fantasy or two. It might be difficult
for you to put these things down in black and white, but this exercise
will teach you to express any unspoken thoughts about sex in a safe
place where you are free from inhibitions. The least self-conscious
starting point for this is a private diary.

One good exercise is to write down all the thoughts and beliefs you
have surrounding sex, such as "Sex shouldn't be talked about," or "I'm
not sexy." Next, spend some time thinking about where those thoughts
come from and how they began to play a role in your life. Once you
discover the root of these thoughts, you can begin to see how false
they are and you will be able to release them more easily.

seeking *therapy*

If sexual anxiety is preventing you from
enjoying sex and is harming your relationship
even after you have talked to your partner, or
if you feel unable to start a conversation about
your concerns, you might want to consider
seeing a therapist. In particular, a sex therapist
can help you understand and trace the roots
of your sexual anxiety, and can work with you
as a couple and as individuals to help heal your
inner spirit and rebuild your sex life.

loving sex is...
seductive

The best sex is built upon thoughtful seduction. Whether you invoke desire through quick, physical exploits or slow and steady gestures of romance, the most seductive acts are deeply personal. Strip, kiss, stroke, embrace, and flirt shamelessly with your partner—part of the beauty of a longstanding relationship is that you will know exactly what actions and words will trigger that irresistible, even unbearable, desire.

creating *sexual desire*

Buddha once said that desire is the root of all suffering. Anyone who has ever been in love can testify to the pain of sexual desire. It can be as intense as other physical pains such as hunger or thirst, and yet it can also be addictively pleasurable and exciting. The trick is to find a way to court and master this physical desire, using it to increase your own sexual pleasure.

rethinking sex To begin with, you have to reset the way you think about sex. Too often people assume that sex has a beginning, a middle, and an end: first comes foreplay, second comes penetration, third comes climax. This might be an efficient way to reach orgasm, but you don't necessarily have to follow this formula—or any formula, for that matter—during sex.

The easiest way to avoid formulaic sex is to stop thinking of orgasm as the end-all, be-all of sexual activity. Yes, the release of pent-up sexual energy can be earth-shattering, but the journey to that climax can be just as pleasurable. In fact, considering that the average male orgasm lasts six seconds and the average female orgasms lasts 23 seconds, the actual act of climaxing is a very small part of the human sexual experience. Delaying climax is a surefire way to increase arousal and satisfaction (for more on the benefits of delaying orgasm, and tips on how to do so, see pages 220–221). Once you get rid of the need to rush through sex toward a "goal line," you might be surprised at how present and fulfilled you feel after sex.

mental seduction Creating desire is about more than delaying climax in the bedroom, or touching your partner in just the right way. Seduction isn't physical. It's primarily a mental game. To maximize desire, the key is to create an environment that inspires sexual fantasy outside the bedroom. This will help do away with the expectation that you will be able to switch instantly into a sexy state of mind in bed, which isn't always realistic. Instead, build those feelings throughout the day or week. Start with the ideas below.

choose an exotic theme Think back to a memorable trip you've taken, or dream up a trip you'd like to take, such as a "Weekend in Paris" night with wine and cheese and plenty of French kissing.

add some R-rated fun Consider doing something that you would normally find taboo or a little intimidating. I don't mean that you should do anything that makes you feel uncomfortable or unsafe, but it is thrillingly sexy to push your boundaries in small ways. For example, try watching an erotic movie together, or read passages from an erotic book out loud, lingering over the sexy parts and acting out the words you read on the page.

using your *words*

One of the simplest ways to create desire is to speak sensually. Verbal encouragement goes a very long way both inside and outside the bedroom. This might feel funny if you've never done it before, but it's a risk worth taking—the sexual energy your words can generate is unbelievable. Let your partner know that you find him or her sexually desirable with compliments like, "I love it when you touch me" or "I can't wait to be with you tonight." By the time you get to the bedroom, you'll both be craving each other's touch.

A girl wearing an open trench coat with nothing underneath is every guy's fantasy—and nothing is more seductive, mentally and physically.

the power of *anticipation*

Author Gustave Flaubert said, "Pleasure is found first in anticipation," and this is particularly true when it comes to intimacy. Just as exciting and pleasurable as sex itself is the anticipation of your lover's touch, and the sense of expectation as you await a romantic evening.

anticipation every day We often think of anticipation as something that is reserved exclusively for special occasions, but the truth is that you can enjoy these feelings at any time. In fact, building anticipation is all part of making sex a more regular and passionate part of your relationship. Below are a few ways you can harness the power of anticipation, even on a typical Tuesday night.

set the mood early Don't wait until night falls to seduce your partner. By then, you will probably both be too tired to truly enjoy each other. Instead, start your seduction early in the morning. Bring her a cup of coffee in bed and greet her with a long kiss. Or keep the kids out of her hair, so she has time to get ready (it's hard to feel in the mood if you haven't had time to shave your legs). Don't have time for all that? Hop in the shower together and spend five minutes washing each other. Then, turn off the news (which can be stressful and a real mood-killer) and play some feel-good music. No matter how rushed you are, take the time to give each other one real, passionate kiss, and try to surprise your partner with a little sexual energy. Slip him the tongue, call her by a name you only use in the bedroom, or flash him some cleavage. The memory of these flirtations will give you a more sensual outlook for the rest of the day.

seduce each other with technology Now that you have your partner in a sexier frame of mind, strike while the iron is hot. After a few hours, send a suggestive text message, such as "Can't wait to see you tonight" or "Let's put the kids to bed early." Letting your partner know that you are thinking about being alone together is a huge turn-on. You can also appeal to your partner's visual sense with a picture message. If you don't feel comfortable taking a nude shot of yourself, try sending a picture of your lacy bra or of the waistband of your boxers with the message "Can't wait for you to take this off me." It's okay if you feel a little shy at first. Once you see how enthusiastically your partner responds, these sexy messages will feel more natural.

feeling sexy It's equally important to reap the feel-good benefits of anticipation for yourself. After all, you are one-half of the sexual equation. Start by taking the time to feel confident and sexy during the day, whether that means wearing your best lingerie underneath your boring work clothes or spending an hour at the gym. Then, try to keep your mood stress-free by tackling your most difficult projects in the morning. Instead of working through lunch, catch up on a good book or take a brisk walk for some fresh air. Using this hour to do something you love will help you feel more balanced and whole, which in turn makes it easier to access your sensual side. Later, keep traffic from ruining your mood by listening to a favorite band on your way home or calling a friend for a good chat (on your Bluetooth, of course!).

The idea is to keep your day as pleasurable and stress-free as possible, which fortunately isn't so difficult to do once you commit to having a good day. Not only will you be less likely to get bogged down in the minutiae of daily life, but you will also be surprised by how sexy and seductive you feel. Whenever stress starts to take over your day, think about your evening plans with your partner and let your anticipation color your whole day with excitement and sex appeal.

Give your partner a true goodbye: lingerie-clad, kiss-giving and all. Stealing moments like these will help you both feel more sensual during the day—and will help prepare you for a romantic evening later.

exciting the senses

Your senses are your tools for experiencing the world around you. Without them, you wouldn't be able to taste the sweet flavors of a strawberry or smell the scent of your partner's hair or feel how smooth and supple her skin is beneath your fingers. Great sex is sensual sex: sex that involves all the senses and has you tasting, smelling, hearing, touching, and seeing your partner in a whole new light.

dwelling in the moment Sensual sex requires that you occasionally put the brakes on your hectic lifestyle. In order to truly experience sensations, you have to slow down and be present. You have to pause to enjoy the flavors of a meal, and the conversation your kids are having down the hall. You have to turn off the television to notice the different shades of yellow and orange in the sunset. Appreciating all these little pieces of your life will help you relax and dwell in the moment. You will feel more restored and more fully yourself—and this is the type of environment in which great sex can thrive.

One simple way to dwell in the moment is to add some variety to your daily experiences. Our senses become dulled to the familiar, which explains why we tend to take everyday things for granted, whether it's a hot cup of coffee, a soft bed, or the warmth of our partner's embrace. Even just a short absence from these familiar blessings can make us more aware and appreciative.

This doesn't mean you have to transform your life to appreciate it. Instead, simply inject a little novelty into your routine. Take a different route home, cook a new cuisine, explore a new restaurant on date night, or add a few pieces to your wardrobe that are out of your usual comfort zone. All of these things will help you to appreciate and find adventure and romance in everyday life.

Then, start living more sensually. Take a long bath with the intention of reveling in each of your senses. Use scented bath oil and slowly slip your body into the water, feeling the heat as it gradually covers your body. Wash yourself with your fingers instead of a washcloth so that you can feel your skin. Dry off with a soft, fluffy towel, and rub lotion over your skin while it is still warm and damp from the bath. You can practice this type of awareness with almost any of your daily rituals, simply by becoming present and listening to what your senses are telling you.

building a sensual environment Once you push yourself to include new experiences in your daily life, you will be surprised at how much more alive your senses become. The next step is to create an environment that cultivates passion. Start with your bedroom, then work your way around the house.

Your bedroom should be a sanctuary for seduction. Set a rule that you won't use this sacred space for watching television, working on your laptop, folding laundry, or any other mundane daily task. A good rule of thumb is this: If it doesn't relate to sleep or sex, it shouldn't be in your bedroom. For this reason, I also recommend moving any family photos to another room. Pictures of your mother-in-law or children aren't going to encourage sex under any circumstances.

As you undergo this cleansing exercise, take a good look at your bedding. If your sheets and comforter have been around almost as long as your relationship, it's time to toss them out. Not only will you sleep better on new, fluffy bedding, but you will also reap the benefits from a sexual standpoint. New bedding livens up your bedroom, and it might just inspire you to add some spice to your sex life, as well. To really add sensuality to your bedroom, choose luxurious fabrics with a high thread-count, like cotton or satin, and avoid colors that are too feminine. One of the most important traits of a sensual bedroom is that it feels like it belongs to both of you.

privacy in the *bedroom*

We don't often think of privacy as an erotic trait, but it's hard to feel intimate if you don't feel like you're alone. Enhance the intimacy of your bedroom by hanging new window treatments that give you plenty of privacy to engage in your wildest fantasies. If you have children, make sure that your bedroom has a good lock on the door. You might also consider investing in a little soundproofing in order to make sure that your private affairs stay private. Take whatever steps feel comfortable to you— just make sure that your bedroom becomes a place where you are able to distance yourself from distractions and focus solely on your partner.

music and lighting There is a reason that music and candles have become a romantic cliché—they work. Adding sound and scent and subtle lighting means adding layers of sensual texture to your space. Any music that gets you in the mood is a good idea, as is relaxing, atmospheric, spa-like music. Choose songs you both like—make a bedroom playlist together, or take turns picking out tunes that match your mood on a special night.

When choosing candles, be careful when it comes to scents. Again, it's important to avoid anything too girly or sweet. Think sexy, earthy, and gender-neutral scents like sage, sandalwood, patchouli, cedar, basil, and clove. Cucumber and licorice are also widely appealing. In fact, a scent study performed by Dr. Alan Hirsch of the Smell and Taste Treatment and Research Foundation in Chicago revealed that scents of cucumber and licorice had the biggest impact on sexual arousal for both men and women. While we don't exactly know how scent impacts arousal, researchers believe that, although scent is processed

Adding a blindfold makes a sensual taste test all the more mysterious. For added sex appeal, feed your partner with your mouth.

through the olfactory bulb (the part of the brain that interprets scent), it might then go on to affect the parts of the brain that control sexual response, creating an aphrodisiac effect.

A dimmer switch for the lights in your bedroom and bathroom can also be a valuable foreplay enhancer. (Nothing ruins the mood like a beaming ray of fluorescent light!) Even more important, having a range of lighting options means you can find a level of visibility that you both feel comfortable with and that allows you to see each other while making love, for greater intimacy and eroticism.

seductive sounds
Use the sound of your voice to seduce your partner. Studies have shown that people instinctively lower their voices when speaking to someone they find attractive—which means that lowering and softening your tone can increase your partner's arousal and subconsciously communicate your desire.

Of course, you can also take a less subtle route, by telling your partner exactly what naughty things are on your mind. You don't have to be crude to be erotically effective. What's truly arousing is simply and specifically expressing why you're looking forward to being alone together (it's easier than you might think!). Whether on the phone or in person, the point of naughty conversation is to spur your partner's imagination along, and build anticipation for the night ahead.

sex and taste
As we've discussed, our sense of taste is closely linked to sexual desire (for more on this, see page 32). Both cooking and eating can be incredibly arousing—especially if you are purposeful about turning your partner on. A sexy, playful way to do this is to plan a sensual picnic, al fresco or in the bedroom. Pour chocolate sauce wherever you desire and have her lick it off, or lay fruit across your stomach that he can nibble. Take turns blindfolding each other for more mysterious, taste-testing arousal.

sensual touch
Touch is an obviously sexy sense, but that doesn't make it any less pleasurable. Use your bodies to awaken each other's sexual appetites; take turns caressing each other in the nude, or simply lie still together, enjoying the sensation of your partner's bare skin. Or alternate the heat of your breath with the cool of an ice cube as you explore his body; the changing sensations add an element of seductive surprise, and will also keep you sexily in control. You can accomplish this same effect by changing the temperature of a glass sex toy. First, warm it in hot water, then chill it in ice.

touch and arousal

There is so much power in physical touch. More than any other sense, touch connects you to your partner and allows you to gauge the pleasure in their response. Set aside time with your partner to revel in touch for touch's sake. It may lead to sex or it may not—either way, the pleasure will be intense.

rub every part of his body Have your partner lie on the bed and get comfortable. Using massage oil, slowly and seductively begin to knead into his trouble spots. Once he's loosened up, turn on some erotic heat. Trail your fingers along his buttocks and massage his thighs with extra attention. By the end of the massage, he will be dying for you to give him a happy ending.

work with props Use props such as feathers, handcuffs, or blindfolds to add spice to your bedroom routine. If you don't find these traditional props naturally appealing, consider looking for more luxurious versions, such as silk blindfolds or peacock feathers.

expose more skin
slowly and sensually

stripping down Part playful, part pure sex appeal, a striptease is an incredibly seductive way to woo your partner. Trail your hands slowly over your body as you remove each piece of clothing, igniting your partner's imagination for how she can please you later. Maintain eye contact as you move, allowing her to guess at all the naughty things on your mind.

let your hands linger
as her longing swells

speak softly
of your desire

dating in a relationship

Many well-meaning couples have scheduled special nights together, only to be disappointed by lackluster results. Truthfully, it's not enough simply to plan a date. In order to increase connection and intimacy, you must plan specifically with your partner and relationship in mind.

planning for romance The first rule of thumb when it comes to dating is this: Don't make date night a regular night out. To be successful, dates need to be romantic, sensual, and thoughtful occasions where you and your partner can connect as lovers. This doesn't mean that you have to indulge in an expensive dinner at a five-star French restaurant every time you go out. What you do need to do is get into the spirit of the evening. The following budget date nights are guaranteed to create sparks without denting your wallet.

• Go ice skating, and flirt over hot chocolate.
• Challenge each other to a game of Scrabble and share a bottle of wine. Set some terms: the loser has to give the winner a massage.
• Hit the roller skating rink and jam out to the old-school music.

Some of the best date conversations have an element of playfulness. Try asking your partner: "What super power do you wish you could have?"

• Keep abreast of online deals. You just might find a bargain on a fancy dinner or discounted tickets to a concert in the park.
• Check out the free things your city has to offer: the zoo, art museums or galleries, street fairs and seasonal festivals.
• Go to a local high school football game. Sit in the stands, dine on hot dogs, and feel the team spirit. (Really buy into the atmosphere by hooking up behind the gym just like you used to do in your wild youth!)
• Snuggle at a drive-in movie. Dress up the occasion by bringing a bottle of champagne to sip while you enjoy your popcorn.

To plan any one of these nights successfully, it's important to decide well in advance who should have what role, as you would with any other important event. If you leave it to the last minute, miscommunication will occur. Perhaps you're in charge of making reservations, and your partner is responsible for booking the babysitter. You can also take turns planning your date night from start to finish, which lends the added element of surprise. What you don't want to do is put off planning until that night—this causes stress, and is a natural starting point for arguments.

restoring conversation Another way to avoid slipping into a dating funk is to change your conversation topics. Talking about the kids and the bills is tempting, especially when it feels like this is the only time that you and your partner have to discuss these things. But don't forget about romance! Talking about stressful household issues is not going to help you relax and reconnect. And while talking about your children might not be stressful, it will put you back into that Mommy-and-Daddy mode. Remember: Tonight you are lovers, not parents. So save all that everyday talk for another time. Instead, engage each other with funny stories, interesting news articles, or plans for the future. You can even talk about sex. (Just the good stuff though! Save complaints for another time.)

To start, try one of the following conversation starters:
• What country would you most like to visit?
• What quality are you most proud of?
• Who was your childhood hero?
• What was your first kiss like?
• What is your favorite part of our relationship?
• What sexual fantasy do you want to fulfill?

preparing for *your date*

One way to relax and focus on the evening ahead is to spend some time getting ready for your date, just like you did when you and your partner first met. If possible, you can even get ready in a separate area of the house, and then meet in the living room to be "picked up" for your date. As you get ready, keep the kids engaged with a board game, or have the babysitter come over an hour before you leave. This serves a double purpose: Not only will your kids have a chance to feel comfortable with the babysitter while you're still home, but you will also have time to breathe, relax, and get ready for your special night. This should make the transition from Mommy-and-Daddy to lovers a little easier on all of you.

the art of *foreplay*

We have all heard how crucial foreplay is for great sex, but people often wonder: How much is enough foreplay? The answer is that it depends on you and your partner. However, a good rule to live by is this: If you have the time, use it! Foreplay not only helps to build passion and intimacy, it also helps ensure that you and your partner truly connect, so you are that much closer to reaching orgasm during lovemaking.

mental foreplay I always say that men are like microwaves and women are like slow-cooking ovens. For most men, all it takes is the mere suggestion of sex and they are ready to go, but women are a little different. Not only do their bodies often take longer to respond, but they also need some time to make the mental switch from "mommy" or "corporate star" to "sex kitten." Men, remember that women are often multitasking machines, which means that they have a million things running through their heads at any given time during the day or night. Letting go of that to-do list and getting into a sexy frame of mind isn't as easy as hitting a switch or donning some lacy lingerie, and that's where foreplay can help.

Begin by making sure that you will have enough time to enjoy foreplay before the main event. You don't need hours for this—in fact, 10 or 15 minutes can make all the difference. Not all of this foreplay needs to be physical. You can also use this time to unwind, cuddle with each other, have a glass of wine, kiss, or talk. (Talking dirty is one of the best ways to get both of you excited.) It will be a lot easier for both of you to feel sexual and enjoy the moment if you aren't still stressed out over work or worrying about the kids. Take a few minutes to put the world on pause, breathe deeply, and reconnect with each other. Think of this as mental foreplay.

physical foreplay Now you can move on to the physical stuff. The best approach is to start slow and engage the senses. Run your fingers gently along your partner's back or between her thighs. Kiss her along her breasts or neck. Spend time engaging the erogenous zones (for more on these, see pages 16–17), and when it's your turn, simply lie back and enjoy the sensations your partner's fingers and tongue create.

Don't feel like you need to always be the "giver" or that you are selfish if you enjoy your partner's advances. In particular, women seem to suffer from this inability to simply lie back and enjoy receiving without giving. If this sounds familiar, it's time to reset your way of thinking. Instead of thinking of receiving pleasure as selfish, think of it as a way for your partner to feel connected and intimate with you. Notice how he enjoys making you feel good, and how much more bonded and sensual you feel when pleasure is a two-way street. In short, think of foreplay as a dance: You each have a role to play and steps to perform, and it shouldn't be a solo routine for either of you.

Women need slow, subtle touch to begin, which can eventually give way to firmer, more direct pressure.

the timing of foreplay
Foreplay doesn't have to begin right before sex, or even in the bedroom. If you know that you don't have time to have sex, or if you are in a place where you can't have sex (such as in a restaurant or at a wedding), you can tease your partner by giving him a taste of what's to come. Give him a deep kiss when no one is looking, lay your hand on his thigh, or whisper to him what you want to do when you get back to your bedroom. Flirt with him like you would when you were first dating—show off your cleavage, cross and re-cross your legs seductively, and be the femme fatale he fell in love with. Remember, great sex doesn't begin when the lights go out—it begins many hours beforehand.

You don't want to rush through foreplay, nor do you want to feel like it needs to last a certain amount of time. If you are in tune with each other's bodies, the switch from foreplay to sex should be organic, smooth, and naturally evident.

afterplay
Though less talked about then foreplay, afterplay can be just as sexy and intimate. Just because your partner has reached climax doesn't mean that your experience has to be over. If you haven't reached climax, ask him to bring you to orgasm manually, or you can do this yourself. Alternately, give each other a chance to cool down, and then slowly begin to arouse each other again with gentle stimulation. If this inspires you to have another go, then by all means, go for it! Or simply enjoy the intimacy and sensuality of afterplay.

foreplay menu
The best foreplay is both physical and mental. It is also tailored to your partner's desires and peak erogenous zones. Expand your foreplay horizons with the suggestions below.

• Challenge her to a game of strip poker.
• Tie his hands to the bedpost with a tie or a pair of panties. Slowly kiss and caress your way down to his genitals, making him anxiously wait for you to touch him there.
• Watch a sexy movie together. Make a pact to act out one of the scenes.
• Play a naughty board game.
• Slip your hands under her skirt at the dinner table when no one is watching.
• Take him to a sexy costume store. Tell him to buy something that he wants you to wear.
• Make out in the back of the movie theater.
• Feed each other chocolate fondue or fruit.
• Offer her an unexpected foot massage.

the *kissing* connection

Kissing is our way of tasting, smelling, and touching our mates. During this intimate act, we use our most primal senses to gauge our partner's sexual framework. Indeed, a kiss really is more than just than a kiss—it helps our bodies read subconscious cues such as chemical makeup and sexual readiness.

kissing and intimacy How did you view kissing while you were growing up? What were your first experiences with kissing? These experiences and memories will have a large impact on your current kissing patterns. If you grew up in a home in which kissing and affection were important, you might find that you still treasure the importance of kissing in your relationship. On the other hand, if you grew up in a home where expressions of intimacy weren't common, you might not always initiate kissing or other forms of affection.

Kissing can have many different uses and different levels of impact in relationships. It can be a source of intimacy that keeps you and your partner bonded, affectionate, and in tune with each other; it can be an erotic way for you to initiate foreplay; or it can be a comforting and sweet path to connecting with your partner. Use kissing for all of these reasons, and it will become an incredible source of bonding, closeness, and romance in your relationship.

long-term kissing Unfortunately, the sparks that are generated by this meeting of lips are often lost in long-term relationships—which means that your connection, intimacy, and sexual inspiration will also suffer. This is especially true for women. Research has shown that women use kissing as a way to determine sexual compatibility, and that kissing is one of the ways that they experience romance and affection most clearly. In fact, if regular kissing is not a part of your relationship, regular sex may very well not be a part of it either! So you can see why you wouldn't want to bypass this important source of intimacy and arousal.

And yet, we do. Kissing is usually a no brainer in a new relationship, when you can't get enough of each other, but once a bit of time passes, the kissing often disappears along with the novelty of new love. Yet women need kisses in order to maintain a sense of sexual connection and desire. In long-term relationships, the only way a woman will maintain her desire for her mate is if she feels emotionally connected to him and if her "slow-burning stove" of desire is quietly and consistently stoked.

everyday kissing So this is important: Think about when you last kissed your partner (and I mean really kissed him!). The answer might surprise or even disturb you. It's hard to imagine that such an intimate, tactile expression of love can so easily be lost in a long-term

Add new sparks to your long-term relationship by experimenting with different kissing styles: soft and sweet, sexily romantic, or bold and passionate.

the *testosterone* transfer

The pressing of lips has a second purpose: It may also help prepare a couple for intercourse. Men, who have higher levels of testosterone in their saliva, might actually use deep French kisses to help transfer testosterone to their mates. This can increase libido and help ensure that both partners are at a similar arousal level. Hence, kissing might do more than get a woman physically primed for sex; it might get her hormonally primed as well.

relationship, but it happens to the best of us. And, fortunately, it doesn't mean that your love or attraction for each other is diminishing. Usually, it simply means that you are busy and have fallen into a habit of forgoing small signs of affection. This is a fairly easy problem to fix, especially once you decide that you really need these kisses in your everyday life.

Making an effort to kiss more often is important because it will help to keep you in a more sensual frame of mind. It is also important because it can help you establish what I call "non-demand" kissing. This type of kissing comes with no strings attached. In other words, you kiss just for the sake of kissing, with no expectation that sex must follow. In long-term relationships, kissing often occurs only before sex, which means that couples sometimes avoid kissing if they don't have the time or energy for intercourse. This is a mistake. Not only is kissing enjoyable in its own right, it can help establish a romantic and intimate mood that will last throughout the day or week until you do have time for sex. (As I've mentioned, this is especially crucial for women, who generally need to build that "slow burn" of arousal over a longer period of time.) Regular deep kisses and make-out sessions that are not part of foreplay and do not lead to expectations of intercourse help her feel ready when a sexual opportunity presents itself.

the 10-second ritual If you are truly out of the habit of kissing, it might feel a bit odd to suddenly start locking lips. Use this nervousness to your advantage. Pretend you and your partner have just started dating and are still in those first throes of awkwardness. When you are out on a date, lean in for a deep, intimate kiss like you would have soon after you met. Your partner will be taken aback by this romantic, erotic gesture, and you will soon find that your initial nervousness is replaced by desire and arousal.

You can also make a pact to kiss each other for 10 seconds each day. Although this might sound unromantic and even forced, it will help you get back into the habit of kissing daily. If it feels awkward or even silly, go ahead and express those feelings to each other, but realize that this practice is only temporary. Once you both get back into the habit of kissing every day, you won't need to "clock in" anymore.

Another benefit of the 10-second kiss routine is that it can give you a chance to experiment with different kinds of kisses. Make it your goal to surprise, titillate, and seduce your partner every time you kiss. Experiment with deep, erotic French kisses; soft, innocent kisses; and playful, nibbling kisses. Let your hands roam to new places as you kiss.

Clasp her face in your hands. Run your fingers through his hair or entwine your hands together. Be open-minded and find out what feels good, what feels sexy, and what makes your heart race.

kissing environment
As you experiment with different types of kissing, you should also explore new places and times to lock lips. Do you usually kiss goodbye in the morning as you leave for work? Make it a habit to wake your partner with a deep kiss first thing in the morning. (Worried about morning breath? Just make sure you have some water by your bed to help freshen up.) Or give your partner a sexy kiss right when she walks in the door from work, pinning her up against the wall before she even has time to put her purse down. She will be blown away by your spontaneity and commanding attitude.

Other good places for a make-out session include: the back of a movie theater, the middle of the produce aisle at the grocery store, waiting in a line, at the dinner table, in the shower, in the coat room at a boring party—basically, anywhere and everywhere!

the whole-body kiss
As all lovers know, kissing isn't just for the lips. One of the most sensual ways to use your mouth is to explore the whole landscape of your partner's body. Kiss her neck, earlobes, breasts, nipples, vulva, inner thighs—anywhere you want to taste and caress with your lips. To jump-start a sensual evening, slowly start kissing your partner, interspersing deep, erotic kisses with light, gentle kisses all over his body. Be creative. Run your hands along his skin as you explore his territory with your mouth, using your lips to seduce and excite him. Move from less intimate erogenous zones (such as the neck and arms) to areas of peak sensation (such as the genitals).

Whether you are making up after a fight or have been too busy to connect lately, these full-body kisses can get both of you on the same page in no time flat. Get into the habit of bringing these kisses back into your love life, whether that means kissing her belly as you wake her up in the morning or getting into a hair-pulling, hickey-giving make-out session when you come home from date night.

As you do this, tell your partner what you like. Giving feedback during kissing serves the same purpose as giving feedback during sex: it ensures that your needs are met and that the experience is enjoyable for both of you. Tell your partner: "I love it when you kiss me softly and slowly," or "Let me show you how I love to be kissed." Talking about kissing is erotic, it renews your intimacy, and it makes the experience feel fresh and new even if you have been together for years.

Grazing her lower abdomen with your lips can be an incredibly erotic intro to sex. You can also use this type of kiss to wake her up in the morning—although it might just keep you in bed for a few more minutes of liplocking!

sexy, sultry embraces

Nothing can replace your partner's embrace. Whether you call it hugging, spooning, or cuddling, most people find that there is no happiness like the feeling of being securely wrapped in their partner's arms. Like a kiss, an embrace can serve many purposes: it can be reassuring, calming, encouraging, tender, playful, or erotic.

physical connection Sometimes a hug at the end of a long day is all you need to get in a more positive, more sensual frame of mind. In fact, studies have shown that physical affection and happiness go hand in hand. One study found that women who were hugged multiple times a day by their partners had lower blood pressure than women who did not receive such expressions of affection. Another study found that people who gave five hugs a day for a month were happier than people who did not offer hugs.

The power of physical embraces can't be overstated, especially in a relationship. Staying connected physically won't necessarily translate into staying connected emotionally, but it is a very good starting point. Begin by slowly incorporating all of those forgotten embraces back into your life. Come to the door when she returns from work and give her a long, powerful hug, rather than simply shouting, "Hey, I'm in here" from the living room. Cuddle in bed before you turn off the lights at night, and lie beside each other on the couch while you watch the news. Take every occasion to offer these embraces and caresses, because this type of touch is the glue that keeps you connected and intimate.

stroking Just as with kissing, there are many techniques for stroking your partner, and each expresses a slightly different emotion. During a standing embrace, stroking adds eroticism, giving you more intimate access to your partner's body. Keep the length of your bodies fully touching and entwined as you embrace. Feel the muscles in his arms and chest with your hands, reach up and nibble on his neck or earlobes, or caress her back and buttocks.

In a lying embrace, stroking can help prime both partners for sex. There are many hot spots to caress as you lie together. Run your hands up and down her body as you caress her from head to toe, spending time on forgotten areas like the small of her back, the soft skin in between her thighs, her neck, or the backs of her thighs.

kama sutra embraces While hugging isn't traditionally thought of as a sexual action in our society, it has the potential to be as erotic as any other act of foreplay. The *Kama Sutra* suggests a number of different embraces for lovers—both new and old—to increase attraction and intimacy, and to show desire. Try these four classic embraces to ignite instant passion.

An embrace can be both playfully flirtatious and intensely erotic, strengthening your bond and your desire for one another.

Straddling your partner in a sitting embrace possesses all the urgency of sex, even if you are fully clothed.

touching With this embrace, you can feel the shape and desire of your partner's body without even taking off your clothes. The act of touching is simple: he moves in close either beside or in front of his partner, and gently presses his body against hers. The unexpected intimacy of this movement is flirtatious and seductive. You can also perform this embrace from behind—try practicing it while you are waiting in line somewhere.

rubbing The rubbing embrace is touching's daring older sister: As your bodies are fully pressed against one another, gently gyrate, moving your bodies together in a rubbing motion. Think of it as dancing without music. Although this embrace is intimate, I dare you to try it in public, at least once. Find an enclave at a restaurant or a darkened room at a party, and see how performing this movement with potential voyeurs might make it that much sexier.

pressing Although only a few seconds long, this embrace offers a strong sexual charge. Here's how to do it: the man presses his body against his partner, pushing her up against a nearby wall. You can add even more intensity by interlacing your fingers and holding her hands against the wall, mimicking the act of lovemaking. Because this move is so sensual, you might prefer to perform it somewhere you have complete privacy to enjoy its erotic undertones fully. Try to incorporate it early in the day or evening, so that you can experience these feelings of desire and eroticism as a taster long before you and your partner enter the bedroom. And, of course, it doesn't have to be the man who takes charge!

milk and water With this embrace, you will tackle even more of your inhibitions—trust me, it will pay off tenfold in the bedroom! The man should be sitting for this embrace, and the woman simply positions herself in his lap facing him, so you can wrap your arms and legs around each other and press your whole bodies together. This embrace simultaneously gives you comfort and intimacy, and a strong sexual thrill as your hot spots press together. Because it's so intimate, it's probably better kept for private spaces rather than public displays of affection, but because it's easy to get into and out of you can use it to grab a few moments of intimacy at odd times, such as while the kids are out of the room, or if you're parked somewhere quiet in the car together. The surge of desire and connectedness that you both feel will be breathtaking.

public *touch*

To stay truly connected, it's also important to incorporate physical touch into your activities outside the home. On a date, hold hands as you walk down the street, or as you are sitting in a restaurant. At the movies, sit in the back row and have an old-fashioned make-out session like teenagers. At a party together, stroke his back while you are standing together, or put your arm around her chair. These actions are not about making the room aware of your coupled-up status, but rather about keeping your physical connection alive, even while in the midst of a crowd. Soon these physical exchanges will become a natural and beloved part of your relationship routine.

undressing to seduce

Being naked is sexy, but undressing is even sexier. In fact, you can actually turn this everyday event into an art form. Slowly disrobing tantalizes the imagination and is the best kind of visual foreplay, which explains why everyone from burlesque dancers to strippers can make so much of such a simple act.

the attire First, you have to prep your costume. You can't do a sexy striptease if you are wearing granny panties or unflattering briefs. Ladies, if you don't love lingerie, you can still add sex appeal by wearing a pair of lacy briefs and a tank top. If you are more daring, try the classic garter belt with a thong and thigh-high nylons. Men, fitted boxer-briefs are a form-fitting option that will show off your shape.

Anticipation is what makes stripping so sexy. The more clothing you have on, the more time you will have to reveal yourself. Classic, sexy options are always a good place to start: think a suit that hides a pair of flattering Y-front briefs or a dress that conceals a sheer bra and revealing panties. For added layers (and sex appeal) incorporate props like a feather boa or a pair of satin gloves that you can slowly peel off. Always remember that the most important thing is for you to feel comfortable and happy with your outer- and underwear. Confidence is crucial for a sexy striptease!

the scene Set the scene with the right lighting and music. Harsh, bright lights are not flattering for anyone, no matter how many hours you spend in the gym. Instead, opt for sexy candlelight, or try strings of lights or colored light bulbs (blue, red, or even pink are soft and seductive).

Choose music that lends itself to slow, purposeful movement, such as classic R&B or atmospheric jazz. If you prefer to have a more upbeat striptease, consider pop or eighties rock, or something else with a beat that will get your partner smiling and in the mood. Songs that have special memories for you both can also be an intimate way to set the mood for your striptease performance.

the moves Once your partner is in position, start the music and get moving. Focus on the beat and the lighting and the knowledge that you're in charge—all of these things will help you feel sexy. Move your hips, seductively remove a layer of clothing, and look your partner in the eye. If it seems difficult to maintain constant eye contact, interrupt intermittently by looking from under your lashes, turning your back and giving your partner a view from behind, or simply closing your eyes and moving with the music.

After a few pieces of clothing have been dropped, include your partner in the act. Be creative with your moves: For instance, incorporate a seductive chair dance by straddling him and gyrating on his lap. Let him look but don't let him touch. Maintain control by using your hands and even your breasts to caress him gently. Have him lie down so you can straddle him. Confidence and desire are what a striptease is all about, and these should be heightened with each layer of clothing you remove.

undressing your partner Finally, it is time to undress your partner! Now that he or she is your willing hostage, begin unbuttoning his shirt and slowly run your hands over his chest. Pull off his shirt and move slowly down to his pants. If you're playing the male stripper, you can slowly unhook her bra and gently massage her breasts, giving her a taste of what's to come.

Next, use your teeth to gently unhook his belt (or your hands if you don't think you can pull this off). Men, use your teeth to gently pull off her panties, allowing your hands to seductively graze her thighs. Throughout this act, remember to maintain eye contact and to share plenty of deep kisses. By the time you are both undressed, the fire will be fully stoked.

Near the end of your striptease, allow your partner the touch he—and you—crave. After building arousal levels for several minutes, it will be all the more satisfying.

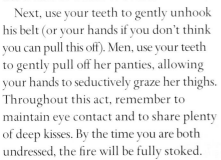

overcoming nervousness

Your partner is guaranteed to love your performance, even if you miss a beat. If you feel shy or embarrassed, remember the mantra "fake it till you make it." False confidence can soon give way to real confidence. Once you see your partner's enthusiasm, you will feel more comfortable. You might not have the skills of someone who strips for a living, but if you are having fun, your partner will enjoy every minute of it—and so will you.

undressing each other Always undress your lover with reverence, as if you are unwrapping the most beautiful present anyone has ever given you. Undo each fastening slowly, and spend time stroking and kissing each piece of skin as it's revealed. Make undressing a part of foreplay, instead of a means to an end, so you won't take each other's bodies for granted.

trace the line of her shoulder
through her blouse

pull her panties
with your teeth

unfasten his pants
oh so slowly

fondling *and stroking*

The right touch can be as intimate and erotic as sex itself. Knowing how to give your partner pleasure with just the flick of your tongue or the tip of your finger is a powerful way to ensure that he or she enjoys every erotic encounter. Fondling is one of the most erotic, seductive, and intimate ways to bring your partner to orgasm.

stroking her Your hands are a potent tool for giving your partner pleasure. Gently rub her body, focusing on erogenous zones like her neck, inner arms, and inner thighs, then slowly work your way to her breasts and genitals. The options for stimulation are endless: caress, nibble, pinch, kiss, lick, and find new ways to use your tongue and hands. Gently stroke around her breasts, then move inward toward her nipples. Do the same with her genitals, following an "advance and repeat" pattern. Use your fingers to stimulate her clitoris and play along her inner and outer labia, exploring every inch of her vulva. The idea is to keep her arousal level high but not yet orgasmic. Bring her to that brink of pleasure and then take her down again by decreasing the intensity of your stimulation—then increase her arousal again by intensifying your rhythm or pressure. The longer you delay her orgasm, the more powerful it will be when it occurs.

Experiment with different intensities and speeds—and don't neglect the rest of her body. While one hand stimulates her genitals, your other hand can rub her breasts. You may also try inserting a finger inside her vagina or anus while you continue to give her plenty of external stimulation (if you need a quick anatomy lesson, see page 27).

stroking him One of the keys to becoming a master of manual stimulation is lubricant. Saliva will work if no lubricant is handy—in fact, there are lots of sexy ways to lubricate with your mouth. You might look him in the eyes as you suck your fingers before touching him, or orally stimulate him for a bit, as a tease of what may follow.

Use a grip that is firm but gentle. Men often complain that women use too soft a grip when pleasuring them. If you're unsure how firm of a touch to use, ask him to show you what kind of grip he likes.

It's important to vary the pressure and speed, which you can do using both hands to create two different sensations. For example, with one hand you can stroke the shaft up and down, while the other hand can be stimulating the glans in a turning motion (as if you were turning a door knob). Continue to tantalize him by bringing him very close to the brink of orgasm. (How do you recognize this? Listen to his breathing and the sounds he makes.) Once he's almost there, slow down for a few moments, and then increase his arousal again. Not only will this delay orgasm and intensify his pleasure, but it can also train him to become a pro at postponing orgasm during intercourse.

manual *stimulation* techniques for her

To gauge her arousal levels, pay close attention to her response. Does her breath quicken? Are her chest and face flushing? Is she starting to perspire? All of these are signals that she's enjoying your touch. Here are more tips:

• Graze your fingers along her inner thighs, stroke her breasts gently, and slowly move to her outer labia. Then, begin to explore her inner labia. Soon, she will be dying for you to touch her clitoris!

• Gently start to rub her clitoris. Use your thumb to apply a soft but firm pressure. As she begins to become more and more aroused, you can increase the intensity of your strokes.

• Insert a finger into her vagina as you keep stimulating her clitoris. The first third of the vagina is the most sensitive, so you can play around the entrance or move on to her G-spot, applying firm, deep pressure.

• Stimulate her clitoris while you apply pressure to her perineum.

manual *stimulation* techniques for him

Stroke up and down his penis with a firm grasp. (Use lubrication, so you don't pull on his skin.)

• Try using both hands, with your thumbs underneath his shaft. With both hands, you will be able to stimulate his entire penis at once.

• Use one hand to stimulate his penis while the other gently massages his testicles.

• Use one finger to apply pressure to his perineum while you stimulate his shaft.

sensual massage

Nothing is better than a relaxing massage—except, perhaps, an erotic one. Massage is truly an art form, and the better you understand the technique, the better you're able to perform. Whether you want to relax, restore, or seduce, the right massage strokes are the path that will lead you to happy fulfillment.

massage techniques Picture your partner's body as a blank canvas on which you can use your fingers to draw, sculpt, and create new sensations from head to toe. Master the basic massage techniques, and all that artistry will be within your grasp. The first five you'll want to learn are effleurage, petrissage, vibration, friction, and tapotement. Combine these with your knowledge of erogenous zones, and you'll be ready to tantalize your lover with touch.

• **effleurage** is a fancy word for stroking. For this technique, use deep, intimate touches across the body to awaken your partner's muscles and help him or her relax.

• **petrissage** is a technique in which the muscles are lifted up and away from the body. (You've probably used this method when giving a shoulder massage.) Use this motion across the body, focusing on sore areas like the hamstrings and arms. You can also gently pull on your partner's legs as he or she lies face down, or on the fingers and toes.

• **friction** uses your fingers to work the muscle tissue in deep circles. This is most effective in areas such as the shoulders, lower back, and thighs, where the muscle is thick and carries a lot of tension. Use your thumbs to generate more power and pressure. (Always remember to ask your partner how much pressure to use.)

• **tapotement** uses your fingers and hands to tap on your partner's body, as the name suggests. Perform chopping motions up and down the body to loosen up the muscles and beat out stress.
• **vibration** imitates the motion of a chair massager. It is similar to tapotement—simply shake the area instead of rapping it. Place your fingers on the muscle, leave your hand flat and firm, and shake the muscle area to release tension.

becoming an expert Start by asking your partner how deep your touch should be. Then, notice the response you get throughout the massage. Mix up the intensity and rhythm to match your partner's response. For extra sensuality, add a few genital strokes to your massage, letting your fingers gently roam and explore these erogenous zones. This is a good way to bridge the gap between massage and sex.

If you don't feel comfortable with the idea of massage, you might consider taking a massage class together at your local spa or massage school. Even easier, test the massage waters by scheduling a couples' massage or a spa date. Afterward, continue the massage at home— while your touch may not have quite the same therapeutic effect, the added seduction of a bedroom massage will more then make up for it.

massage oils

As you become more experienced with massage, it's a good idea to invest in a few massage oils. There are a number of different aromas and ingredients to choose from, including oils that warm and tingle, and even ones that are edible. Some massage oils double as lubricant, and most of these can be found at your local drug store. One word of warning: Remember that not all oils can be used as lubricant with latex condoms, including household products like petroleum jelly. Oil-based lubricants can break down the latex. For the same reason, never use silicone-based lubricants with silicone sex toys.

Utilize the five basic massage techniques— effleurage, petrissage, vibration, friction, and tapotement—to seduce your partner and make foreplay even more irresistible.

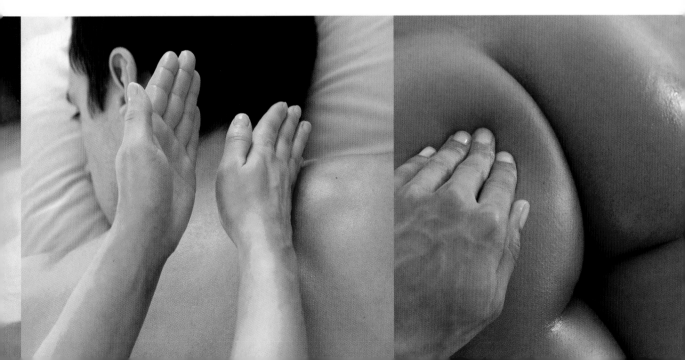

non-penetrative sex

We often think of sex in very limited terms. Oral sex, intercourse, and perhaps anal sex are as far as our imaginations take us. However, there is so much more to sex than penetration—more intimacy, more arousal, and more creative fun. That's the idea behind "Very Erotic Non-Insertive Sex," otherwise known as VENIS.

the rules VENIS essentially turns what most of us think of as foreplay into the main event. The basic rule for VENIS is this: no vaginal, anal, or oral intercourse. Anything else goes. Orgasm is not necessary, but completely permitted—and since just 30 percent of women reach orgasm through intercourse, VENIS is a wonderful way to engage with one another sexually. This is true whether you are with a new partner and want to postpone intercourse, or in a committed relationship and want to try something new. It's also useful for couples that struggle with erectile dysfunction (for more on this, see page 249).

One of the best things about VENIS is that it is just as intimate—perhaps even more intimate—than traditional intercourse. This is because communication and connection are essential to making VENIS work. You have to communicate to explore ideas beyond intercourse, which helps you connect both emotionally and physically. At the same time, your body feels more visible and exposed when you aren't pressed up against each other, and the vulnerability is higher because you can't simply bury your head in your partner's neck.

practicing non-penetrative sex An evening of VENIS allows you to engage in a way that is highly erotic. Orgasm doesn't have to be the goal unless you wish it to be. Instead, focus on experimenting, creating new sensations, and slowing down your sexual experience. Ready to give it a try? Try these as a starting point.

draw a hot bath Place candles around the tub and use some sensuous bath oils. Invite your partner into the tub and bathe her gently. Wash her hair and give her a relaxing scalp massage. Take your time bathing her from head to toe, moving slowly and purposefully over all of her erogenous zones. But remember: no penetration! Instead, find other ways to give pleasure, whether that is with your tongue, your hands, or the showerhead. You can even use a waterproof vibrator or another waterproof toy (for more on sex toys, see pages 180–185).

pull out the sex toys A vibrator can be highly erotic for both men and women. If you haven't ever used a sex toy as a couple before, incorporating one into a night of VENIS is a simple and non-threatening way to begin, because the man won't risk feeling "replaced" by a toy, since you're not leading up to penetration.

expand your fantasies Act out a personal fantasy you share, perhaps even adding a costume or a sexy striptease as part of the act. Maybe you're the policeman (carrying handcuffs and a blindfold) who pulls her over and, instead of a giving her a ticket, stimulates her until she reaches orgasm. Perhaps you are the teacher and you've kept a naughty pupil after school. You get the idea. Let go of your inhibitions, and see how arousing creativity can be.

spend your time together in the nude Sleep nude, put your makeup on in the nude, prepare dinner in the nude. Being naked together without engaging in intercourse will be a new and erotic experience for both of you. Turn up the heat a notch by engaging in sexy activities, like lying in a sexy position on the couch.

try erotic wrestling Gather some towels and a plastic tarp or latex sheets (easily found online or at sex toy boutiques) and place them somewhere private, like the floor of your bedroom. Disrobe, and then oil each other up slowly and sensually before engaging in a slippery and erotic wrestling match.

compose a sexy passage together Describe all the naughty things that you want to do to each other. Or, write your fantasies separately and then read them aloud. You might also watch an erotic movie together, stroking and caressing each other during the action (for some suggestions, see pages 188–189).

VENIS is all about touch, both innocent and erotic. Bringing in props like this strand of pearls adds a feeling of sensual naughtiness.

loving sex is...

ecstatic

We crave sex in part because of its ability to deliver blissful satisfaction and fulfillment. Climax is the pinnacle of sexual pleasure, and it celebrates not only our unique physical chemistry as lovers, but also our mental and spiritual bond. To reach these heights, you must understand how your body works and what brings you pleasure. Experimenting —alone and with your lover—can help you learn what touches will bring the deepest sexual thrill.

the anatomy of *orgasm*

Have you ever wondered what happens to your mind during an orgasm? What causes that pleasurable sense of release, and how does your body process these feelings of arousal and gratification? Understanding what happens to your body—and your partner's body—during the peak of sexual satisfaction can help you to reach new levels of fulfillment and intimacy together.

the orgasmic brain Orgasm is nature's way of encouraging and rewarding us for mating, crucial for the proliferation of the species and for our very identity as humans. Yet while most of us know why we seek out orgasm, we may not know what actually happens during these few sensual seconds. The changes our bodies and minds undergo help explain the unique beauty of human sexuality.

During orgasm, the brain is flooded with information, both from our emotional response and from millions of nerve endings in our genital region. When stimulated, these nerve endings send messages to the pleasure center of the brain—the same area that lights up when we eat something delicious, like dark chocolate. In turn, feelings of pleasure are transmitted throughout our bodies. (This pleasure center can also be activated by more illicit activities such as drug use—which gives some weight to the idea that you can become addicted to love.)

Not only does orgasm activate the pleasure center, but it also causes our minds to lose control temporarily. A recent study from the University of Groningen in the Netherlands found that when men and women reach orgasm, the lateral orbitofrontal cortex—the region of the brain responsible for behavior control—temporarily shuts down. This is partly why we make so much of orgasm—not only is it one of the most intense sources of physical pleasure, but it also gives our brains a chance to let go. Orgasm is one erotic way to recharge and refresh.

orgasm and intimacy During orgasm, our brains are also flooded with oxytocin, a powerful chemical that inspires feelings of intimacy. Known as the "cuddle hormone," oxytocin helps you feel connected to your partner. Both men and women experience this hormone to a degree, although men have higher levels of testosterone in their

Oxytocin, or the "cuddle hormone," is what helps you feel connected and intimate with your partner after sex.

brains, which may minimize its impact. These differing hormone levels might explain why the old stereotype is sometimes true: women like to cuddle after sex, while men often want to go to sleep. It might also explain why men, more often than women, are able to have casual sex without developing feelings of attachment.

This isn't the only post-orgasm difference in the male and female brain. Studies have found that women experience decreased activity in the amgydala (the part of the brain that helps with memory and processing emotions) and the hippocampus (another area that contributes to memory processing) during orgasm, both of which help monitor fear and anxiety. It may be that these parts of the brain are deactivated because women need to feel safe and relaxed in order to reach orgasm, something that seems to be less important for male orgasm. In fact, studies suggest that feeling safe may be the most important factor in determining whether or not a woman reaches orgasm.

orgasm in the wild

Scientists and researchers believe that many animals—or mammals, at least—experience orgasm. Although it's impossible to ask a cat or a wolf if they enjoyed last night's hook-up, researchers believe that animal body language, such as muscle relaxation and facial expressions, indicate that orgasm is likely not only a human pleasure, but also one that extends into the wild.

types of *orgasm*

Orgasms are the ultimate in sexual gratification. In fact, many of us equate this peak experience with total nirvana. Less celebrated, but just as true, is that our sexual responses are as fluid as our relationships themselves. This means that no two orgasms are exactly alike and—even more important—that you should never stop exploring your sexuality and redefining your experiences of pleasure.

single orgasm The single orgasm follows the traditional sexual response pattern that we are familiar with: desire, arousal, plateau, orgasm, and resolution (for more on these stages of response, see pages 12–13). Men experience orgasm in this sequence, although time spent on each stage can vary widely. For instance, a man who practices Tantric sex might spend hours moving through the excitement and plateau stages, climbing up and down the pleasure scale, before he allows himself to attain orgasm. On the other hand, in the middle of a quickie, a man can zip through all five stages in as little as 10 minutes.

Women experience single orgasm much as men do, and can spend a varied amount of time on the excitement and plateau stages, postponing orgasm for as long as they like. Delaying your orgasm can increase the pleasure by heightening the intensity of sensation (and certainly the anticipation), which explains why many of us enjoy pushing the limits of orgasm and seeing how long we can go before giving in to pleasure. This is one of the true joys of sex.

multiple orgasms Women are lucky creatures, because single orgasms are just the beginning. Unlike men, women don't require a refractory period in between sexual experiences. Instead, they can jump right back into the plateau or excitement stage, and can often build their way up to another orgasm in minutes.

Of course, just because women have the ability to be multi-orgasmic doesn't mean that they always are. It takes a good amount of practice and awareness to be able to tap into this ability, and it won't always be possible. Fortunately, there are techniques you can practice that will help you master this power. (For more information on how to orgasm, alone and with a partner, see pages 98–103.)

Not only do women have the ability to experience orgasms in quick succession, but they can also experience different types of orgasm: vaginal, clitoral, and a combination of the two, known as a blended orgasm. A vaginal orgasm is one that happens within the vagina, as the result of penetration. A clitoral orgasm (the most common type of orgasm for women to achieve) happens outside the vagina through direct or indirect stimulation to the clitoris. When you combine the two, you get what it is called a blended orgasm, which encompasses the vagina and the clitoris, and which some people describe as the Holy Grail of female sexual satisfaction.

which type of female *orgasm* is best?

First things first: never judge your orgasms. Freud himself once slipped into this trap, calling clitoral orgasms "immature" and stating that vaginal orgasms were the mark of an adult female sexual experience. This is simply not true. In my opinion, an orgasm is always wonderful and, while they are all different, no one kind is any better than another.

Second, by most counts, women experience clitoral orgasm most often and most easily, since stimulation of the clitoris is fairly straightforward. Vaginal orgasm is equally powerful, and is certainly something you and your partner can try and achieve. The most important thing to remember—whether you achieve an orgasm clitorally or vaginally; one time or multiple times; before, during, or after intercourse—is simply to enjoy it. Explore all the possibilities in your pursuit of sexual pleasure, but don't allow the destination to become more important than the journey.

embracing *self-touch*

Masturbation is good for your sex life because it helps you to get in touch with your own sexual response. It also keeps you in an amorous frame of mind, and can help to contribute to that slow burn I keep talking about. Newcomers to the world of self-touch sometimes think just the opposite—that they will expend their sexual energy on themselves—but fortunately for all of us, sex is the gift that keeps on giving. It's one of the few hard and fast sexual rules: The more you enjoy your sexuality, the more sexual energy you produce.

masturbation for him Masturbation is one of the best ways for men to explore their bodies, improve their stamina, and increase their sexual pleasure. It is also downright fun—a fact that few men need to be convinced of! The more open and secure you can be about masturbation for yourself and for your partner, the more connected you will feel to your body as something sensual and sexy. This pays off in the bedroom—the sexual energy that you create will spill right over into your experiences with your partner, turning your lovemaking sessions into a time of free, fantasy-fueled exploration. Here's how to start.

• **use different types of touch** Masturbation is a natural time to discover new techniques and strokes that you prefer. Run your hands up and down your shaft, feeling your arousal intensify with each touch. Use your other hand to massage and stimulate your testicles, and notice how they respond by becoming tight and full. Twist and tickle the top of your penis, paying particular attention to your frenulum, which is often particularly sensitive.

• **be playful** Written or visual, erotica can feed your sexual fantasies in ways you could never dream up alone (for more on erotica, see pages 188–191). Sex toys can add a host of new sensations to your solo play. Consider using a vibrator to stimulate your scrotum and perineum, or a sleeve to re-create the sensation of being inside your partner.

• **embrace flavor** Lubricants can also spice up your usual routine: experiment with different flavors and materials, including those that warm or tingle on contact. And speaking of flavors, you might consider tasting your own semen to really push your sexual exploration. After all, if you want your partner to taste it, it makes sense that you should also give this a try. Masturbation is a time for you to let your mind run wild and explore your body without any inhibitions.

• **build endurance** There's no need to make every session about how long you last, but it's a good idea to make this your focus every once in a while. To do this, stimulate yourself slowly, stopping before you reach orgasm. (Think of it this way: if orgasm is a 10 on the pleasure scale, allow yourself to reach only a 5 or a 6.) Then, bring yourself down to a lower arousal level, taking deep breaths as you go. Keep yourself stimulated and then begin climbing back up the pleasure scale again. Do this a few times. It might help to give yourself a set limit on the clock—perhaps you start masturbating at 9 p.m., delaying orgasm until 9:20 p.m.

masturbation for her As we've just discussed, when a woman reaches orgasm there is decreased action in the parts of her brain that control fear and anxiety. This means that in order for her to reach orgasm (even while masturbating) she needs to be relaxed and free of stress. If you are new to masturbation, this will be of special importance. Follow these tips to get started.

• **make some space** Find a time and a place when you can be alone and are truly able to enjoy and explore yourself, such as in the bathtub or in your bedroom when no one else is home. Set the scene to help yourself get in the mood. It might feel silly to "romance" yourself, but you will be more likely to reach orgasm if you light some candles and play mood music. Woody Allen once said, "I like masturbation because it's sex with someone I love," and this is the general mood that you should try to create for yourself while masturbating: a mood of love, acceptance, and comfort with your own body.

• **clear your head** This is not a time to think about how you want to lose weight, how you need to mow the lawn, or even how the idea of masturbating makes you feel silly. Of course, it's okay (and sometimes unavoidable) to think about all of those things—the trick is to notice when your thoughts start wandering, and bring your focus back to the present. The act of touching yourself is called self-love for a reason— it's a time to let go of anxieties and insecurities and simply love and celebrate who you are as a sexual being. Seducing yourself, loving yourself, and feeling the different sensations that radiate throughout your body are all part of the program.

• **engage in mental foreplay** Women often need mental stimulation in order to respond to physical stimulation, so it's a good idea to keep a few favorite fantasies at your disposal. This way, you can flick through your mental rolodex whenever you have the time or inclination to self-stimulate. These fantasies can be as wild as you prefer, whether they're sparked by your sexy neighbor, a well-built celebrity, or even a long-ago ex-boyfriend. Nothing is off limits in the fantasy realm.

If dreaming up your own fantasies is difficult, look for inspiration in a collection of erotic stories or a good old-fashioned Harlequin romance novel. A recent study performed at Boise State University found that women who read romance novels have a higher libido than women who do not, which means that a great sex life and an erotic book collection often go hand-in-hand.

ending *embarrassment*

You won't be able to enjoy yourself and reach orgasm if you can't stop thinking about how silly you feel, or how embarrassing it would be if someone walked in on you. Try to replace these negative thoughts with more positive statements: think about how sexy you feel, or how it would turn your partner on if he or she could see you touching yourself. Remember, everyone masturbates, and it's a completely healthy and normal activity, not one that you should feel embarrassed or ashamed of. The more you do it, the more you will be able to think in these sexually confident terms.

Be creative as you explore your body's most intimate parts, following your intuition to learn what touch will feel best.

• **explore everywhere** With these sexy thoughts at the front of your mind, it's time to move onto physical foreplay. Start slowly by exploring your whole body, stroking, squeezing, or massaging your breasts and nipples, running your fingers along your inner thighs and labia, and finally stimulating your clitoris. Use your index finger to begin lightly applying pressure to your clitoris, slowly and rhythmically rubbing yourself. As you begin to get more aroused, you can intensify your pressure and increase your pace.

• **touch erogenous zones** As you touch your genitals, continue stimulating other erogenous zones. Massage your breasts or use your hand to stimulate your peri-urethral area, applying different kinds of pressure to see what you like best.

• **use props** For a full list of bedroom toys, see pages 180–185—and if you don't have a sex toy handy, don't despair. Common household items, such as a handheld showerhead in the bathroom, can apply tons of feel-good sensations on your clitoris and genitals. A clean, tapered wax candle or cucumber can also work wonders (if you are using produce, make sure it is washed thoroughly before). Or you can try common bathroom tools such as a hairbrush handle or an electric toothbrush. With any of these tools, be careful that there are no sharp edges, and if you plan to use them regularly, make sure that you have a dedicated set for your sexual pleasure only. This will ensure that you avoid bacteria that can cause vaginal infection.

• **focus on the inside** Insert your fingers into your vagina and deeply penetrate yourself, feeling the sensations of softness and warmth. Notice the soft ridges of your vulva, and pay particular attention to your G-spot (for tips on how to find this, see pages 27–28). As you explore, use your other hand to stimulate your clitoris. Feel how the pleasure radiates throughout your body, and how your arousal level builds. Use pressure that is intense, then gentle, to keep yourself on the brink of orgasm for as long as you can bear.

• **dream big** If you want to explore multiple orgasm, masturbation is a great place to start. Here's what you do: Once you have reached orgasm, stay present in your body. Continue to stroke your erogenous zones and even your clitoris and labia, but much more softly and indirectly. Keep the erotic thoughts going. The clitoris is typically hypersensitive immediately following orgasm so it can be uncomfortable to continue to stimulate it right away. After about 30 seconds, slowly start direct stimulation of the clitoris or G-spot again. You'll notice that each progressive orgasm feels more intense and that multiple orgasm gets easier and easier with practice. Experience will teach you how to bring yourself up and down the pleasure scale in order to master your multi-orgasmic abilities.

mutual masturbation Once you become comfortable touching yourself, consider a mutual masturbation session. This can be one of the most erotic experiences you'll have with your lover. Whether you both demonstrate your favorite techniques or you simply let your partner watch as you slowly touch and arouse yourself, mutual masturbation can bring a new, adventurous dynamic into the bedroom. Consider the following tips to get started.

• **Start by masturbating alone** You must feel comfortable with the idea of self-touch before you'll feel comfortable doing it with an audience. Follow the above tips if you aren't yet at this point.

• **Next, masturbate when your partner is home** Whisper into his or her ear that you are going to take some private time, sharing a few erotic details so your partner will be able to visualize your plans. This thrilling secret will get your partner's libido revved up, too.

• **Touch yourselves side-by-side** Keep your focus on yourself and enjoy the sexual energy that you can create without even touching each other. Close your eyes or glance at your lover from time to time, but remember to make your own enjoyment the focus.

• **Face each other** Once you have embraced this intimate part of your sexual self, share the experience more fully with your partner. If looking into each other's eyes feels awkward, try watching your partner's hands. Not only is it incredibly sexy to watch each other during this act of pleasure, but it is also an easy way to understand the types of touch that turn your partner on the most.

talking about *desire*

Because it is such an intimate act, mutual masturbation is a good time to talk about your own unique wants and needs in the bedroom. Even if you have a relatively happy and satisfying sex life, there are likely a few desires that you haven't shared with your partner, either due to embarrassment or because you are worried it might hurt his or her feelings. Rest assured, your partner wants to fulfill your every desire, and likely has a few requests to share as well. Creating an open and safe environment in which you can discuss these needs can be a little awkward at first, but by using the tips found on pages 50–51, you can be sure that your first conversations about sex will go smoothly (and perhaps even sexily).

enjoying *orgasm together*

Sometimes orgasm is so powerful and intense that it feels as though every cell in your body has come alive at once, while other times it might be just a blip on the screen of your sexual history. You won't feel fireworks every time, but even a little bit of pleasure can be enough to satisfy your desire and keep you connected to your partner.

stress-free sex While it is also more special, having an orgasm with your partner can be more difficult than having one alone. First of all, even if you've talked about the type of touch you like (and I encourage you to do so), your partner may not be able to replicate the exact stimulation you want or need. Second, it can be harder to relax and focus on your arousal when you are also focused on someone else's pleasure. This is especially true for women, who are nurturers by nature and tend to be more comfortable giving than receiving. In bedroom terms, this means that if a woman feels like her sexual pleasure is requiring too much work from her partner, she will feel pressure to reach orgasm quickly. This type of stress can cause the blood vessels to constrict (including those to the genitals), which can make it difficult to achieve and maintain the arousal levels needed for orgasm.

Thankfully, if you're connected to your partner and open about your needs, you can avoid all of this stress.

First, it's important to remember that men and

If you talk about the touch you need before lovemaking, you will be much more likely to experience pleasure in the act.

women experience orgasm differently. As discussed on page 50, women need to feel comfortable and relaxed in order to enjoy sex. Depending on the woman, this can mean a lot of different things. Perhaps it means taking the time to ensure that the kids are asleep, that your bedroom door has a lock, or that you have cleared away any clutter (for tips on how to do this, see page 65). Or maybe it simply means having some time alone with your partner to relax and enjoy each other's company instead of jumping instantly into the act of sex.

changing your focus
Many of us also need to rethink how we view sex before we can feel free in the bedroom. In our society, women receive so many conflicting messages about their sexuality and their bodies. On the one hand, we are told that sex is dirty and that only "bad" girls engage in sexual activity. However, once we are married or in a monogamous relationship, these messages are reversed. Suddenly, we are supposed to be sexual goddesses, well-versed in our own pleasure and able to orgasm at the drop a hat. Of course, it isn't as easy as all that. For many women, discomfort and embarrassment can translate into an inability to let go and enjoy yourself, even if you have been with your partner for years.

The truth is that only 30 percent of women experience orgasm from sex alone. This is no surprise, considering that many sex positions don't stimulate the main female hot spots, such as the clitoris and the G-spot. The majority of women find that they need clitoral stimulation before, during, or after intercourse in order to reach orgasm. As her partner, it's important to accept that sometimes she'll reach orgasm and other times she won't.

In other words, stop trying so hard. When you let go of the intense focus on the goal, the performance anxiety decreases and you are more present in your body. An orgasm-only focus makes you a spectator rather than a participant in the sexual experience. Instead, simply enjoy the intimacy of being close to your partner. Focus on a specific physical sensation, such as the way his mouth feels on yours, or how soft and smooth her skin is underneath your body. The connection generated by your mutual affection and sensuality is much more than the sum of its parts, so enjoy every touch, lick, kiss, and caress for what it is, rather than trying to make them all add up to orgasm as quickly as possible. This will help ensure that sex builds intimacy, not stress.

simultaneous *orgasm*

Redirecting your focus doesn't mean that you can't set sexual goals. When you're ready, strive for simultaneous orgasm. This can be an explosive lovemaking experience that has true bonding power. Begin by masturbating together and timing your orgasms to come together. It usually works best if the man paces his orgasm to match the woman's, since men typically reach climax much earlier and easier than women. As she's moving through the plateau phase, he can slow down or speed up the stimulation to match her arousal.

Once you've mastered the masturbatory simultaneous orgasm, you can use the same skills during intercourse. As with self-stimulation, he should match his pace to hers, Try these tips, too:
• Spend plenty of time on foreplay. Ask your partner to tell you when she feels close to orgasm, then move on to intercourse.
• Make sure that your position affords plenty of stimulation. Manually stimulate her clitoris as you thrust, or move her hands there so she can see that you want her to stimulate herself.
• Use a clitoral stimulator (for a list of sex toys, see pages 180–185) to stimulate her during sex.
• Perform mutual oral sex, timing your pace so that you reach climax at the same time.

when *orgasm* is hard

Orgasm isn't always easy. Many people suffer from an inability to reach orgasm, whether it is the result of negative messages or experiences from childhood, poor body image, relationship woes, stress, or physical difficulties such as sexual dysfunction. If you are struggling to reach orgasm, remember that it isn't a reflection on your relationship. And don't lose heart: with communication and openness, your orgasmic potential can still be realized in all its glory.

the relationship factor Much of this chapter has been about the physical and mental things you can do to help reach orgasm, but it's also important to make sure that your relationship is primed to its full orgasmic potential. Touching each other in ways you both enjoy isn't enough. Respect and trust are just as key to your relationship satisfaction, both inside and outside the bedroom. To build this trust, you must feel safe expressing your sexual needs and desires. This includes being able to talk about when sex isn't working.

Many people find it daunting to talk about sexual pleasure, which is understandable, considering that sex isn't something that most of us grew up discussing openly. However, there is nothing more important than being able to talk to your partner openly and honestly about sex.

faking orgasm Talking is especially important if you haven't been having orgasms—or worse, if you've been faking orgasms. I don't need to tell you how devastating fake orgasms can be for your sex life. Not only are you cheating yourself out of sexual pleasure, but you are also chipping away at the trust between you and your partner. It may seem like a small thing in the moment, but faked orgasms can make your partner feel deceived and insecure.

If you have been faking orgasm, the best thing to do is to be honest. Start by talking openly with your partner about your sexual pleasure. For example, you might ask, "Is there something you want me to do in the bedroom that I haven't been doing?" When it's your turn to share, you can confess that orgasm isn't always easy for you, and that you have sometimes tried to hide behind a fake orgasm. Emphasize that it is not your partner's fault and that your attraction has not diminished. Then, follow the specific points below.

when she is faking For many men, it can be difficult not to take this news personally. Men love to give pleasure, and part of their sexual enjoyment and self-esteem comes from knowing that they have fully satisfied their partner. On some level, women know this, which is part of the reason that fake orgasms are so common.

Men, if you find yourselves in this situation, remember that her lack of orgasm is not a reflection of your sexual abilities. Quite the opposite—it reflects what is happening for your partner, both physically and mentally, and can stem from factors that are entirely beyond your

Describing what works for you in the bedroom can be the missing link between a mediocre love life and one that is passionate and fulfilling.

seeking *therapy*

Once you start talking about what's really going on in the bedroom, you can start to pinpoint where the trouble might lie. Is it a new issue that started happening after a recent relationship rift? Could the trouble stem from aging or a health issue? When you figure out when the difficulty started and how often it's been happening, you can decide what the next step should be. If it's an ongoing issue, you might consider seeing a doctor. Therapy, even sex therapy, may also be a good option. A sex therapist can help you work through any trust issues, and suggest sexual tips and techniques that can lead you on the road to better sex. (For more on sex therapy, see page 57.)

control. Your partner needs to be the ringleader in accomplishing her own sexual pleasure. You can help by taking the focus off orgasm, and encourage her simply to enjoy the different strokes and touches of sex. Once she knows that you are there to please and not pressure her, she will be much more likely to relax enough to reach orgasm.

when he is faking Up to half the male population has confessed to faking orgasm at some point or another. Unlike the media's sexually ravenous male stereotype, real men are susceptible to sexual difficulties, just as women are. If your partner is struggling with this, it will be a very sensitive topic for him to discuss. It is perfectly acceptable—and often healthy—for you to express that you feel sad or concerned that you aren't meeting his sexual needs. However, remember that support is the most important thing. Listen to his thoughts, share how you're feeling, and then try telling him you are here to support him, and you want to talk about this, even though you know it is a difficult topic.

mutual manual touch Your fingers are an amazingly sensual and precise tool, which is why touching your partner's genitals can be so arousing for you both. Vary the pace for a tantalizingly intimate experience: use long, firm strokes, a whisper-soft brush of the fingernails, and pleasure-building circles to create the deepest orgasm.

play with touch *all night long*

an arched back reveals pleasure

feel the excitement *between her thighs*

loving sex is...
intimate

Certain positions are made for intimacy. Missionary allows for full-body caresses, woman-on-top positions throw inhibitions to the wind, and side-by-side sex is inherently close and cuddly. Each of these positions—and their multiple sexy variations—are satisfying staples for nights when you want to focus exclusively on your partner. Keep them as part of your sexual routine and you'll see your relationship soar to new heights of intimacy.

going down on him

Oral pleasure is an intimate sexual gift. A well-known male favorite, it's simply one of the sexiest ways to make love. And it's easy to see why: the sensations your mouth can give are rich, exhilarating, and incredibly versatile. Performed on its own or alongside penetration, oral is a sensual sex staple.

acclimating to oral Despite all these pros to oral, the idea of it makes many women uncomfortable. There are numerous reasons for this—perhaps you don't feel confident in your performance, or you have had a bad experience in the past, or you just plain don't like it—but almost all of them can be fixed by rethinking your perspective. First, it's important to become comfortable with the basic idea of the act. If you think oral sex is gross, dirty, or wrong, your discomfort will affect your performance. This can make your partner embarrassed or insecure about his own sexuality—not really a turn-on!

To increase your comfort level, begin by identifying your negative thoughts and their possible sources. For instance, did childhood lessons teach you that sex was wrong or dirty? Do you remember this message most strongly during oral sex? (See page 43 for advice on how to confront these issues.) Or do you feel unskilled and out of your element? If so, you are not alone. Many women grapple with insecurities about oral sex. Unfortunately, and unhelpfully, the most common way of dealing with this insecurity is to avoid oral altogether. The truth is that the best way to overcome inhibitions is to be bold and try it out—just enjoy the pleasure you can give your partner.

getting into the act Oral pleasuring can be highly erotic for you as the giver, allowing you to access every bit of sexual power and prowess, and play the role of seducer. If it's hard for you to get in this mindset, remember that your partner doesn't expect you to act like the star of a pornographic film. You don't have to take his entire penis in your mouth or perform all of the feats you see onscreen. Instead, listen to your body and do what feels comfortable and pleasurable for you—these are usually the moves that will also feel pleasurable for him. To ease into the act, you might also start by using a condom, which promotes safer sex and can help you feel less intimidated.

Above all, don't forget the importance of attitude. Oral is most erotic if your partner feels like you are enjoying the experience as much as he is. You can share your arousal in whatever way feels natural for you: look up flirtatiously while you are stimulating him, or tease him by kissing up and down his body, stimulating his penis every so often and leaving him begging for more. Or, simply moan or gasp to express your enjoyment. All of these gestures will increase your confidence and take his pleasure off the charts.

expert techniques While so much of the oral experience is intimate and individual, there are a few classic techniques that are nearly guaranteed to take your partner beyond the brink of pleasure. Before you begin, consider the following tips.

• **Start slowly** A leisurely pace helps you feel more comfortable, and is unbearably erotic for your partner. Tease him by licking the shaft of his penis, or kissing and sucking his glans (try blowing and humming, too). Use your tongue to stimulate his frenulum, an area that is highly sensitive. You can also gently lick or suck his testicles or scrotum.

• **Use your lips** Some men enjoy gentle nibbles during oral sex, but this is a highly personal preference that, if unwanted, can lead to pain instead of pleasure. In general, the rule is pretty simple: No teeth. To ensure that your teeth aren't exposed, cover them very slightly with your lips. Before you do this, jump-start his arousal by licking your lips, or by licking your hand and running it along the shaft of his penis.

• **Use your hands** Combining mouth and handwork gives your mouth a break and extends your partner's pleasure. Use one hand to stimulate the base of his penis while your mouth stimulates the glans. Or grasp his penis with your hand next to your mouth and move the two in tandem (if your hand is wet, it will feel like your mouth is encasing all of him). You can also try gently pulling down on the base of the shaft. This pulls any excess skin taut, giving greater sensation.

• **Stimulate his anus and perineum** Make sure he is comfortable with this idea, then start by stimulating these areas manually. Use your finger to apply firm pressure to his perineum, or insert one finger into his anus while you orally stimulate his penis. You can also lick or suck his perineum, or even use your tongue along his anus.

• **Don't worry about gagging** And if you do, don't feel embarrassed. It happens to everyone at some point, and it doesn't mean that you aren't talented at pleasing your partner. What it does mean is that you should tweak your experience to make it more comfortable. Use your hands alongside your mouth, be purposeful about breathing through your nose so you get enough air, or try using an edible, flavored lubricant.

• **Swallow only if you want to** It can be highly erotic for your partner to see you enjoying this experience, which might be motivation to try it out (if you do, remember that semen doesn't have much of a taste and it's perfectly healthy to ingest it). If you prefer to spit it out, simply use a nearby tissue to dispose of it.

special treat

While one traditional way to give oral pleasure is to kneel on the bed, kneeling on the floor gives you an easier angle for stimulation, and can give you greater confidence. Grasp the sides of your partner's buttocks for support; he can caress the back of your head to keep you close.

going down on her

Female sexual anatomy is famously less straightforward than the male anatomy, which can make it hard to know where to begin with oral pleasure. And, even once you figure it out, there might still be another obstacle in your way: your partner. Many women aren't comfortable receiving oral pleasure, often because they are embarrassed at the thought of their partners being up-close and personal with their genitals. Fortunately, you have the power to change this.

the first step You can help your partner relax and achieve pleasure by starting slowly. Give her a massage, or gently kiss and stimulate other parts of her body. Start with less sensitive erogenous zones: massage her breasts slowly or kiss her inner thighs before you stimulate the clitoris or G-spot. You can also help her relax by reassuring her that you love the way she looks, smells, and tastes, and that you consider it a privilege to be this intimate with her. And remember the other key trait of a great lover: help keep her mind on the moment. Say that you want her simply to lie back and enjoy the experience, and that giving her pleasure is something that you look forward to, not something you want to rush. When you seduce her body and mind, she will be so much more ready for sexual intimacy.

perfecting your technique Once you are both comfortable with the idea of oral sex, indulge in it regularly. Oral sex is not just for foreplay. Especially for women who have trouble climaxing during penetrative sex, oral can be one of the most erotic tools in your sexual repertoire. Follow the tips below to become a master.

• **Use indirect stimulation** Begin by kissing her body, working your way down to her genitals. Then orally stimulate her through her panties—she will revel in the feel of your breath and tongue through silk or lace. Heighten her arousal levels even more by delaying the moment when you finally pull them aside and make direct contact.

• **Flex your tongue** Stimulate her clitoris with soft, slow motions, gaining momentum and intensity over time. Intermittently lick and suck her inner and outer labia (the most sensitive part of the female genitals, after the clitoris). Gently suck on her clitoris as you slowly move your head from side to side, or in circles. You can also flatten your tongue against her clitoris and move it slightly back and forth

passionate gift

The classic oral sex position has her lying back on the bed, while he kneels in front of her and bends over to give pleasure. If she struggles to relax during oral, this is the best position to try—not only is it the most comfortable for her, but it also makes it easy for him to stroke and caress other parts of her body.

or up and down. Switch your rhythm and intensity, but give her time to enjoy each sensation. As you use your tongue, move your hands along her labia and perineum for added arousal.

• **Be deliberate** The most arousing tongue motions follow a plan. Some men swear by tracing the alphabet, while others concentrate on moving their tongue in a circular motion. Cue into her moans and breathing patterns, and take note of the physical changes in her genitals.

• **Keep things interesting** Just because she enjoys one touch or technique doesn't mean that it should become your only go-to move. The same stimulation can become boring or even irritating on an area as sensitive as the vulva, so make sure to explore different parts of the genitals. Stay in one spot for a longer time only if you can tell she is close to orgasm and your motions are about to send her over the edge.

• **Don't forget about your hands** Explore her body with your fingers as your mouth stimulates her genitals. Insert a finger into her vagina and penetrate her, or locate and stimulate her G-spot. You can also rub her perineum with your fingers, or insert a finger into her anus while you are using your mouth to stimulate her.

• **Find the right positions** There are so many positions that can make oral sex comfortable—not to mention sexier—for both of you. Have your partner lie on her back while you give her pleasure. She can also sit in a chair or on the edge of the bed, surrounded by pillows, or even on the kitchen counter while you kneel before her.

kneeling pleasure

This more active position moves her to the edge of the bed (or a chair, or a couch—oral is not just for the bedroom!) while he kneels before her on a pillow. Kneeling at her level gives him easier access to her genitals and puts less strain on his neck—so she gets maximum pleasure.

69 positions

Positions in 69 hold an incredible promise of intimacy. The sensual mystique of this formation—the man's mouth at the woman's genitals; the woman's mouth at the man's—is celebrated for good reason. These positions are the ultimate in sexual pleasure because they allow both partners to enjoy giving and receiving at the same time.

getting comfortable with 69 Part of the reason 69 is so sexy is that it brings your two most intimate areas together. The other part of its appeal is that it requires a total release of inhibitions, which helps prime both of you for pleasure. It almost goes without saying that the bonding that comes with this level of trust and this desire to be so intimate is incredibly powerful. And, if you have a hard time lying back and accepting pleasure without feelings of guilt, 69 is the ideal option because it allows both partners to receive pleasure at the same time.

All those pros aside, this position requires a degree of bravery because it is so unconventional. If you have never tried it with your partner before, it's understandable to feel nervous or even a little embarrassed the first time. In 69, there is no shrinking away from physical intimacy or from full exposure of your most intimate parts. If this sounds daunting, I promise that the sensual benefits, both physical and emotional, make it worth fighting your inhibitions.

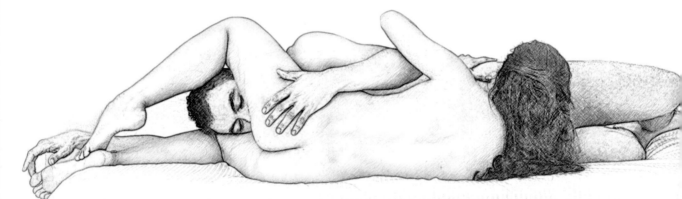

head-to-toe

A gentler style of 69 is performed side-by-side, where each of you rests your head on your partner's inner thigh. The set-up can be a little trickier, since you will have to angle your bodies toward each other, but it is also more comfortable, since one of you won't have to kneel or worry about resting too much weight on your partner. In addition, it frees up one hand to add manual stimulation into the mix, for an extra level of orgasmic pleasure.

becoming an expert There are a number of different positions that lend themselves to 69 and, as with any sexual selection, the only way to find out which ones you like best is to experiment. As you practice, the first rule is this: don't get hung up on whether you are pleasuring your partner in the "right" way. This adds stress, and one of the keys to 69 is staying relaxed enough to enjoy your own pleasure.

Instead of overthinking every movement, focus on becoming "one" with each other. Notice the strokes, licks, and touches that your partner gives you, and try to imitate that rhythm and intensity. If she is pleasuring you softly and slowly, use your tongue to do the same for her. When he picks up intensity, do the same; 69 is one of the best ways to sync your sexual pleasure and intimacy, and it will give you a chance to reach orgasm together. If you are using 69 as foreplay, watch for when you are almost at your climax level, and then switch to intercourse or another form of sexual play.

props for pleasure

You can add even more spice to these positions by trying a few new elements. Use a flavored lube to help decrease friction and make 69 even more pleasurable and erotic (try piña colada, cherry, chocolate, or any other flavor that appeals), or use a lubricant that has warming or tingling properties. You can also use pillows as props: 69 will be more comfortable for both of you—and will last longer—if you place a pillow under your head or under your partner's hips.

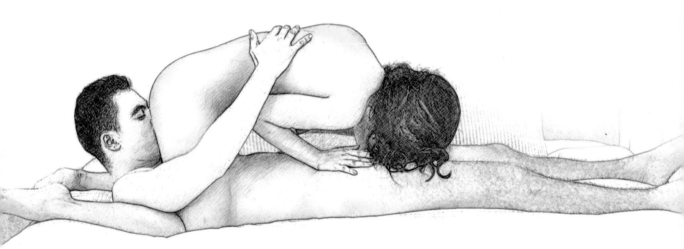

yin and yang

He lies on his back, while she kneels on top, supporting herself on her knees and hands (or forearms). This gives her easy access to his penis and allows her to stimulate his scrotum and perineum orally and manually, while he can bend forward to kiss and lick her genitals. Alternatively, try this position with him on top while she lies on her back beneath him, to reverse the sexual dynamic completely.

the *missionary* position

Creative couples are forever finding new and sexy ways to contort their bodies, but sometimes there is simply no need to reinvent the wheel. Despite the innocence of the name, the classic missionary position is one of the absolute sexiest positions a couple can perform. Time and time again, it has proved to be fulfilling for both partners, delivering a degree of comfortable intimacy that is unrivaled.

why it's a favorite The missionary position is timeless for many reasons. For one thing, it's comfortable for both partners. There are no complicated acrobatic routines involved, and no strain or pressure on the joints. For another, it gives both of you incredible stimulation. The male partner can penetrate deeply for intense pleasure, and can also excite peak female erogenous zones as he thrusts. This position is also inherently intimate because couples can maintain eye contact, kiss deeply, or nuzzle each other's necks.

In addition, there are a number of variations of the missionary that can add an extra dose of eroticism. She can use her hands to stimulate her clitoris and her breasts during intercourse, exciting both her own pleasure spots and her partner's fantasies. He can change his depth and rhythm of penetration by adjusting the angle of his body, whether that means resting on his knees, supporting himself on his elbows, or laying his entire body flat on top of hers. And with CAT—short for coital alignment technique (see page 120)—missionary is reinterpreted with a steady, rocking technique that hits all of her sensitive hot spots and increases her chances of having an orgasm.

Perfecting these positions keeps your love life intimate, and gives equal pleasure to him and her. There are so many ways to enjoy the missionary position that it always feels fresh, while maintaining that sense of tried-and-tested comfort. For all of these reasons, the missionary position holds a sensual spot in every lover's repertoire.

when to do it At once intimate and erotic, this position can fulfill just about any bedroom desire. In its simplest form—man-on-top, her legs wrapped around him—it is the perfect position for nights when you are tired but crave sexual connection. No acrobatics are involved in this quieter technique, and because it puts you face-to-face, it is incredibly bonding and satisfying.

Missionary is also a favorite position for sex with a new partner. Less exhibitionist than many other positions, especially for her, the familiarity of missionary can help make new partners less nervous together. For men, it also meets a desire to be in a more dominant role, and for women, the chance to look into his eyes and see his desire makes missionary deeply romantic. Later on in your relationship, missionary can be the perfect sexual staple to rely on in new situations: try it when you want to get intimate in a new place, such as your lounge, or even discreetly outdoors (such as your backyard or, for the truly bold, an empty beach). Just don't let your passion run afoul of any public indecency laws in the area.

techniques to try

As with all sex positions, a slight switch of the hips can revamp the missionary—and your entire sexual experience. The philosophy here is simple: Just as switching kissing styles can maximize arousal and keep your interest during a make-out session, so can a combination of thrusting styles during sex. Men, try penetrating her very deeply, then using shallow thrusts to stimulate her whole vulva (this will also help you last longer). You can also move your hips in a rocking or circular motion, which increases clitoral friction. Women can vary sensation, too, by practicing Kegel exercises to tighten the pelvic floor and intensify sensation for both of you (for more on how to do this, see pages 34–35).

props for missionary

One of the most useful bedroom props is something you already have in your home—a pillow. This simple tool can help intensify the depth of penetration—and thus the intimacy—of the missionary position. Place it under her hips to assist with orgasm, or underneath his knees to increase comfort.

Sex toys can also be an orgasmic addition to the standard missionary. A small vibrator can fit between you and your partner during intercourse, raising pleasure to new levels for both of you. Or you might try fitting a vibrating ring around his penis, which will stimulate her clitoris as he penetrates. (For more on using sex toys during intercourse, see pages 186–187.)

Missionary can be playful as well as intimate. Looking into each other's eyes and sharing a private joke strengthens your bond just as much as orgasm does.

loving twine

In this classic missionary position, he kneels between her legs to penetrate as deeply as he desires. The opportunities for intimacy here are many: He can caress her breasts, grasp her hand, or bend down to kiss her neck and lips. The only thing this position doesn't offer, it seems, is much clitoral stimulation. She can fix this by wrapping her legs more tightly around him and raising her hips to meet his thrusts, or by reaching down to stimulate this hot spot, or inserting a small vibrator between them.

deep caress

In this raised-leg missionary, he can thrust freely, while she can pull him even closer by tightening the grip of her legs. His legs stay stretched out behind him, which puts his pelvic bone at the perfect angle to rub against her clitoris—making this position a favorite for female orgasm. The emotional bond is incredibly strong with this position, too—both partners can caress to their hearts' content while they watch the mounting lust and pleasure on their lover's face.

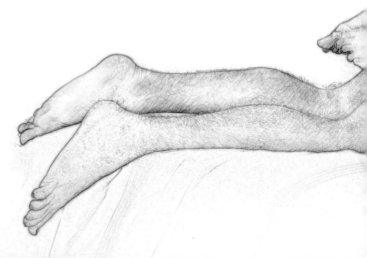

pull him close

This emotional position lets both couples lead. While he's in the dominant role, she can use her leg to dictate the depth and pace of his thrusts, pressing him gently with her heel when she wants him more deeply inside her. Bending her leg in this way also adjusts the angle of her vaginal opening, allowing for more intense penetration. Just as sexy, this position allows full access to just about every other erogenous zone, and lets you gaze into each other's eyes as you climax.

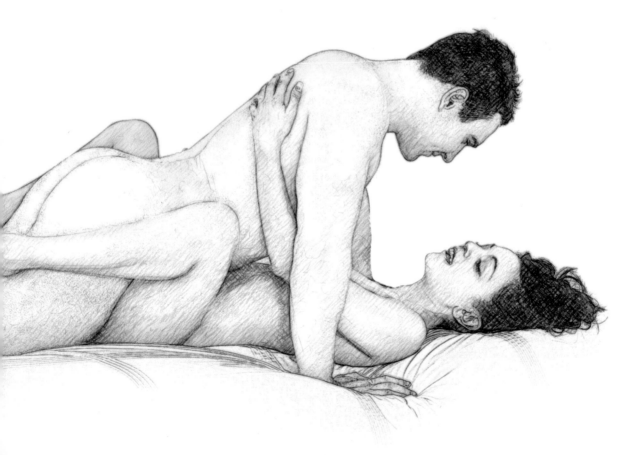

good connection

A *Kama Sutra* classic, this position brings you extra close. He lies on top, while she bends her legs around his waist, encircling him with her body. This whole-body contact builds extreme intimacy, and also allows perfect coital alignment, which means that he can rub against her clitoris as he thrusts.

eager lover

Men love this position for its inherent expression of female desire. She spreads her legs, arches her back, and offers her body by thrusting her hips up to meet him as he penetrates (place a pillow under her hips for a closer contact). For greater friction, she can exercise her Kegel muscles, squeezing his penis each time she drops her hips back down.

sweet and simple

She creates a sensual "lock" between her body and her partner's body by squeezing him between her thighs, fixing them both in place. He can feel the urgency of her desire by how tightly she squeezes.

seductive pose

This is another male favorite, since she opens herself up to him completely. He will love the feeling of the length of her legs exposed to him. Surrendering yourself to your partner's passion can be very sexy, and you can always relax your legs by resting your heels on his bottom to take control back again.

wrapped together

For maximum intimacy, stay tightly entwined. Here, the male partner is on top of the female, while she stretches one leg straight in front of her on the bed. She wraps her other leg around her partner, creating leverage for him to penetrate her deeply.

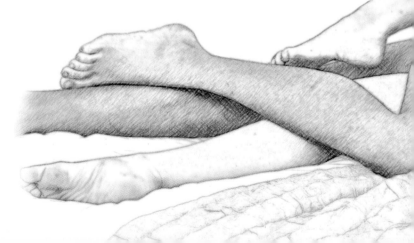

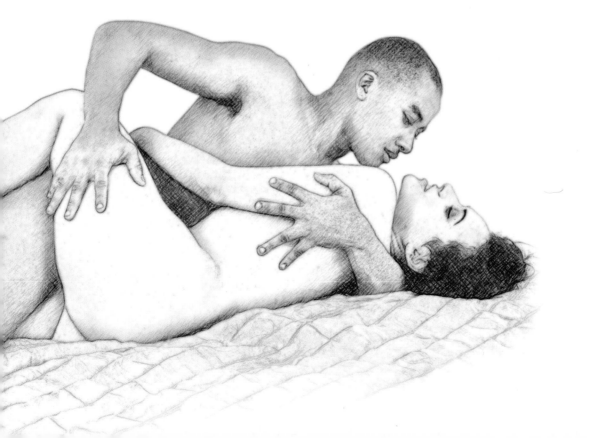

pressing close

This supremely sensual position helps align your sexual hot spots. To start, assume the missionary position. She brings her knees to her chest and he positions himself slightly higher than usual. Instead of penetrating in traditional "in-and-out" fashion, rock back and forth together. This will allow for greater clitoral stimulation, and can also help him to last longer—making it a true female favorite.

positions for emotional intimacy

We often seem to get hung up on the physical side of sex, but the fact is that, for many couples, the emotional intimacy of making love is just as important as the physical pleasure. The closeness and bonding that we share with our partners during good sex are vital to our lives, our well-being, and our relationships.

intimacy and relationships In your relationship, intimacy is what keeps you and your partner bonded. It's the glue that keeps you connected, during good times and bad. And relationship intimacy is closely tied to intimacy in the bedroom. If you and your partner feel disconnected emotionally, your sex life will suffer, and so will your relationship. Creating intimacy takes work, but once it gets going intimacy is self-generating. The more you work to grow closer, by communicating your needs to each other and making your relationship a priority, the more intimacy will grow organically between you. So make sure you stay in the habit of emotional and physical intimacy as part of your day-to-day life together.

Intimacy translates to better sex because it leads to honesty and openness, both of which are crucial when it comes to creating a great sex life and lasting connection. You need to be able to express your needs and desires to your partner throughout your relationship, especially when it comes to sexual needs, and feeling comfortable with each other allows you to bridge this gap and talk about the things that really matter without feeling shy or embarrassed. This can help to safeguard your relationship long into the future.

intimacy and sex Intimacy in sex is an extension of intimacy in your relationship—it's built on closeness and consideration for your partner, as well as desire. Intimate positions may not provide the most intense physical stimulation, but they allow you and your partner to connect through the whole of your bodies, so you can concentrate on physical and emotional closeness as much as pleasure and orgasm.

The good old missionary position is great for intimacy. The whole length of your body is pressed against your lover, and your faces are close together so you can kiss, whisper, and see the pleasure you are giving and taking. The classic spoons position also offers plenty of full-body contact, and while you can't gaze into your lover's eyes in this position, your faces are close enough to talk and to kiss.

Seated positions, where you wrap your limbs around each other, such as Yab Yum, are ideal for intimacy, partly because neither partner has much freedom of movement. This means you have to stop focusing on thrusting toward orgasm and live in the moment, pressing your bodies close together and really feeling every sensation that your partner gives you. And, since you're not lying down, these positions give you options for intimate lovemaking outside the bedroom.

the *position* list

Try these other positions when you and your partner desire slow, intimate lovemaking:

- Loving Twine (page 118)
- Pull Him Close (page 119)
- Good Connection (page 120)
- Sweet and Simple (page 121)
- Wrapped Together (page 122)
- Loving Embrace (page 128)
- Tight Squeeze (page 130)
- Legs Entwined (page 136)
- Yab Yum (page 222)

woman-on-top positions

Simply put, woman-on-top is one of the best ways to achieve sexual pleasure. Particularly stimulating for women, these positions give her the reins in the bedroom, allowing her to control the depth and rhythm of penetration and to maximize clitoral stimulation. This means that women (and their lovers) learn what often seems elusive: how to reach ultimate, orgasmic satisfaction.

finding your rhythm As with the missionary position, varying your pace and rhythm during woman-on-top will help you both reach maximum arousal levels—so make sure to mix things up. Give him just a taste of pleasure with shallow penetration that requires him to lift his hips to meet you. Then, become more forceful with your thrusts, allowing him the deep contact he craves. Teasing him in this way will play up your sexy dominatrix side. (One caveat: Be careful when you are thrusting at full force. If you come down wrong and miss your mark, you can seriously injure his penis.)

As you move, show him how much you enjoy the feel of his body beneath yours by moaning or catching his eye seductively. And get him involved in the stimulation. Place his hand on your breast or your clitoris, so he can see where you want to be touched and what will bring you closer to climax. You can also generate clitoral stimulation organically, since his body rubs against yours as you move. Experiment with different techniques and types of movement to see what brings both of you pleasure in this position.

woman-on-top variations There are many ways you can play with woman-on-top. Consider reversing positions, so that you are facing away from your partner (looking toward his feet). Situated like this, you can lean forward and use his legs for support as you gyrate up and down, while he can enjoy a saucy view of your backside. Or you might sit facing him with your arms resting on his legs behind you. This will encourage your back to arch more sharply, providing a different angle of penetration and giving you the chance to play the exhibitionist, overtly expressing your desire. Another variation is to rest on your legs, or to sit and rest on the balls of your feet, moving up and down as you do so. Penetration in this position will be shallow, but will tease the sensitive tip of his penis and the whole of your labia, which can build up to a mind-blowing climax.

Despite the fact—and perhaps partly because of it—that woman-on-top is a female-dominant role, each of these variations is incredibly arousing for men. The primary reason for this may be that these positions provide men with the visual stimulation that is so crucial to the male sexual appetite (one of the reasons men love porn so much). A man's arousal is linked to what he sees, and enjoying your assets up close and personal as you take control and move against him is incredibly erotic.

For men, part of the pleasure of woman-on-top is seeing you take control. Pounce on him when he arrives home from work, leaving no question as to what you want.

tailor made

He lies flat on the bed while she sits on top, facing him, with her legs crossed in his lap. In this cross-legged position, she can move up and down, using his body to help support and balance her. This allows her to control the angle of penetration, directing his penis to where she wants it.

loving embrace

This is the classic missionary position reversed, but with the same capacity for building intimacy. The woman lies on top and controls the thrusting. He will enjoy the sensation of her swiveling hips, a sensual change from the usual thrust of man-on-top intercourse.

driver's seat

The woman is all-powerful in this position! To start, he lies flat on his back as she squats over him and guides his penis inside her. Then, she leans back, grasping his legs for support and swiveling her hips in a churning motion, providing the aggressive force he craves while also meeting her own need for clitoral stimulation.

the upper hand

Few things say dominatrix like this position. He lies down while she kneels on top of him, gyrating and moving her hips in order to control the penetration. He can reach up and stimulate her breasts or clitoris, or reach behind and stimulate her perineum. This position requires her to have very strong quads, so until you work up your strength it will be an exciting, but not a long-lasting, position—great to finish off a more lengthy lovemaking session.

tight squeeze

In this quieter version of the classic cowgirl, he lies back with his legs stretched together in front of him. She then sits astride him, guides his penis inside her, and bounces up and down, gently at first and then with greater intensity as she comes close to climax. As she enjoys these moments of control, she can lean down to whisper, kiss, and seduce.

loving tease

This intimate embrace is also thrillingly erotic. He lies flat on his back, while she straddles him, lowers herself slowly onto his penis, and keeps her calves close to his body. On all fours like this, she can find the right pace and rhythm of thrusting that will bring her to climax, while he can lie back and enjoy an intimate view of her pleasure, with unlimited access to her breasts and bottom. This position is perfect for nights when he is tired and she wants intimacy— although it's pretty satisfying when he's full of sexual energy, too.

do this when . . .
you want to reach orgasm together

Woman-on-top can be one of the best positions for mutual orgasm, because it allows the woman to set a pace that gives her greater stimulation and pleasure. Try placing a small vibrator on your clitoris, to stimulate this peak pleasure point as you move from shallow thrusts to deeper, more intense ones. If you sense him getting close to climax before you're ready, take a break from penetration and rock gently back and forth together—you'll continue to get prime stimulation that will prepare you for a mind-blowing mutual orgasm.

teasing pleasure Our bodies have unlimited capacity for pleasure, and the key to unlocking all of this potential is to play with sensation. Good sex becomes great sex when you knowingly seduce: Inspire shivers of pleasure with the soft brush of a feather, relish the sight of lips encircling a popsicle, rub an ice cube slowly across hot skin. Each of these acts leads to pleasure—and pleasure to intimacy.

wet his lips *with icy sweetness*

tempt her desire
with soft, light strokes

massage her breasts
with scented oils

side-by-side positions

Side-by-side sex is intimate and comfortable for both partners. These positions create deep emotional intimacy, since you can gaze into each other's eyes, but they're not just about sweetness. Sideways positions allow you to twist your bodies in ways that gravity prevents during missionary and woman-on-top sex, and also afford plenty of opportunities for manual stimulation, since you won't need to use your hands for support as you thrust.

the strengths of sideways Perhaps less common, but just as intimate as the missionary position, sideways sex has earned its place as a bedroom favorite. These positions give you unlimited access to your partner's body, help align your hot spots, and allow the whole of your bodies to touch at once, meaning that you will feel more of each other as you make love. This explains why side-by-side positions are so good for creating intimacy and for helping reestablish closeness after time apart. The *Kama Sutra* even recommends sideways positions as the best choice for first-time lovers.

Unlike missionary or woman-on-top positions, sideways sex puts both lovers on an equal footing. Without one dominant partner, making love side-by-side tends to be gentler and slower than other favorite positions—which also means that it can feel more spiritual. These positions are all about sharing sexual energy, and lovers often come away feeling renewed and truly connected.

And yet, for all its quietness, making love side-by-side is one of the best ways to reach simultaneous orgasm. One of the prime benefits of sideways positions is that they make it easy for her to receive clitoral stimulation, either from her partner or herself. He can also stimulate her breasts, and both partners can run their hands across their lover's body, feeling every hot spot as they move together.

when it works Because no one partner supports a great deal of body weight when lying side-by-side, and because the act of thrusting is less forceful, these positions are ideal for times when one partner is recovering from illness or injury, or for during pregnancy. The natural cuddliness of lying side-by-side makes it perfect for morning sex, and it is also an erotic solution for nights when you are both too tired to get on top or perform a kneeling or standing position. In fact, sideways sex is amazing for what I like to call maintenance sex—those times when you don't have the energy or the creativity to try new or unique positions, and simply want to bond through close, sensual contact (for more on intimate sex, see pages 50–51).

However, side-by-side positions are not just for quiet nights. These positions provide incredible freedom and flexibility, allowing you to wrestle, roll, and wind your way across the bed. Take full advantage of these versatile positions and try them on nights when you want raucous, playful lovemaking, too.

Turn a spooning embrace into a steamy lovemaking session: Begin by kissing and caressing your partner's body, then work your way up to sultry, satisfying penetration from behind.

sweet spoons

Although you are facing away from each other, this position is deeply intimate. Both partners lie on their sides facing the same direction. His thigh is pressed against the back of her leg as he penetrates. For added sex appeal, she can reach back and grab his bottom to pull him in, or he can lean down to kiss her neck.

legs entwined

This is a teasing position that dramatically boosts desire. To start, she lies on her back as her partner props himself up next to her. Then, she drapes both of her legs over his waist, opening them slightly to allow him to penetrate. The close friction is intensely pleasurable, but penetration can be difficult, so this position may be best used for delicious foreplay before moving on to something that allows for deeper stimulation.

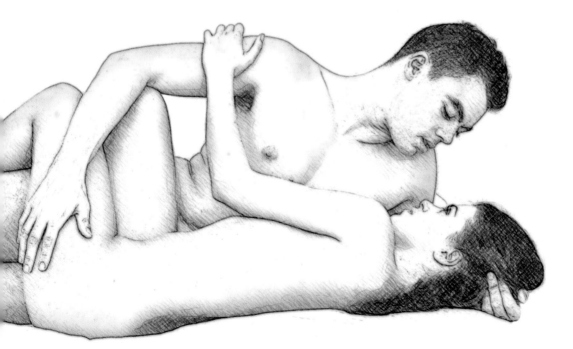

gentle touch

In this position, you lie facing each other. Keeping your legs straight and your bodies parallel to each other, he penetrates her. The natural equality of this position means that either of you can lead—and also that you can use your hands and your lips to stimulate a number of other erogenous zones as you thrust.

positions for making up after a fight

All couples fight. The important thing is to fight constructively, and not to let petty arguments get in the way of a deep and loving connection. Loving sex can help remind you both that the joy and pleasure you find in each other is more important than anything else.

sex and fighting Some couples find the passion of arguing naturally shades into passionate sex, and more power to them. But it's important not to use sex as an outlet for negative feelings. Sex based on anger or frustration can be exciting, but can also become bitter, with one partner feeling exploited or even abused. Instead, think of sex as a way of reestablishing your bond with your partner after a fight. If you don't want to jump right into sex after an argument, there are other routines you might consider, such as taking a walk together, sharing a hot bath, or watching a funny movie to get you both laughing again. Whatever you choose, make sure it gets you on the same page again, free of tension and any lingering sadness or anger.

the best positions Face-to-face positions are some of the best for makeup sex because they give you the opportunity to reestablish the intimacy and affection that was lost during your argument. These positions are also often ones where both couples have equal control, so there's no risk of one partner feeling dominated or exploited. Woman on top positions, such as Tight Squeeze and Seated Seduction, allow for slow, gentle movements and lots of intimate full-body contact. Standing positions such as Twined Together can be fun as well as sexy, helping you go from argumental to playful. You might also try lying side by side to enhance feelings of closeness as you look into each other's eyes and wrap your body around your lover.

the *position* list

Try these other positions for times when you and your partner need to get back in tune with each other:

- Deep Caress (page 119)
- Good Connection (page 120)
- Pressing Close (page 123)
- Tight Squeeze (page 130)
- Sweet Spoons (page 136)
- Seated Seduction (page 143)
- Kneeling Comfort (page 154)
- Twined Together (page 168)

sitting positions

Want to have amazing, intimate sex? The only prop you need is a chair. There are so many wonderful positions that involve sitting—and they aren't only comfortable, but they are also highly erotic. These are excellent positions to practice when you want to have sex outside the bedroom—consider the living room, the kitchen, or even the car. (Just make sure you are safely parked, of course!)

sensual sitting Inherently sexy, sitting positions are also great for when you crave physical intimacy (for example, after a fight). Even more intimate than missionary in many ways, sitting positions allow you to cuddle like no other type of sex, and also give you full access to each other's bodies with minimal obstruction from the bed. Thrusting is not as easy in these positions, so what works best is to focus on a gentle rocking or bouncing motion—and on each other. You can look deep into your partner's eyes as you slowly move in unison together, speeding up and moving faster as the pleasure begins to spread across your bodies. And while your lower parts might not have quite the freedom you'll find in other positions, your hands and lips will, so use them to the fullest.

For women, these straddling positions can be intensely pleasurable because they align his pelvic bone with her clitoris, ensuring you get extra stimulation each time you touch. And if you crave something deeper than gentle gyrating, have him pull your bottom up and toward him as you move, for a more powerful thrust.

location, location, location Sitting
positions are perfect for when you want to have sex comfortably outside the bedroom, and they give you the chance to be creative and spontaneous. Try it in the car, sitting on his lap and gyrating up and down (lay his seat back, so you have more room). Or use these positions in the living room to spice things up while you are watching television on the couch. Seated positions can also work well with countertops, which you can use to indulge in some spur-of-the-moment lovemaking in the kitchen or bathroom.

One of the most pleasurable parts of seated sex is that it lends itself to spontaneity. Try it at the breakfast table for an unforgettably sexy start to your day.

do this when . . . you want to initiate intimacy

A flirtatious and fun sexual stunt is to initiate intimacy by straddling your partner spontaneously. Try it, and see where it leads. For example, you might casually sit on his lap while he is watching TV, leaning down to kiss his neck and undo a couple of the buttons on his shirt, or to take off his belt. If you aren't able to have sex right then and there, this type of playful touch can be a sensual way to stay connected and keep that slow burn alive. If you can have sex, even better—you'll earn double eroticism points for having made the first move and for being in a sexy new location.

ankle wrap

This position is absolute seduction, and it starts with him. He presses his legs together beneath her bottom, then pulls her on top of him, gently guiding her on to his penis. From this position, she can gyrate up and down at whatever pace she pleases, and also lean in to seduce him with kisses—teasing at first, then rough and ravenous. Locking her ankles behind him pulls him closer and may also increase the friction between his pelvic bone and her clitoris. She can also stretch her arms out behind her, moving her hips to alter the angle of penetration.

loving lean

This position is pure, slippery sensuality. Called The Snake Trap in the traditional *Kama Sutra*, it's less about thrusting—which is difficult to do with your bodies positioned this way—and more about writhing and wiggling against each other's pleasure spots. Start with a healthy dose of massage oil to make friction more pleasurable, then use your hands to pin your partner's ankles so that you are truly trapped in this tempting tussle. This playful position is the perfect way to revel in, and then release, any pent-up sexual tension. And all that writhing feels deliciously naughty.

seated seduction

He sits in a chair, while she straddles his lap and faces him. Resting her arms on his shoulders for support, she can move her body up and down as he penetrates her. He will enjoy her dominant posture in this position, and she can kiss to her heart's content, beginning with soft lip grazes and ending in deep, orgasm-enhancing tongue twirls.

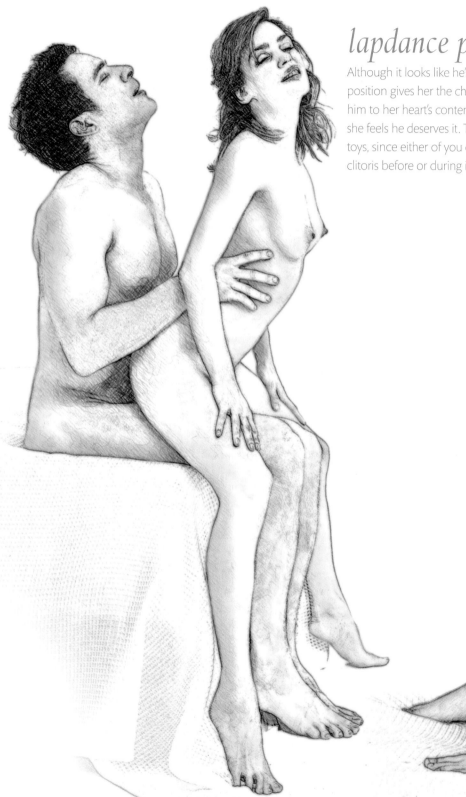

lapdance plus

Although it looks like he's having all the fun here, in fact, this position gives her the chance to take charge. She can tease him to her heart's content, only letting him enter her when she feels he deserves it. This position is also great for using toys, since either of you can hold a small vibrator to her clitoris before or during intercourse.

tangled limbs

He sits on the bed or in a chair with her in his lap, then hooks his elbows under her legs to pull her close for penetration. (If you are worried about being able to keep your balance, use a chair with arms, so that you can hold on more easily, or stick to the bed for this one.) Rock from side to side, enjoying the growing friction between his shaft and the walls of her vagina.

deep desire

He sits while she lies back with her legs spread wide and bent, her feet resting on the floor behind his back. This position allows for the deepest penetration, and lets you try different angles (he can even pull her toward him as he thrusts). He is in control here, so she can lie back and abandon herself to the moment and the sense of vulnerable intimacy.

erotic picnic Combine two of life's greatest pleasures—eating and sex—for a truly decadent bedroom experience. Lick, suck, nibble, and taste sweet, succulent fruit from your favorite parts of your lover's body, stopping only to indulge your desire to kiss and caress unobstructed skin. By the time you're finished, both of your erotic appetites will be piqued.

brush your lips *against sweet skin*

take her nipple
in your mouth

nibble lightly
along her thigh

loving sex is...

passionate

Indulging in moments of unbridled passion is the lover's privilege. Though it's true that, in long-term relationships, passion can sometimes seem scarce, there are plenty of positions that will bring it back to the bedroom in full, fervent force. Try kneeling, standing, or making love from behind to release your most animalistic desires. Whether you have all night to explore or just minutes for an erotic quickie, these positions will ensure that sex is never dull.

from-behind positions

Man-from-behind, or "doggy-style," as it is commonly known, is an incredibly satisfying and exciting position for him and her. Not only does it give both partners plenty of stimulation in just the right places, but it also feels almost animalistic in its eroticism. In all its forms, this bedroom favorite encourages you to relinquish inhibitions, relish the moment, and wholly embrace passion.

why it's a favorite Man-from-behind positions are physically rewarding because they give both partners ample stimulation for all of their hot spots. For women, the angle of the position can help to stimulate her G-spot, and it also gives her partner an easy opportunity to touch her clitoris or breasts, or even her perineum or anus. (She can also stimulate these areas herself.) Men also receive plenty of pleasure because the angle allows them to penetrate very deeply—and to watch the act of penetration, which can be quite a turn-on.

Versatility is also a strength of man-from-behind. These positions work whether you are sitting, standing, or kneeling, which means you can try them just about anywhere. It can also be highly sensual while you are both lying flat—the woman on her stomach; the man stretched out on top of her, supporting himself on his hands or outstretched forearms. This erotic arrangement allows the whole length of your bodies to touch, and she can get clitoral stimulation from the sheets or by rubbing her hand against her genitals.

As you experiment with these positions, play into their natural animalism and embrace true sexual release. Grab her hips and direct the angle of her movement, or gyrate against him and moan seductively. Spank her bottom (start lightly at first to gauge her threshold for pain and pleasure), nuzzle her neck, or gently pull her hair. Let your inner animal out in whatever way appeals to you, and be ready for a wild, passionate night—that's what these positions are all about.

when to do it Men especially seem to crave doggy-style sex for its exhibitionist nature and for the pure, unadulterated arousal of watching the act of sexual pleasure. For women, this means that from-behind positions are perfect for nights when you want to seduce your partner and indulge his fantasies. And, because they also offer easy access to the clitoris and G-spot, these positions can also be good for nights when she is feeling adventurous. Try them after an especially sexy date night, or on an evening when you want to feel the thrill that comes from a new sexual experience. Because you are not face-to-face in this position, it lends itself nicely to playing out sexual fantasies of first-time sex, sex with a new partner, or even sex with a stranger, all of which can boost feelings of passion for both of you.

feminine power

Man-from-behind often seems like a male-dominated position, but with a few slight variations in movement, women can also control the rhythm of stimulation. She can move her hips dramatically, arching her back and thrusting her pelvis back to meet him each time he thrusts toward her. Or she can thrust back while he remains still, which puts her in the dominant position and shows him just how eager she is for pleasure—a huge turn-on.

Most men love the sight of their partner's bottoms, and she can take pleasure in seducing him with the promise of this position.

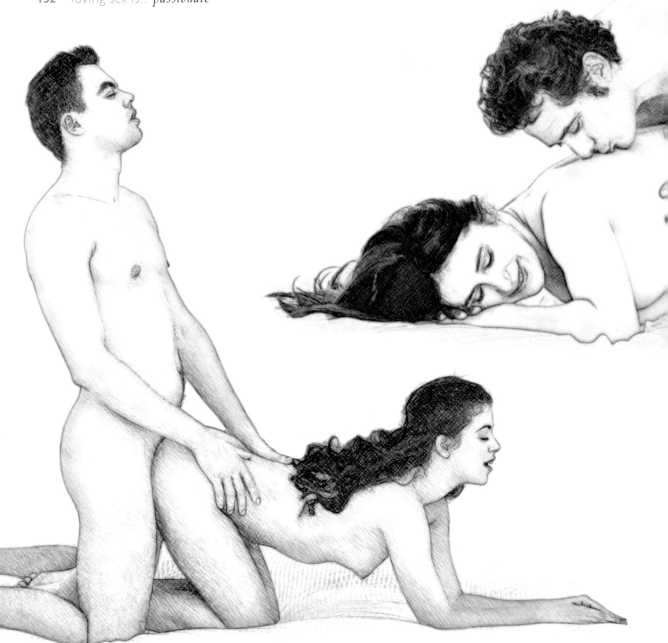

passionate surrender

This is classic doggy-style: She gets on all fours, while he stands on the floor or kneels on the bed and enters her. He can use his hands to direct the motion of her hips and mix up the rhythm to keep things interesting. She can arch her back deeply to improve the angle of penetration—and if he keeps his thrusts shallow, he will be perfectly placed to hit her G-spot.

small but beautiful

In this position, both partners kneel on the bed or floor as he guides his penis into her and she leans forward to create a smoother angle for penetration. Spice things up by letting your hands roam freely—she can even reach around and stroke his thigh. One of the most romantic doggy-style positions, this also allows him to kiss and caress her neck, back, and breasts.

full-body friction

To start, she lies flat on the bed with a pillow beneath her hips, as her partner penetrates her from behind. He can support himself on his knees or lie flat across her body and support himself on his palms. This latter position is especially erotic because it allows your bodies to touch from tip to toe. It also gives the female partner a perfect angle for G-spot stimulation and indirect clitoral stimulation from the sheets underneath her (or from her own hand or a sex toy).

kneeling comfort

This gentle kneeling position is comfortable for both partners—and it can also be extremely orgasmic. To start, he kneels and she lowers herself onto his penis. From this position, she can gyrate up and down on top of him, or he can bounce her up and down while she rocks back and forth, building pressure on his frenulum and her G-spot.

tail spin

This classic kneeling position fulfills many male fantasies. She stands leaning forward against the edge of a bed, supporting herself with her hands, while he stands behind her and bends his knees slightly to penetrate. If he holds onto her waist for support, he can thrust deeply from this position and, best of all, watch his penis moving in and out of her. He can also easily stimulate her G-spot from this angle—and, for extra stimulation, she can pull his hands around to stroke her clitoris.

arc de triomphe

This position is absolutely no-holds-barred—use it when you are so turned on that you don't have time to make it to the bed! Both partners stand, while she bends forward at the waist, using her hands or her elbows to support herself on a countertop, a chair, a desk, or, if very flexible, the floor. He then enters from behind, placing his hands on her waist to keep his balance as he thrusts.

positions for g-spot stimulation

As we've discussed, the G-spot is one of two peak female hot spots that lead straight to orgasm. And, unlike the clitoris, this pleasure zone is best reached by penetration. Understanding which positions will take you there is one of the secrets of being a great lover.

exploring sensation Of course, you can't expect your lover to know how to pleasure you there if you don't know yourself, so the woman should explore her own anatomy first (for more information, see pages 26–29). You can then guide him to the right place, first using his fingers, then during intercourse.

Don't forget that the G-spot is fairly close to the entrance of the vagina—you're more likely to stimulate it through shallow penetration, so that the head of his penis rubs against it, than through deep intercourse, where the shaft of his penis only skims across it.

G-spot orgasms generally require long, sustained stimulation, especially when you're first starting to explore them, so don't necessarily expect to achieve one during penetration. Instead, just enjoy the new and exciting sensations positions like this can offer—and make sure he gives her the additional stimulation she needs to reach orgasm before or afterward with his fingers, tongue, or a toy.

the best positions Simply put, man-from-behind positions are great for G-spot stimulation. The G-spot is on the belly-button side of the vagina, so he needs to penetrate at an angle that pushes his penis against the front wall in order to stimulate it.

One of the best of these positions is Passionate Surrender, in which you both kneel on the bed. The woman can then lay her hands on the bed to support herself while the man penetrates her deeply. Another position to try is Full-body Friction, where she lies full length on her front and he penetrates from behind. If you prefer to make love face-to-face, leaning away from each other angles his penis upward, so that it pushes against the G-spot as he thrusts. Or you could try a woman-on-top position, such as Deep Desire, where she is kneeling over him and leaning back, which allows her to control the angle and speed of penetration. She might have to wriggle a little to bring his penis to the right place, but that only adds to the fun!

The *position* list

Try these other positions for the best chance of stimulating her G-spot during intercourse:

- Eager Lover (page 121)
- Driver's Seat (page 129)
- Sweet Spoons (page 136)
- Loving Lean (page 143)
- Lapdance Plus (page 144)
- Deep Desire (page 145)
- Passionate Surrender (page 152)
- Full-body Friction (page 153)
- Kneeling Comfort (page 154)
- Coming Together (page 163)

kneeling positions

Kneeling positions are a sensual way to add variety to your sexual repertoire. They offer couples an erotic assortment of penetration angles, and each new variation creates a different type of pleasure. These positions are ideal when you want to take your sexual show on the road because you don't have to worry about having access to a bed. Whether you are in the bathtub, living room, or any other room of the house, kneeling sex positions are passionate, erotic, and deeply intimate for both partners.

whole-body pleasure Kneeling positions ignite passion quickly because they allow you to touch each other from head to toe. He might wrap his arms around her waist and fondle her breasts, while she reaches back and grabs on to his bottom or snuggles into his chest. You can also suck on each other's necks easily in this position: Create a youthful thrill with an old-fashioned hickey, or simply kiss and bite the neck lightly to give that erotic rush of pain and pleasure. And, as a bonus, kneeling positions can be very comfortable if you arrange some pillows on the floor, or perform them on your bed.

for him and her Like doggy-style positions, kneeling sex is incredibly erotic for both partners. Sexual pleasure is often all about angles, and kneeling postures are naturally good at this. For women, these positions can be excellent for G-spot stimulation, putting him in just the right place to hit this often elusive pleasure point. The challenge is that it is hard for her to direct him—kneeling positions don't give her much control over penetration or the direction of thrust. Fortunately, there's a simple fix for this: She'll have more control if she kneels but remains on her knees instead of leaning forward on her hands. Just as important, this arrangement gives you lots of skin-to-skin contact, and allows him to easily stimulate her breasts and clitoris. As he does this, you can lean against his body to help direct his gyrations against your G-spot, increasing your pleasure and making climax more likely.

For him, the most erotic element of kneeling positions is the no-holds-barred access to her body and the sense of urgency that they bring. Thrusting can be more difficult and generally happens at a slower pace when kneeling because he is less supported than in, say, missionary—however, the mental arousal these positions bring can more than make up for this.

Add to this the natural connection between kneeling and quick, steamy sex and these positions can truly become favorites with both men and women. Incredibly flexible, kneeling requires no bed, no props, and can be done anywhere and in very little time. Try it when partially clothed to create that must-have-you-now quality that defines all the most passionate sex positions. Or, try it in the tub, kneeling in warm water, with him entering her from behind while she uses the water flow from the showerhead to stimulate her clitoris.

Kneeling positions are perfect for quickies because they don't require a bed.

tightly pressed

She crosses her legs tightly, then rolls back on the bed, exposing herself to him as he kneels over her. Some women find the slightly constricting shape of this position exciting, and he will love the way her intimate areas are exposed to him. If she feels too vulnerable—positions like this with the legs raised can be bruising to her cervix if he is well-endowed—she can wrap her legs around him to slow the pace.

rising passion

He kneels and she lies on her back before him, bending one leg at a 90-degree angle, so that she can place a foot on his chest. Her other leg can rest on his shoulder. As he thrusts, he can hold her leg for balance, and to help him control the depth and rhythm of movement. He can also run his hands up and down her leg, savoring its shape, and even suck or kiss her foot.

kneeling close

In this simple but sexy position, he kneels on the bed or chair while she straddles him. This position is ideal for sex with a toy tucked in between you to stimulate her clitoris, or for passionate sex in unusual places, such as the bathtub. Women, make it even more sensual by pulling yourself as close to him as you can, to intensify the pressure of penetration.

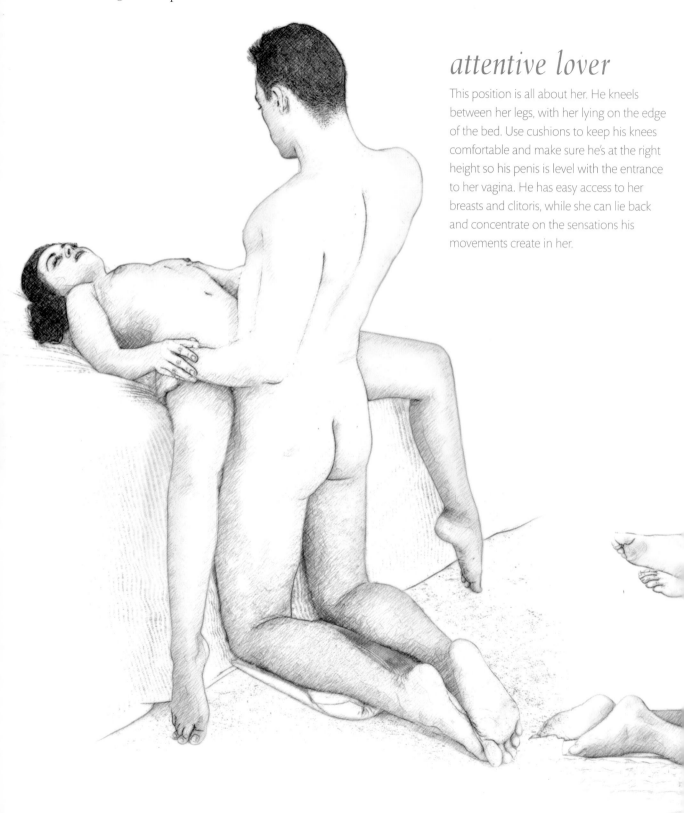

attentive lover

This position is all about her. He kneels between her legs, with her lying on the edge of the bed. Use cushions to keep his knees comfortable and make sure he's at the right height so his penis is level with the entrance to her vagina. He has easy access to her breasts and clitoris, while she can lie back and concentrate on the sensations his movements create in her.

the perfect angle

He kneels, while she lies before him with her hips propped up on cushions. This opens her up to him, directing his penis toward the front wall of her vagina (good for G-spot stimulation) and allowing easy access for passionate thrusts. This position is also good if she has problems with back or hip pain (see pages 270–271).

coming together

He kneels on the bed and she lies flat in front of him, wrapping her legs around his waist and locking her legs in place to create a circle shape around his body. With this frame in place, she can lift her hips off the bed and move with him as he penetrates her. This gives her a satisfying angle for G-spot stimulation, and lets him hold on to her bottom as he penetrates her.

grasp her thigh
as you press between her legs

heat of the moment For pure, unbridled passion, nothing beats spontaneous sex. Its ability to capture and express desire, its innate creativity, and the thrill of trying a new position or location fuel many of our fantasies. Not to mention, these quick sex sessions help us fit great sex into our otherwise busy schedules, transforming us into ardent, inspired lovers.

pull him toward you *rough with desire*

let your lips drift
across her skin

standing positions

Most couples rarely have sex standing up, which makes it new, daring, and highly sensual. Even better, you don't have to be an acrobat or have amazing upper-body strength to perform these positions. There are a number of standing positions that are fulfilling regardless of your age and fitness level—and so many places where you can use these positions to spice up your connection and enhance passion.

uninhibited desire One of the best things about standing positions is that you can make the experience as rough as you want. Like doggy-style, these are wild and uninhibited positions. Keep some of your clothes on or undress each other, ripping clothing off as you go. Give each other bruising kisses as you become wrapped up in the intensity of the moment. Help him unbutton his pants and then reach down and stimulate his penis, showing how you can't wait to touch him. The goal is to create a moment with so much passion that you have no time to get in bed or assume a traditional position—you need to have each other right then and there!

There are so many ways to work these passionate positions into your sex lives. For example, when your partner comes home from work, you can take each other, still partly clothed, right there in the living room or kitchen, leaning up against a wall or countertop. Or use a standing position to perform a daring daylight escapade in the semi-privacy of your balcony or backyard. (Standing positions are great for discreet outdoor sex because neither partner has to lie on the ground and get dirty.) These are also good positions for having sex in the shower or even in the pool—just make sure that you have a firm grip on each other, since water often makes things quite slippery.

the techniques For all the pleasure they bring, standing positions can be a bit challenging if they're new for you. They require strength and balance, and they work best if you and your partner are similar in height (if you're not, simply have the shorter partner stand on a stool or a step so that your bodies will fit together more easily).

Once you're at nearly the same height, he can bend his legs slightly to get the right angle for penetration. A rocking motion can bring waves of pleasure, and can also be easier than thrusting, as you may not have a good amount of leverage. This will also bring his pelvic bone in contact with her clitoris, which is guaranteed to generate orgasmic sparks for both of you.

If you do try thrusting in this position, and if you have enough balance, she can wrap one leg behind him to pull him closer and increase the intensity of his thrusts. As you do this, don't forget to make good use of your hands: He can grip her thigh for support, while she can let her fingers roam from erogenous zone to erogenous zone across his body—or down to her own clitoris.

A huge part of the appeal of standing sex is that it feels so driven by desire: Whether you're in your bedroom, another spot in the house, or somewhere more unusual, the "must-have-you-now" appeal of these positions is irreplaceable.

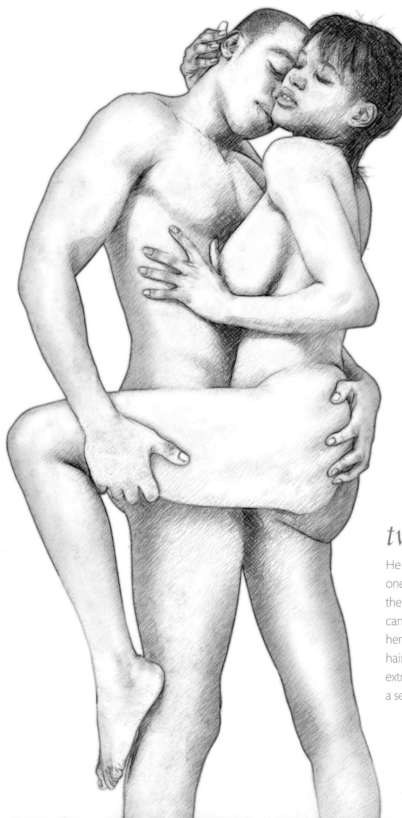

clinging embrace

This position requires a bit of flexibility, but its arousal factor is high. With both partners standing, the woman wraps both her legs around his waist. Try this position near a wall, so that the woman can brace her back against it for support, rather than putting all of her weight on her partner. For even more support, she can sit on another piece of furniture (try a chair, desk, or bed) that puts her at the right height and angle for penetration.

twined together

He stands, while she faces him and wraps one leg around him. For additional support, the woman can lean against the wall, or he can encircle her with his body to support her as she gyrates up and down. Pulling his hair gently or nibbling on his neck will add extra erotic effect, or add a pair of heels for a sexy height boost.

quickie heaven

Both partners stand facing the wall. She places her hands on the wall and bends forward slightly, exposing her genitals to him so that he can guide his penis into her. The wall provides leverage as she moves back and forth with her partner.

positions for passion

Passion is a crucial element in every great relationship. It is the key ingredient that enhances your bond and sets your partner apart from every other important person in your life. A passionate relationship is what we all dream of: something that provides security, intimacy, and adventure.

proof of passion When you think of a passionate couple, you might think of people who can't keep their hands off each other, or who make everyone uncomfortable with over-the-top public displays of affection. However, passion doesn't always look like this. A passionate couple won't necessarily be the ones at the party who make out in the corner. Instead, they are the couple who arrive in a good mood, allow the other to speak without interrupting, encourage one another to share stories, and enjoy each other's company. They seem bonded and connected, even when they are standing a room apart. Reaching this level of passion requires honesty, openness, and a commitment to putting each other first, but it creates sparks that people can see from a mile away.

When making love, passion is the ability to lose yourself in your partner and the moment. Sharing pleasure with each other is the heart of passion, and by taking time to bring passion back into your sex life you can help those sparks to fly in every aspect of your relationship.

passionate positions Remember your early days of dating, when you just couldn't get enough of each other? Rediscovering the positions you tried then will remind you of that electric connection. Passion and creativity go hand in hand, so you may find the best positions are ones that let you move around and try new things. Try Coming Together, where you can easily change the angle of his body or the position of her legs to vary your sensations, or The Upper Hand, where she takes control to achieve the stimulation she wants. Man-from-behind positions encourage passion since they allow deep penetration, and standing sex positions are equally exciting because they have a sense of urgency, as if you can't wait to ravish your partner. Indulge in a few sessions like this every month and you will find that the rest of your lovemaking takes on new creativity, connection, and life.

The truth is that almost any position can become a passionate frenzy if the mood takes you. Passion is spontaneous, joyful, and exciting, and when it strikes you should let yourselves go and just enjoy the ride.

The *position* list

Try these other positions when you want to bring some extra passion into the bedroom:

- Deep Caress (page 119)
- Seductive Pose (page 122)
- The Upper Hand (page 130)
- Lapdance Plus (page 144)
- Passionate Surrender (page 152)
- Tail Spin (page 154)
- Arc de Triomphe (page 155)
- Coming Together (page 163)

mastering *the quickie*

Do you ever feel like you don't have time for sex? If so, you aren't alone. Juggling kids, careers, and other responsibilities often leaves couples feeling as if they don't have a free moment—or enough energy—for sex. If you're committed to creating excitement and sexual connection in your relationship, without a doubt, the quickie is one of the best ways to do this.

creating sexual energy Sex doesn't always have to be a marathon or involve hours of planning and preparation. A "quickie" is the affectionate term used to describe sex that is as fast as it is fulfilling. These passionate sex sessions can last mere minutes, and they can be done just about anywhere. Even better, the more you practice, the more satisfying your quickies will grow to be.

Of course, the most important part of the quickie is ensuring that you are both able to enjoy pleasure even though you are short on time. One of the best ways to do this is to generate sexual energy constantly and create that slow burn of desire (for more on this, see pages 62–63). Taking your sexual energy level from 0–60 mph can be very difficult to do quickly, especially for women, who generally become aroused more slowly than men. However, if you are both always hovering around 30–40 mph, it is much easier to accelerate on the pleasure scale. And guess what? One of the best ways to keep at these higher levels of arousal is to rely on the quickie. Sex feeds sexual energy, so the more sex that you have, the more sex you will want. This is just one reason why quickies can transform your relationship.

techniques and toys As you maintain that slow burn, it is essential that you are well aware of your sexual response and what types of strokes and touches you enjoy. If you can't reach orgasm on your own, then it will be difficult to do with your partner, especially if you are short on time. As we've discussed, masturbation is a great way to get in tune with your personal preferences in the bedroom—in fact, you might even consider "testing" yourself by seeing how quickly you can reach orgasm on your own. (For more on masturbation techniques and tips, see pages 98–101.)

Sex toys can also be critical to a satisfying quickie. Use them to become aroused quickly, or play with them during sex to help give both of you maximum (and fast) arousal and enjoyment. This can be especially useful for women. In fact, it might even be a good idea to help yourself along before your partner even enters the room. For example, if you know that you are going to have a quickie when he comes home from work, try using a sex toy to arouse yourself before he comes home. This way you will already be close to orgasm when he walks in the door—and if he finds you using it, all the better to jump-start his own arousal!

the *best* quickie positions

Another way to get the most out of the quickie is to try positions that are mutually satisfying. Woman-on-top is a great quickie move, because it makes it easy to stimulate her clitoris manually. Standing sex positions are also great for quickies because you can perform them in the shower or in another less traditional spot. Find the quickie position that you know works for you and then keep it in your sexual arsenal, ready to be pulled out whenever you want a quick burst of pleasure.

Sneak away from the kids every so often for 10 minutes of steamy, relationship-restoring sex.

when, where, and why Once you've become comfortable with the idea of integrating quickies into your sex life, you can move on to become a real master of this speedy sexual art. Quickies truly fulfill all of their potential if you perform them at a time or in a place where you might get caught. The element of secrecy increases adrenaline and eroticism, and you will feel deeply bonded knowing that you are sharing this intimate risk. In fact, one of the most appealing things about the quickie is that it increases your dopamine levels—the same hormone that caused your heart to beat faster and your stomach to flip-flop in the early days of dating. This is proof that quickies can make your relationship feel new all over again.

So find yourselves a secret location where you won't be disturbed and get to it. Pull your partner into the coatroom at a party and have a quickie while the rest of the guests are milling around outside. Slip away while your kids are safely absorbed watching cartoons and create your own entertainment in another room. Heat things up in a restaurant bathroom, or become official members of the "Mile High Club". The only rules are to use your imagination, be creative, and keep local laws about public indecency in mind. Live out your fantasies, whether that means fast-and-furious sex in the kitchen, or snatching the chance to make love under the stars in your own backyard. Just make sure, wherever you go, that you'll be safe from prying eyes and unwelcome interruptions!

And while you're seducing one another, talk. More than any other type of sex, quickies require communication in order to give maximum pleasure. So, tell your partner what you want. Since you have limited time to reach climax during a quickie, it's important to be completely open about what type of stimulation you desire. For example, ask him to stimulate your clitoris while he penetrates you, or tell her to gyrate fast and hard against you.

quickies in context As pleasurable as these moments are, remember: Quickies are only a useful way to revamp your sex life when you don't have time for other remedies, such as a couples-only vacation or a romantic date night. However, they can't and shouldn't completely replace longer sex sessions. Think of a quickie as a "snack" and a more intimate sex session as a "meal." Snacks can keep you going and give you energy and motivation, but you can't live on snacks alone. The best approach is to use quickies to tide you over when you don't have time for more intimate sex, and then to indulge in longer sex sessions when your schedule and energy levels allow.

too *tired* for sex?

Your partner might not be as tired as you think! While 44 percent of women reported believing that their partners were too tired to have sex, only 14 percent of men say that this is true. This is an excellent reminder that sex can be the perfect reward at the end of a hard day, and also a motivator to take the plunge and initiate sex, whether it is a quickie or a longer sex session. Women especially are often guilty of waiting for their partner to make the first move, but the truth is that a man needs to be reminded that you desire him and that you crave intimacy. This is crucial to the male sexual self-esteem and to the strength of your relationship. So, next time you are on the fence about asking for sex, just do it. A little bedroom initiative can truly revolutionize your relationship.

claw his skin,
ravenous with lust

trace light circles
beneath her panties

playful passion The most memorably intimate sex sessions are both playful and passionate. One of the best parts of being in a longstanding relationship is that you know exactly what turns your partner on—which means you can play to every temptation. Tease him by stroking just below his waistband, then drawing your fingers away, or playfully pinch her nipples before lavishing her whole body in soft, seductive strokes.

loving sex is...
insatiable

The more we have sex, the more we want it. This is true for lovers new and old alike, and it means that our sex lives can get better and better as we age. Keep your relationship electrifying with tools that will prime you for pleasure and excite your imagination. Sex toys and erotica can turn your bedroom into a passionate playground, lending your lovemaking a brand new shine of seduction and sexy satisfaction.

sex toys

Sex toys help increase and enhance our sexual response. Often thought of strictly as a tool for self-pleasuring, these erotic devices can revolutionize your lovemaking together, too. For women especially, sex toys keep sexual drive strong and can add limitless excitement to your bedroom experience.

historical sex toys No matter how much we want to enhance our sexual experiences, many of us shy away from the use of sexual aids and devices, thinking that they are only for the exhaustively adventurous. On the surface, sex toys don't seem very intimate, and it can be hard to get used to them in the context of a relationship. If this sounds familiar, it might help to know that these aids are not an invention of the modern era. In fact, they have been a part of the human sexual experience for thousands of years. From dildos to lubricants, sex toys have long been used to help spice up sexual encounters and enhance couples' intimacy. Time and time again, archeologists have unearthed ancient artifacts that appear to have erotic purpose, and similar erotic undertones have been found in art, literature, and stone carvings.

All of these erotic findings seem to suggest one thing: Humans have always been interested in sex, and in improving and enhancing their sexual experience with outside tools—tools that are very much like our modern sex toys.

Using a sex toy together is incredibly arousing—he can see every bit of pleasure on her face, while she is much more likely to reach orgasm with it.

sex toy myths If you have never used a sex toy before, you may have a somewhat skewed idea of what they are all about. Many of us have negative thoughts about vibrators and wrongly think that they can get in the way of our sexual response or our connection with a partner. The truth, however, is that these thoughts are mostly urban legends.

It's time to set the record straight! Here are some of the common myths that you may have believed when it comes to sex toys.

myth 1: Sex toys are for wild and swinging singles False! In fact, an overwhelming number of couples use sex toys. Women in committed relationships are actually the largest demographic to own and use sex toys: 78 percent of them do so. In addition, 25 percent of couples report having used a sex toy during lovemaking.

So, clearly sex toys aren't just for singles. As many couples have found, they are particularly useful in long-term, committed relationships because they help bring passion back into the bedroom. Additionally,

how to use a vibrator

Turn on the vibrator and lay it against your clitoris (or slip the vibrating ring around your penis). You might consider applying some lubricant, perhaps even a warming or tingling variety to help awaken your senses. Play with the different speeds and settings of your particular toy, and notice how your body responds with pleasure. You can also use the vibrator on other parts of your body, such as on your breasts and nipples, or in between your thighs or against your perineum (remember to wash toys if swapping between your genitals and anus).

all-over *touch*

Although sex toys are traditionally used on the genitals, you can increase arousal and make foreplay even more fun by using them in a variety of other erogenous zones, too. Try rubbing a vibrator or vibrating dildo gently across the breasts, the lower stomach, or the thighs, and watch your partner's pleasure explode. For couples that are new to sex toys, this can be a comfortable way to get acquainted with the vibrating sensation— not to mention a thrillingly erotic one.

sex toys can be helpful when life throws a curveball at a couple's sex life, such as menopause, andropause, orgasmic dysfunction, or even just plain old stress. (For more on these challenges, see pages 246–257.)

myth 2: Sex toys are a replacement for a man It's understandable that men often feel a little intimidated by the vibrator. After all, vibrators are built to touch a woman in all the right places, and they never get tired (and if they do, you can simply replace the battery!). These pros aside, however, a vibrator can never come close to replacing the human experience of lovemaking. A vibrator can give a woman pleasure, but it can't give her intimacy, sensuality, excitement, or passion, all of which are crucial to her sexual satisfaction. Those are inherently human experiences, and could never be rivaled by a buzzing, battery-operated toy.

A sex toy can be useful in other ways, however. First, it can help decrease the pleasure gap between men and women, enhancing a woman's sexual response so that her arousal is on par with her partner's arousal. Using a toy before or during sex means that lovemaking will bring more mutual satisfaction and will require less foreplay. Toys also make for excellent afterplay if he reaches orgasm first. She can hold the vibrator against her clitoris or ask him to do this, or she can have him penetrate her with a dildo while she stimulates her breasts or clitoris. This can help her to stay aroused and orgasmic if he wants to rest before having another sex session, or it can be an erotic way to help her reach orgasm.

Of course, sex toys can also simply be used to increase sexual pleasure and add novelty to the boudoir. And they aren't just for a woman's pleasure. There are many sex aids that can help to increase a man's arousal, such as cock rings, sleeves, pumps, and prostate toys (for more on male sex toys, keep reading). So, men, if you feel intimidated by the thought of your partner using a sex toy, consider getting one of your own to help you understand both the pleasure a toy can bring, and that it's never a replacement for true intimacy.

myth 3: Sex toys can desensitize the genitals This myth likely shares roots with the fear that sex toys can replace men. The truth, however, is that no study has ever found that women (or men, for that matter) lose genital sensation due to vibrator use, although it's worth noting that frequent use of a vibrator with deep settings may cause human stimulation to feel less intense. This doesn't mean that you are numb or that you have suffered any kind of nerve damage. What it does mean is that after a marathon session with a strong vibrator you might feel less sensation for a temporary period of time. Rest assured, your full range of sensation will return.

If you feel nervous about this, use your toys only on their lowest settings and for shorter periods of time. Along these same lines, if you are worried about becoming addicted to your favorite toy, make sure to spend an equal amount of time having orgasms the "old-fashioned" way with your partner. This will help to keep that human contact intact and integral to your sexual pleasure, while still allowing your sex toy to enhance your sexual response.

types of vibrator The vibrator was originally invented as a
medical treatment. In the 19th century, "pelvic massage" was thought to be a treatment for female hysteria. We have certainly come a long way since those early doctor's visits: In the past five years especially, the sex toy industry has exploded, making bedroom toys popular and socially acceptable across the board. Our Victorian ancestors would have been shocked to discover that the vibrator has now become popular in the majority of couples' bedrooms.

Now that you know sex toys are a safe, healthy, and normal way to increase your sexual pleasure, you might wonder: Which sex toy is right for me? There are many possible answers.

vibrators The most common female vibrators stimulate the clitoris. These make for good introductory toys, since they don't feel invasive, and offer effective, targeted stimulation. More advanced vibrators include a dildo that can be inserted in the vagina, with an external apparatus attached that stimulates the clitoris.

Male vibrators can be used to stimulate the perineum, or can be inserted in the anus to stimulate the prostate. There are also vibrating cock rings (a ring that you slip around your penis) and vibrating sleeves (a sleeve that covers your penis, made of sensual material created to feel like a woman's genitals). Whichever option you choose, vibrators are one of the easiest ways to feel intense pleasure in a short amount of time, whether you are self-stimulating or using a toy with your partner.
• **For the novice user** Try a clitoral vibrator that is discreet and not intimidating. Or try a large massager that can cover a large part of your genitals and doesn't require any guesswork.
• **For the advanced user** Choose a vibrator that can fit between you and your partner during sex, to help you reach orgasm simultaneously.
• **For the expert** A waterproof vibrator is great for shower sessions; or try a vibrator with attachments that you can insert into your vagina or anus.

male vibrators

Vibrators get so much attention for their ability to bring a woman to orgasm that we often forget they can also be incredibly pleasurable for men. If your partner has never tried a male vibrator, consider buying one for him as a sexy surprise. Nothing stirs up extra adventure in the bedroom like a sexual gift!

For men new to the pleasures of a good vibrator, a vibrating ring is a good place to start. It can be placed around the penis either during sex or during self-stimulation and many men find that it greatly intensifies sensation (you can also try this to spice things up during oral sex). A silicone sleeve to masturbate with can also be a sexy gift.

To get used to the sensation of a specific sex toy, try using it for self-pleasure before you introduce it to a sex session.

more *sex toys*

Vibrators aren't the only tools that bring intense bedroom pleasure. Dildos, G-spot stimulators, and prostate stimulators are also highly erotic, and can teach you and your partner so much about how the body responds to different types of stimulation and touch. Experiment with these toys alone or together and bring your sexual pleasure to the next level.

dildos Dildos are phallus-shaped sex aids that can be inserted into the vagina or anus. They often come with features for extra stimulation, such as pleasure dots or vibration, but they can be simple and straightforward. They come in a wide range of materials, including silicone, glass, and acrylic—or you can even make your own dildo with a kit that uses your partner's penis as a cast. (This revolutionizes phone sex! Even when your partner is away on a business trip, you will still be able to stimulate yourself with his penis.)

Dildos can satisfy a variety of sexual needs, and you can use them solo or during foreplay. In fact, you can even use them during intercourse. He can penetrate her vaginally with a dildo while you perform 69 together, or she can stimulate herself clitorally while he penetrates her with a dildo. Both men and women can also have their partner insert a dildo into the anus. A word of warning, however: always make sure to clean your toys after use, and never use a toy in the vagina after it's been used in the anus. Sharing bacteria from the anus to the vagina can lead to vaginal infection. In addition, any toy used for anal play should have a flared base.

- **For the novice user** Try a silicone dildo during foreplay or afterplay. Silicone dildos feel and look the most like an actual penis, which makes them the most comfortable for beginners.
    - **For the advanced user** Choose a dildo that comes with a clitoral stimulator, and ask your partner to help you use it for pleasure during foreplay.
        - **For the expert user** A glass dildo can be heated or cooled. Play with the temperature by warming it up in warm water and then inserting it into your vagina.

g-spot stimulators and prostate stimulators G-spot stimulators are toys that are designed to bring pleasure to your G-spot, through vibration or some other type of stimulation. They are perfectly curved to locate and stimulate your G-spot in just the right way. These toys come in a wide range of sizes, varying from small, handheld toys to large, vibrating ones. If you have never been able to locate your G-spot, these toys can be highly useful—simply insert one in your vagina and let it do the work! They come in a variety of different materials— everything from stainless steel to glass to medical-grade silicone—and some of them come with vibrating attachments that can stimulate the clitoris or perineum simultaneously.

Prostate stimulators can be thought of as a male counterpart to G-spot stimulators, since they are also built to locate and stimulate a specific pleasure spot. These toys are inserted in the anus, where they stimulate the P-spot and can create a prostate orgasm. It's okay to be a little hesitant to use this type of toy, especially if you have never engaged in anal play before. If you feel nervous, remember that it's a pleasurable type of stimulation that many men (gay, straight, or somewhere in between) find highly stimulating.

- **For the novice user** Women, use a G-spot locator to help find your G-spot. Men, use a prostate vibrator for your first foray into anal play.
- **For the advanced user** Women, ask your partner to use a G-spot vibrator on you during foreplay. He can stimulate your clitoris orally as he does so, or insert a finger into your anus. Men, have your partner insert a prostate stimulator into your anus as she performs oral sex on you.
- **For the expert user** Perform 69 using a G-spot stimulator and prostate stimulator at the same time. This really brings oral sex to the next level of adventure.

using *glass dildos*

Many women (and men, for that matter) find the thought of a glass dildo intimidating. This is mostly due to the idea of breaking glass, and I can understand how putting what is traditionally a very fragile material inside such an intimate part of your body can be scary. However, the truth is that glass dildos are some of the safest toys out there, made only from the very best materials. (In fact, even if you were to bang a glass dildo against a hard surface multiple times, it would have very little chance of breaking!) Just as important, glass dildos don't hold bacteria the way other sex toy materials sometimes do, and they are blissfully easy to clean.

One of the most appealing parts of the glass dildo is that it can be heated up to mimic the body temperature of a lover. To do this, simply run it under warm water for a few minutes prior to using—then, enjoy!

positions with sex toys

Every couple has its own preferences regarding types of sex toys and how to use them. Missionary, woman-on-top, sideways, standing positions—any of these can be injected with new, erotic life by adding a toy. To find out which work best for you, indulge in a night (or a string of nights) of sultry exploration.

using toys together If you have never used a toy during lovemaking before, broach the topic carefully by letting your partner know that this doesn't mean they're not satisfying you. Instead, it just means that you want to electrify your pleasure and bring a new level of adventure and eroticism to the bedroom. Say something like, "I saw this toy online the other day. I couldn't stop fantasizing about you using it on me and all the fun we would have with it." Let your partner imagine pleasuring you with the toy, and make sure they know that using it is a way to enhance your time together for both of you, and not just to boost your own pleasure.

A few toys are an essential part of any couple's love life, and you shouldn't feel embarrassed about experimenting. But at the same time, it's important to remember that they're an added extra, not a mainstay. Use them as treats to enhance your sex life, but don't let them replace the simple pleasure you take in each other's bodies.

the best positions Most man-from-behind positions offer easy
opportunities for adding a toy, since he can reach around and hold
a vibrator against her clitoris. A standard vibrator is ideal, especially
if she reaches down to position it exactly where she wants it.

You can also try using a sex toy in woman-on-top positions. A small,
bullet-style vibrator works well here since it can fit in between you.
Some couples feel this removes the connection of the man bringing
his partner to orgasm, but on the other hand he gets a ring-side seat
as she uses the toy on herself, something most men will love.

Another option is a vibrating cock ring (a dual ring that vibrates
against him and you is ideal), which will offer a hands-free approach
and can be used in almost any position. There are also plenty of
waterproof toys to spice up your bath time together, and you might
try an anal plug or prostate stimulator during intercourse or oral sex
to help spice up your experience and try something new.

the *position* list

Try these other positions to get the most
out of bringing a sex toy into your love play:

- Tailor Made (page 128)
- Sweet Spoons (page 136)
- Lapdance Plus (page 144)
- Passionate Surrender (page 152)
- Kneeling Comfort (page 154)
- Attentive Lover (page 162)

embracing *erotica*

Erotica is a term derived from the Greek word Eros, meaning intimate desire. Eros was the Ancient Greek god of sexual love and beauty, and is also associated with creativity. For many couples, this passion for creativity and sexuality comes together in the form of modern erotica—both visual and verbal.

about erotica If you are new to erotica, you might have a few misconceptions about it. Although it is traditionally known as pornography, I prefer to call it erotica since the term "pornography" often elicits discomfort and negativity in our society. Truthfully, erotica isn't for everyone, but it can be a fun and sexy way to spice up your sex life if you are both open to the idea.

Erotica ranges from "hardcore," in which you get to see everything, to "softcore," in which male genitals and penetration aren't actually shown. (It's perhaps a little sexist that softcore erotica will show female genitals up-close, but that's just how it works in the pornography field.) To get your feet wet, try watching a softcore erotic film together (for suggestions on where to start, see the resources on page 282). If this titillates you, you can try a more revealing film.

There are many different subcategories of erotica. There is lesbian and gay erotica, and heterosexual erotica, but even in traditional mainstream pornography, there are often "girl-on-girl" scenes and plenty of threesomes. This seems natural when you consider that most erotica is made with men in mind, and one of the most common male fantasies is being with multiple women at once (for more on this and other male fantasies, see pages 206–207 and 226–227).

Women, on the other hand, tend to crave erotica that comes with a plotline to follow. This act of telling a story makes it more like a traditional movie, as opposed to strictly sexual stimulation scene after scene without any context. Thankfully, the market is no longer targeted toward men alone. In fact, many production companies now gear their movies toward women or even couples. Candida Royalle, for example, produces a number of movies that fall under the umbrella of "female-friendly" erotica. These still include plenty of sex, but they keep the female viewer in mind. Many include women with more realistic looking bodies (not just extra-large breasts), and they also follow plotlines and include more varied sex acts. This makes erotica easier for women to relate to, and it also makes the erotica experience one that can be enjoyed whether you plan to jump right into sex or simply want to increase arousal and get some ideas for later.

making your own erotica Couples often find it incredibly sexy to perform for the camera. One word of warning, however: If you are going to make your own erotic film, I recommend that you erase the video after you watch it together. You need look no further than the news headlines to see what can happen when sex tapes or pictures fall into the wrong hands, and deleting bedroom footage also guarantees that your kids won't have any opportunity to discover it.

Once you've agreed not to keep a record, go ahead and tap into your inner actor. Enter the experience wholeheartedly by playing sexy music, lighting candles or using a dimmer (lighting is everything, no matter what kind of movie you are shooting), and dressing up in your sexiest lingerie or role-play costume. Plan a plotline that you can follow, whether it's a sexy nurse and patient, schoolgirl and teacher, a police officer and offender, a superhero and damsel in distress, or any other fantasy you want to bring to life.

For the best results, set the camera somewhere fairly high, so that you can get a good angle—shooting from a higher angle is more flattering than a direct or low angle—and keep your scene simple and focused in one location. Moving around the room or trying to do too much at once will complicate the scene unnecessarily. Make sure that you are facing the camera and that you are close enough to show some detail. For especially close action, one partner can hold the camera and film the other. For example, your partner can film you giving him oral pleasure, or he can hold the camera close with one hand while he penetrates you. Remember to film with the sound turned on, so that you can hear every moan and sigh, and to think in advance about what will make for a super-sexy ending.

written erotica
One of the main differences between male and female tastes in erotica is that women are highly verbal and can become aroused simply by reading and fantasizing. No wonder romance books are notoriously popular among women. Nancy Friday and Violet Blue offer a range of sexy stories that you can read alone or with your partner (for more on these books, see the resources on page 282). If you prefer erotica with a touch of romance, there are plenty of sexy romance novels that will certainly get you in the mood—and you don't have to rely on the traditional Harlequin romance. Erotic romance novels are as varied and unique as the women who read them, so whether you love vampires or cowboys, there is a romance collection for you. Even better, you can purchase these books discreetly and easily online, so that your reading material can be kept private.

erotica in the real world
As you watch an erotic film, it's important to keep in mind that what you see on-screen is not truly indicative of what women want or need, or even of what they experience in the bedroom. Most women don't have screaming, intense orgasms as a result of penetration alone, nor do they necessarily enjoy having their partners ejaculate all over their bodies or faces. Take these scenes with a grain of salt so that erotica doesn't give you false expectations about performance or sexuality. It is fantasy, after all! Instead, rely on real-world knowledge and experience as your primary teaching tools for what to do in the bedroom.

Filming yourselves can be a great turn-on, and help you to feel infinitely sexy and creative in the bedroom. Use these moments to live out your deepest fantasies.

One of the great things about written erotica is that it is portable. It's easy to bring a book with you on a romantic vacation, or to keep one near your bed for whenever you need inspiration. To make the most of this material, try these tips.

• **Read a chapter** of your favorite erotic author in the tub before date night to get those sexy feelings flowing.

• **Highlight a few sexy chapters** and leave them sitting out for your partner to read. You can even sneak part of a story into his briefcase. He will be thinking about you and that sexy story all day long.

• **Draw on this erotic material** to get your own creative juices going. Take inspiration from your favorite books and pen your partner a short erotic scene starring the two of you, sharing all the things you want to do to him, or reflecting on one of your favorite encounters in exquisite, tantalizing detail.

erotica addiction

As enjoyable as erotica can be, it can also become a crutch or even an addiction. With the advent of the internet, many people have found themselves struggling with an addiction to this type of pleasure. As with most things, it's important to enjoy erotica in moderation. If you use erotica obsessively or find that you must be stimulated by it in order to reach orgasm, then you might be struggling with an addiction.

Symptoms of addiction include: spending hours looking at online erotica, hiding your erotica use from your partner, or engaging in cybersex activities with strangers online. If you feel out of control when it comes to your use of erotica, or if it is interfering with your relationship, seek help from a therapist, particularly someone who specializes in sex addiction (for more information on how to find a therapist, see the resources on page 282). The good news is that you are not alone. There are many resources to help you overcome your addiction and reestablish a healthy relationship with your partner.

If you believe that your partner is struggling with this form of addiction, talk about your concerns openly and honestly. For example, you can say, "I want you to know that I love you and I am here for you no matter what. Lately, I have noticed that you are spending a lot of time looking at erotic websites. You seem distracted and unhappy, and I know that this is something that a lot of couples go through. There are people who can help you and it's something we can do together." Mention that there are 12-step programs designed to help people who suffer from sex addiction or from erotica addiction, and that these can be a good first step on the road to recovery.

the appeal of female-female sex scenes

Female-friendly erotica often includes scenes of girl-on-girl pleasure, and this is not just because men might be viewing these films—many women find watching female-female sex scenes to be highly erotic. In fact, a recent study performed by Northwestern University found that women are often aroused by erotic content featuring same-sex interaction, even if those women don't identify themselves as homosexual or bisexual. The opposite was also true: Women who identified as homosexual were aroused by heterosexual pornography. In contrast, whether they were gay or straight, men generally became aroused only by movies that followed their own sexual interests (although heterosexual men often do enjoy watching female-female sex scenes).

This shows how fluid female sexuality is, especially when compared to male sexuality. I think this is partly because women have received greater social permission from an early age to identify and express their sexuality, while men aren't given much leeway when it comes to this type of exploration. This explains why male-geared erotica can be so simplistic and repetitive—and also why it's so wonderful to have a burgeoning market of female-friendly erotica to enjoy with your partner.

loving sex: round two

The great thing about amazing sex is that you aren't limited to one serving a night. Having another round after you have had time to relax and recharge is incredibly sexy, and it's part of what gives new lovers that enviable "honeymoon" high. So spend a few hours exploring. Occasional nights like this will keep the flames of passion sexily stoked.

preparing for passion To be ready for a marathon sex session, it's important to keep your arousal levels at a simmer—in other words, that slow burn I keep promoting. It will be much easier for you to get in the mood organically if you are continually creating and harnessing sexual energy. While you can't be on a sexual high all the time, it's important to make sure that your light is never completely out. When you keep your sexual stove set to simmer, you don't have to reignite the flame every time you want to be sexual—you just have to stoke the already sparking fire.

There are several habits that will help you create and maintain this sexual energy. One of the best is to make sure that you never stop treating each other as desirable and sexual individuals. Prioritizing your relationship, putting effort into your appearance, and treating each other like lovers rather than roommates can really keep that slow burn going. All of these habits will add more sensuality and attraction to your relationship every day, but the most important thing is to find time to connect as partners away from the kids, errands, and minutiae of the day. Touching each other spontaneously and sexually can also keep you connected as lovers, and can keep sensual thoughts flowing between you. Try grabbing her

Stroking your partner's nipples and other erogenous zones after sex can help him prepare for round two.

bottom when you pass behind her, tousling his hair sensually, or pulling your hips close to his when you are kissing. (For more ideas on how to keep things sensual, see pages 52–53.)

Once you have mastered the slow burn, remember how important it is to understand your sexual response and your partner's sexual response. As we've discussed, women are capable of multiple orgasms while men typically need a refractory period in which their bodies recharge (for more on this, see page 13). In order to keep sexual thoughts and feelings alive during this refractory period, continue stimulation at a gentler pace. She can continue to stroke herself and bring herself to orgasm as her partner watches, or she can kiss and massage her partner as he relaxes. Or he can touch her and bring her to orgasm, or perform oral sex on her. The key is to make sure that you keep your sexual energy alight by kissing and cuddling. You can also try talking to each other in sexual ways, such as, "That was amazing. When we go again, I'll be on top so we can try a new position," or "How do you want me to touch you next time?"

Finally, remember that sex doesn't have to have a beginning, middle, and end, and neither do all sexual experiences have to be defined by penetration. If you want to have another round but don't necessarily want to have intercourse, try performing oral sex simultaneously or stimulating each other manually or with sex toys. You can also try a VENIS exercise in which you keep sexual energy burning by caressing and stroking each other in unexpected, exploratory ways (for more on this, see pages 90–91).

reading your partner's mood
If you are eager for more sex, but aren't sure if your partner is up for it, feel him or her out by nuzzling and cuddling as you both relax. This will help you gauge your partner's readiness for sex, and can ignite additional sparks. Keep your sensual connection alive by rubbing her back, playing with his hair, or complimenting the way she smells or the way he kisses. Staying physically close to your partner will keep you in the present, and will also keep the oxytocin (that "cuddle hormone") flowing. Women especially love the seduction and sexual tension that comes before the act of sex, and this buildup of feelings can be just as pleasurable as the lovemaking experience itself. Keeping this tension alive can go a long way toward increasing her desire for more sex.

releasing expectations

If you are concerned about making your second session as passionate as your first, remember that it's important not to compare each sexual experience, especially if doing so makes you feel stressed about lasting long enough or about being able to reach orgasm again. Going for round two is simply a great way to build intimacy and passion, and to express your desire for each other. It doesn't mean that you have to reach some impossible sexual goal, or even that you have to have multiple orgasms. Instead, just think of it as a way to enjoy each other's bodies and increase your intimate bond. Leave the pressure and the "shoulds" at the door. The whole point of a round two is doubling your pleasure—not doubling the stress and performance anxiety.

loving sex is...
adventurous

It's been said that the mind is the most important sex organ, which is probably why sharing our fantasies is so arousing. Exploring your deepest desires is one of the most intimate acts of love— and one of the most fun. As you do this, use touch, sight, taste, and every other sense to create an experience that is full of color, passion, and tantalizing exoticism. This sense of adventure will spill over into every part of your life together.

exotic positions

When you want to add variety and spice to your bedroom routine, look no further than a new sex position. Exotic—even acrobatic—positions are just the antidote when you and your partner are stuck in a rut, and they aren't always as complicated as you might think. With just a few tweaks, you can change what's become a humdrum position into an erotic, sensual experience.

embracing exoticism Exotic positions are all about excitement and adventure. They push you to discover new sides of your sexual self and new realms of sexual pleasure. And these positions allow you to see both yourself and your partner in a new light. In a long-term relationship, the occasional night of exoticism reminds you that there is still uncharted territory to discover as lovers, and that you are both powerfully sensual beings.

Discovering the "wild thing" within may be daunting at first, but it is so important to take this step to have a fully realized, satisfying sex life. By taking charge and trying something completely out of the box, you and your partner can reconnect in a way that is passionate, daring—and *fun*. Many of these positions are difficult to get right, but the act of trying is truly bonding and sometimes even amusing. As they say, laughter is the best medicine, and this goes for relationships, too. Embracing those moments of humor in the bedroom is incredibly restorative, and it's part of what great sex is all about.

when to turn exotic Use these exotic positions whenever you want to bring a little adventure into the bedroom. You can either plan ahead or be spontaneous, though you may want to have a reference on hand to learn how to master some of the more difficult positions. Unlike missionary or from-behind positions, these acrobatic adventures aren't always purely intuitive.

Exotic positions can be perfect for those times when you are stuck in a sexual rut. Partly, this is because they require communication—as you move your bodies in new ways you'll need to talk to each other to find pleasure. In addition, as we've discussed, these positions can make your relationship feel thrillingly new, and can help you and your partner appreciate each other all over again as skillful, desirable lovers.

For these same reasons, exotic positions can be the perfect choice for nights when you are celebrating a special occasion, such as an anniversary. These positions take time and energy—and, ideally, can be used to initiate an entire evening of lovemaking. Because it can be more difficult to reach climax when your body is being stretched to its limits, you may want to start in one of these challenging positions and then move into something more classically stimulating and intimate, such as missionary or woman-on-top. One of the perks of exotic positions is that they are the perfect foundation for long-lasting sex.

exotic challenges Although it might not sound romantic, it's important to have realistic expectations with this type of sex. Exotic positions can bring a brand-new level of excitement and passion to the bedroom, but they can also bring complications. You might discover that the crazy position you have been dying to try doesn't actually provide the stimulation you need, or that it is uncomfortable or awkward to perform. If that's the case, simply try something different, whether it's adjusting the position slightly, bringing in a pillow for support, or exploring a new position entirely. Exotic positions require a little trial and error— but when you are willing to explore, the rewards will be truly unforgettable. You will come away feeling bonded, intimate, and completely in touch with your partner.

preparing for *adventure*

For the best exotic evening, begin the act of seduction before you enter the bedroom. You will have more fun and generally experience more pleasure if you already feel aroused by your partner. Cook a special meal together, enjoy a glass of wine, indulge in a massage or a long, relaxing walk to watch the sunset, and flirt shamelessly. All of these little moments will help prime you for pleasure later.

As always, when you experiment in the bedroom, communication is extremely important. When you try these new positions, ask your partner to tell you what feels good.

height of passion

In this playfully erotic position, she lies on her back, then lifts her legs as high as she can, holding on to her calves for support. He kneels in front of her and leans over to enter, resting his weight on his palms. Her raised legs allow for deep penetration. While it may not be easy to reach orgasm in this position, it is a seductive way to start sex; he'll have an arousing view of her lower assets, and can keep his movements slow and steady while her desire heats up. As you move toward climax, she can wrap her legs around his body for a more cozy finish.

arched arousal

Accomplishing this position is a bedroom triumph! It takes flexibility (for her) and strength (for him), but it's pure, sexy fun. To start, he sits on a chair, and she straddles him, guiding his penis inside her. She grasps his arms and leans back slightly, then arches her back while he supports her at the waist and lowers her to the floor. This is not a position you can hold for long periods of time, so it's best to try it when she is already aroused and he can start thrusting deeply right away. For added eroticism, film yourselves, so you can enjoy this athletic sexual achievement again and again.

sensual scissors

This position looks complicated, but is actually quite gentle. To start, he lies on his back and she straddles him, facing his feet, and guides his penis into her. Next, he grasps her tightly and rolls 90 degrees into a sideways position. From here he can thrust while she rocks—and you both have access to multiple other hot spots. She can caress his thighs while he rubs her shoulders or grabs her bottom. For even greater intensity, she can raise her leg straight up in the air, allowing him to penetrate her to the core.

positions for a challenge

Although tenderness and intimacy are essential in any relationship, loving sex doesn't always have to be slow and passionate. Sometimes the best way to celebrate your connection to each other is to try something new, and maybe a bit silly. After all, one of the best parts about a loving relationship is that you can feel free to be a little ridiculous now and then.

boost your relationship The fastest passion-killer in the world is boredom, so you should never be afraid to get out of your rut and try something new. A sex position that's different, exciting—maybe even a little challenging—is a great way to do this. Try it when you're both relaxed and have plenty of time, and preferably on a soft surface like a king-sized bed!

For centuries, the *Kama Sutra* has been a by-word for acrobatic sex positions, and it's always fun to look at old prints and drawings for inspiration. Be careful not to strain yourselves, and don't get hung up on replicating the acrobatics exactly. Just experiment, have fun, and enjoy the different sensations that sex in an unusual position can give you. You never know, you might come across a new favorite.

the best positions One of the easiest ways to vary sensations is simply to change the angle of penetration. You can do this by leaning forward or backward during sex, or by the woman moving her legs into different positions, which alters the shape of her vagina.

Standing positions feel instantly exciting and different, especially if she can hold herself up with her legs wrapped around him. For the arched position below, start sitting in a chair, with her facing him, then slowly leaning back to touch the floor. If you feel stable in this position, he can then try slowly standing up. Treat this kind of play as a fun experiment. You can always revert to a normal favorite position to finish off. Above all, avoid positions that put too much strain on anyone's back or on his penis.

the *position* list

When you're feeling frisky and up for a challenge, try some of these positions:
- Eager Lover (page 121)
- Tightly Pressed (page 160)
- Rising Passion (page 160)
- Clinging Embrace (page 168)
- Height of Passion (page 198)
- Arched Arousal (page 198)
- Sensual Scissors (page 199)

sex outside the bedroom

Moving sex out of the bedroom is an erotic thrill; stepping outside of our comfort zones changes and heightens our sexual response. To take your first adventurous step, find a place that still feels safe (the sofa; the kitchen) or venture into semi-public territory (a restaurant restroom; your backyard) for some ultra-steamy stimulation.

the hormone factor In the early stages of a relationship, your body generates dopamine and adrenaline, which create feelings of excitement and arousal. These hormone levels tend to subside over time—a good thing, since it signals that you are moving into a deeper and more stable relationship. As the relationship progresses, however, many of us miss those early butterflies. Luckily, you can bring them back to your relationship by engaging in the occasional act of daring.

One of the sexiest ways to do this is to make love outside the bedroom. Having sex in a new place causes adrenaline to pump through your body in a way that mimics the excitement you felt at the start of your relationship. Even better, an inventive location might unleash a sexual voracity you didn't know you possessed.

The bathtub is a slippery, sensual place for sex—and it's also nice and private, so you won't be disturbed.

If this seems intimidating or unappealing to you, start slowly. You can create spontaneity and excitement outside the bedroom simply by bringing more touch into your daily public routines with each other. Hold hands as you walk through the grocery store, or rub his back as you wait in line at the movie theater. Cuddle against him on an outdoor picnic, or pull her onto your lap when you are entertaining in your backyard. Find new and surprising ways to keep that physical connection alive and sizzling. You can be as bold as you prefer, and even if you aren't comfortable with overly extravagant public displays of affection, you can still find modest and appropriate ways to touch each other that will stoke your sexual fires and make your relationship feel exciting and fresh.

around the house If the familial coast is clear, your entire house can become an erotic playground. The bathroom is an obvious place to start—it's likely that one or both of you have fantasized about spending time naked and wet together in the tub. (Its close proximity to the bedroom also makes it less intimidating than other, more public rooms.) If you have a small shower, opt for standing positions. From-behind positions are great for small spaces: she can lean forward and rest her elbows against the shower wall, or reach down and hold on to her ankles to keep her balance secure. If your shower permits, she can also sit on the floor, while he kneels between her legs, lifting her hips as he gently rocks back and forth. Turn up the heat a notch by using a handheld shower to stimulate yourselves, or use your bodies to create a sudsy lather between the two of you.

Whether you spontaneously join your partner for a mid-shower surprise, or set a sexy scene with candles and music, making love in the shower is a good way to spice up your connection and get you touching each other in new ways. For extra lubrication, try a non-water-based lubricant that won't wash away when the shower is turned on. (Remember, however, that not every lubricant is safe for use with condoms. Silicone-based lubricants are safe for latex condoms, but oil-based lubricants are not.)

The kitchen and dining room can be equally sensual places for sex. More open and less intimate than the bathroom, they deliver an extra dose of lustful, must-have-you-now appeal. The kitchen counter or table are convenient surfaces for support. Try a seated position on the

safe spontaneity

If you are planning to make love in a new part of your house, you will probably feel more comfortable if you are sure that no one will walk in on you. While the possibility of getting caught in the act can be exciting, for most people this excitement doesn't extend to their own flesh and blood. To create your best sexual experience, choose a time and location where you will be safe from any interruptions.

This doesn't mean that you can't keep that sense of novelty and risk that makes sex outside the bedroom so sensual. The idea is to pretend that someone might walk in on you without actually risking embarrassment—or potential arrest if you are in a public place! In order to help create this illusion, let your spontaneity take the lead. If you are returning home from a date night, don't wait to start touching until you're in the bedroom. Make out in the car, and perhaps pull over in a safe location where you can explore a little motor vehicle foreplay. Or, try performing oral sex once you are safely ensconced in your garage, or pulling each other's clothes off in the hallway as you walk toward the bedroom.

should we express *affection* around the kids?

Don't worry about your kids groaning when they see Mommy and Daddy kissing. The truth is that it's both healthy and appropriate to express intimacy: besides keeping your bond intact, it gives your kids a strong relationship model that will impact their own future relationships.

For deeper expressions of intimacy, it is also completely appropriate to make sure your private time stays private by investing in a lock or even soundproofing your bedroom. Remember, you are the example that your children will use when building their own relationships in the future, and it's important for them to know that couples need to prioritize alone time and intimacy in order to stay strong, committed, and in love.

counter with him standing between her legs, or make love to her from behind as she leans forward against the worktop. The surprise factor is an eloquent way to express your desire. Approach your partner from behind as they are making dinner, and kiss and nuzzle at their neck and shoulders to show them what you have in mind.

If you have stairs in your house, then you have an amazingly erotic place to make love. In this spot, you'll have plenty of options for different angles of penetration, and you can try anything from man-from-behind to kneeling, standing, or sitting positions. Consider these ideas: She can kneel on her hands and knees above, while he enters her from behind in a standing position, or she can lie across the stairs while he spreads his body on top and penetrates her. She can also sit on top as he lies back on the stairs, using the handrail for support as she gyrates on top. The flexibility of this location means that you can easily switch positions mid session, and that you can share the dominant role as your mood dictates.

The laundry room can also be an incredibly erotic place to make love. She can prop herself up on the washer or dryer, spreading her legs wide and allowing him to penetrate her deeply. Switch on the machine so that it is shaking while you are on top of it, then hold on for the ride.

sex away from the house Sex outside is a common fantasy, and one that is easily realized at home. Few places are more romantic than a starlit backyard. If you are worried about spying neighbors, try this deceptively simple trick: she wears a dress without panties and sits on her partner's lap. Wrapping up in an outer layer keeps things private, while still letting you enjoy the thrill of outdoor sex. This position unleashes your inner animal and increases adrenaline, making sex more enjoyable and unforgettable for you both.

And remember—you aren't limited to your own abode. You can christen every place from the bathroom at your favorite restaurant to your office boardroom. (In fact, the office is a very popular spot to get busy! One in five people say they have engaged in sexual activity at their workplace.) If your partner is working late, surprise him with a sexy visit in which you wear a coat with nothing underneath but a lacy bra and panties. Hop on his desk and challenge him to a sexy session right then and there. Part of the beauty of this is the planning it requires: beyond the pure sexiness of showing up half-nude in a public setting, making the move to initiate sex in this way shows your partner that you fantasize about your time together. For both men and women, this type of mental seduction can be one of the biggest turn-ons.

Sex in the kitchen brings arousal to a whole new level. It is at once private and deliciously naughty—and the countertop provides the perfect support.

indulging your *fantasies*

A world without fantasy would be very dull indeed, especially when it comes to the bedroom. Our minds are capable of coming up with imaginative, deeply personal scenarios that can make sex one of the most vital and rewarding parts of our lives. In fact, every one of us has a hidden fantasy (perhaps even an alter-ego) that is dying to come out and take center stage in the bedroom. If this sounds familiar, it's time to put any shyness aside and start adding a little more magic, adventure, and color to your relationship.

fantasies by gender

Male and female fantasies tend to differ (for more on this, see page 188). For men, the idea of multiple hands, breasts, and mouths is highly erotic, which is why the threesome is a popular fantasy (for more on threesomes, see page 226). Another common turn-on for many men is the idea of being with a new partner, someone mysterious and unfamiliar. In addition to the tantalizing rush of the unknown, this may also speak to a man's desire to seduce—the fact that a woman he doesn't know desires him in this way gives him confidence in his allure and sexual prowess.

Women, on the other hand, tend to fantasize about having sex with a partner who is powerful, either physically or socially. In fact, a recent study on sex dreams from the University of Montreal discovered that men tend to dream about unknown people or multiple partners at once, while women tend to dream about having sex with someone powerful, such as a celebrity or a politician. Again, this probably goes back to our ancestral cues. Unlike men, women historically have not wanted to have sex with everyone in their community. More important to them was making love with someone who was in a position of power, and thus able to guarantee their own security and that of a child.

practicing your fantasies

Knowing about these gender differences, how can you satisfy both partners' fantasies in a modern relationship? First, examine what is sexy to you about your own specific fantasy. Do you like the idea of being with a powerful man because you crave the feeling of being dominated? It is not anti-feminist to feel that way by any means—and, in fact, it's very common among strong-willed women. Many women like being dominated in the bedroom, not only because it feels sexy, but also because it gives them a chance to relinquish control and accept pleasure for pleasure's sake.

In part, the idea of being taken by a powerful lover speaks to a woman's inner desires because it is popular in romance novels and other female-friendly erotica, making it easily associated with sexual pleasure. Another reason this fantasy is so popular is that it works with the way that women experience sex, maximizing their natural capacity for pleasure. Having a dominant partner allows "good girls"—who often don't know how to relax and enjoy sex—simply to let go. A woman acting out this fantasy can tell herself, "I didn't have a choice; he took me against my will!" This gives her a chance to relinquish her fears and inhibitions and simply dwell in the moment. It also relieves her of the responsibility of acting as a driving seductive force during sex.

Fortunately, this is one area where the sexes agree: Men often fantasize about being the active partner in the bedroom and controlling their partner's pleasure, so this is an easy and mutually satisfying fantasy to tap into. This doesn't mean, however, that men don't enjoy being sexually dominated, especially if they are ambitious and like to be in control in most areas of their lives. A strange truth is that people tend to play out behavior in the bedroom that is the opposite of the way they behave in real life. This means that a person who is dominant in the workplace often enjoys being dominated in the bedroom, while a person who is passive and easygoing might enjoy taking control in the bedroom. In reality, we know that neither men nor women crave submissive real-life roles, but it's fun and normal to play that way in the bedroom. A healthy approach for both partners is for each of you to have a chance to be in control and a chance to be submissive.

evolving desires Sexual behavior and desire often evolve as we age and grow into our relationships. For example, you might initially have enjoyed taking a passive role and letting your partner command your body, but as you evolve into your sexuality and your relationship, you might find that you enjoy being the initiator in the bedroom.

Similarly, your sexual appetites might change over time. Perhaps you used to prefer sex that was more "vanilla," with slow, passionate timing, but now you love indulging in wild, spontaneous quickies, or even trying sex in new, slightly risky places. This is completely normal, both for men and women. Your partner's desires will change alongside yours, which is why it's important to communicate about your sexual needs throughout your relationship.

Many women who are conservative in everyday life crave a more dramatic role in the bedroom.

embrace erotic,
mysterious roleplay

softly whisper *secret desires*

explore your fantasies Sharing fantasies just might
become your favorite part of foreplay. Express your desires through
dirty talk, whispering oh-so-seductively the naughty things you
want in bed. Fantasy is about freedom and imagination, so don't
limit yourself with inhibitions or judgmental thoughts. Instead,
simply speak your mind and see where it leads.

use his tie
to seduce and bind

the act of *roleplay*

Roleplay is a defining piece of the fantasy puzzle. When you act out a fantasy role, you are able to tap into your secret desires and release sexual inhibitions. There are no rules when it comes to this incredibly fun part of sex. As long as you and your partner are both enjoying yourselves, you can be as wild and original as you want.

why roleplay works Whether you have a favorite roleplay routine or have never practiced roleplay before, every fantasy encounter can be a new and sexy experience. In fact, the best part of roleplay is that you are completely free to let go of who you are outside the bedroom, including any inhibitions, and step into a new persona who is sexy and bold. You might find that you enjoy sex on a whole new level with this mindset. For many of us, the chance to leave all of our fears and hang-ups at the bedroom door revolutionizes sex.

If you have never tried roleplay before, it is normal to feel hesitant or even a little embarrassed. The truth is that the only way to get over these inhibitions is simply to accept your discomfort and throw yourself into the act. Over time, roleplay will become a more comfortable part of your relationship—although (fortunately) it rarely loses the adventurous thrill that makes it so much fun.

One caveat: Discomfort in the form of performance anxiety is normal, but if it's the actual scenario that you are uncomfortable with, then it's important to speak up and switch gears. You should never feel scared or unhappy during roleplay.

planning your roles Talk to your partner about what types of roles you both want to explore. Simply having this conversation can be very erotic and sensual—try it during a date while you are sharing a drink, or while you are cuddling in bed together. If you don't know where to start, consider the classics. Some popular scenarios include: boss/secretary, superhero/damsel in distress, super-heroine/fan boy, nurse/patient, schoolteacher/schoolgirl/boy, massage therapist/client, and the ever-popular French maid scenario. These are good roles to use in the beginning of your roleplay experience because it's likely that you both know the general character ideas, which will make it easier to plan your dialogue and actions. You can also go online or visit a local sex shop to explore other options.

Once you feel comfortable talking about roleplay together, you can up the erotic factor even more by alternating who chooses your roleplay scenario. Perhaps he stops by a sex shop after work and chooses a costume he is dying to see you in, or you order sexy attire to be delivered in time for date night. You don't have to spend a lot of money on this. In fact, instead of going shopping, you can get creative and use things you already have in the house, such as a kitchen apron (wear nothing underneath and play the sexy chef), or cutoff jeans (wear a tight flannel shirt with your bra exposed and be a sexy cowgirl). The best part? As roleplay becomes an integral part of your sex life, your fantasies will become more and more creative and expressive. Over time, this can become one of the most intimate and personal parts of your shared sexual story.

getting started Jump into your role by pretending that you are acting. You can think in advance about some lines your persona might say, or you can be more spontaneous. One of the best things about roleplay is that there is no right or wrong way to do it.

Of course, a key element of any successful story is drama. Consider what your character might do in real life and blow it out of proportion in order to introduce an element of dramatic surprise. As you do this, focus on creating a strong sexual charge. For instance, a nurse is nurturing, but she might also give you a gentle reprimand if you don't follow her directions. Bring that element to your persona in whatever way feels natural and sexy to you. If you still feel stuck, consider these ideas that our sassy nurse might use:

• **Tease your partner by reprimanding him** for being naughty when he tries to touch you. Then, give him a set of rules that shows him you're in charge, such as "You can only touch me with your mouth, not your hands" or "You can only touch me from the waist up."
• **If he breaks the rules,** "punish" him by gently biting him, or forcing him down and straddling him.

A blindfold is an essential roleplay prop, adding mystery and an arousing element of power-play to your lovemaking.

Try seducing him spontaneously during the middle of the date. If you already have an active fantasy life, you can do this simply by giving him an erotic glance and calling him by a private, bedroom-only name.

• **Make him wait before he can touch you,** titillating him with just a little of what he craves, whether it's a few moments of oral pleasure or the chance to view your breasts. Get him wanting more until he just can't stand it! Anticipation is one of the reasons roleplay is so sexy.

personalized roleplay
Once you have mastered the roleplay basics, you can start to put a personalized spin on your fantasy sex sessions by creating characters and dialogue that are completely your own. To make this more meaningful—and to create perfect fodder for future fantasies—spend some time acting out your roles, instead of just donning your costumes and having sex. Allow these characters to have ongoing roles in your bedroom, and adopt names that go with your new identities. Then, whenever you want to act out your fantasy, you can text your partner, "Jane has to stay after class tonight," or something similarly suggestive.

For some ideas on where to start, consider the possibilities below.

• **Play the massage therapist and client** Act out the scene by having your partner lie down on the table in the nude. Come into the room as you would if you were an actual massage therapist, keeping your conversation and tone professional for a while. Then, as the massage progresses, begin moving your hands closer and closer to her genitals until you have finally crossed the line of professionalism. As the temperature rises, slip off your clothing piece by piece, until you are also naked and the massage takes an even more intimate turn.

• **Act out schoolteacher and pupil** Set up a desk in your bedroom, or lay out some books and papers for pretend homework. As the teacher, you can pretend to give criticism on his assignment, while he acts the part of a wayward pupil, flirting outrageously and ignoring his homework. After he has tried your patience to the limit (and sent your arousal through the roof), you can then teach him a lesson that he won't soon forget!

• **Perform the sexy maid scenario** For this one, it might behoove you to send the kids off to Grandma's for the night. That way you can really act out your character by having access to the whole house. Strut your stuff in a sultry French maid costume, or simply don an apron with nothing underneath except a sheer thong or bra. Play with different variations of this theme: Perhaps he takes her against her will when she least expects it, or she plays the sexy seductress who convinces the homeowner to mix business and pleasure. (Switch up this scenario by having him play a sexy handyman—think overalls and a baseball hat— while she plays the bored housewife who can't keep her hands off him.)

the *play* chest
Store your roleplay props in a sexy play chest (with a lock, of course) inside your closet. Having a place set aside to contain these items will make it easier to incorporate roleplay into your lovemaking more often, and can lend a greater sense of erotic playfulness to the experience—as if you have private access to a grown-up treasure chest. In addition, having this chest means that you will always have a few staples handy for spontaneous nights of roleplay. Include whatever pieces turn you and your partner on: perhaps glasses for a sultry schoolteacher, a police hat for a stern but sexy cop, or a riding crop or whip for the classic, takes-no-prisoners dominatrix.

loving sex is...

experimental

It's a fact of life that we crave variety, and this is especially true in the bedroom. Experimental lovers are satisfied lovers, so leave no stone unturned in your quest for sexual pleasure. Sharing your unspoken desires can enhance your intimacy ten-fold. And don't forget about the spiritual side of sex: Indulge in slow, Tantric lovemaking every now and then to explore new degrees of intimacy.

exploring *fetishism*

Experimentation in the bedroom keeps things fresh, fun, and feisty. Without this pursuit of novelty, it's easy for dullness to set in—and dull is the last thing a satisfying sex life should be. Fortunately, there are many simple, sexy ways to breathe new life into your sexual experiences, including fetishism and BDSM. All you have to do is open your mind to exploration and leave your inhibitions at the door.

what is fetishism? Sometimes the sexiest activities are also the ones that are most taboo to discuss. This is certainly the case when it comes to fetishism, an oft-misunderstood sexual fixation that can range in intensity from erotic interest to erotic obsession. There are many varieties of fetish, but by definition sexual fetishism is when a person has a sexual reaction to a traditionally non-erotic body part or object. This might be someone who feels aroused by the sight of a beautiful pair of feet, or someone who responds sexually to the touch of latex.

The most common fetishes include hands, feet, tattoos, piercings, high heels, hair, and materials such as latex, rubber, or nylon. In fact, these fetishes are so common that in many ways they already contribute to the general definition of what is sexy. For example, an erotic scene in a movie might feature an actress wearing a pair of silk stockings with a black garter belt and high heels.

An image like this is easy to conjure up because it is an accepted expression of sexuality, yet at its core it sexualizes certain nonsexual things. As our definition shows, this is what makes it a fetish. This does not mean that fetishes are weird or unusual. Although people often tend to hide their fetishes from their partners and even themselves, the truth is that it is not uncommon to enjoy this behavior in some form or another.

discovering fetishism There are many ways to explore fetishism in your sex life. To start, talk to your partner about whether fetishized images turn you on, and if so what it is about the idea that appeals, whether it's the thought of her clad in leather or him with a naughty tattoo. It's surprisingly easy to turn these images into sexy fantasies that you make into reality for each other.

If materials like latex or nylon turn you on, try switching to latex sheets for an evening, or give your partner manual pleasure using silk panties or nylons. You can also incorporate other erotic textures, such as tickling feathers, patent leather high heels, or fishnet stockings. Be as risqué or as conventional as you like, but remember, the idea is to give the senses a visual feast that feels as erotic as it looks.

If you have a specific fetish that brings arousal and pleasure, there is also a variety of fetish erotica you can explore with your partner. These books and films feature both fetishized behavior (such as spanking or urination during sex) and fetishized items (such as leather or chains).

sharing *fetishism*

If your partner isn't well-versed in the world of fetish, he or she might be scared or even ashamed of the idea. If this is the case, it's important that you work to establish sexual standards that meet both of your needs.

To start, it may help to describe your fetish in as much detail as possible. If you can, say why it turns you on, and try to help your partner understand this part of your sexual nature. You can also help your partner open up to the idea through a number of books and films that explore this intimate, passionate part of human sexuality. (For specific suggestions, see Resources, page 282).

For many lovers, touch is an important part of fetish exploration.

setting boundaries As long as you aren't hurting yourself or your partner, there is no reason not to explore a fetish. There are instances, however, when fetishism becomes a dangerous—even an uncontrollable—obsession, in which a person goes to unhealthy extremes to satisfy his or her desires. Then it is time to seek help.

A fetish becomes dangerous when it negatively impacts a person's health and well-being. The difference between healthy fetish behavior and unhealthy behavior is the difference between an oenophile and an alcoholic. The former enjoys exploring and enjoying a specific interest, while the latter has no control over their actions. It isn't always an easy line to walk, but if you sense that your behavior is becoming uncontrollable, obsessive, or hurtful, then it is time to make some changes.

A fetish that is compulsive and dangerous will stand in the way of safety and intimacy. A trained sex therapist can work with you to modify your behavior enough to support your personal health and the health of your relationships. (For more on finding a therapist in your area, see Resources, page 282.)

experimenting with BDSM

BDSM is an acronym that encompasses a range of sexual activities, including bondage, discipline, domination, submission, sadism, and masochism. In each of these behaviors, the individual derives pleasure from pain, or pleasure from being completely dominated or completely dominant. BDSM is all about power, and exploring this part of your sexual self can be a sensory eye-opener.

BDSM for beginners It makes sense that people enjoy these activities given our understanding of how the brain works. Because the pleasure and pain centers of the brain are closely related, there are times when pain really does create pleasure (for more on this, see page 208). In addition, because playing with roles of power can allow us to step out of our usual (perhaps restrictive) personas, BDSM can be very freeing.

As you begin experimenting with BDSM, it's important that you first establish some ground rules with your partner. In the heat of the moment, it's easy to lose touch with whether your partner is truly enjoying the pain and domination, so your first step is to create a "safe" word that will be an unmistakable signal that you want the session to stop immediately. Make sure it's not a word that might be confused in the heat of the moment, such as moaning the word "stop"

Begin an evening of erotic power-play by tying your partner to the bed (use silk scarves for added eroticism).

or "no," both of which can be mistaken for part of the roleplay. Instead, use a completely benign word like "horse" or "carpet," or something else to that effect.

experimentation Once you have established your safe word, you are now free to fantasize and let your minds run wild. Begin asking questions: What types of BDSM behavior appeal to you and your partner? Do you like the idea of her tying you up? Do you want him to spank you? Do you want to play the role of a sex slave and have your partner command you? Brainstorm together and let your imaginations run wild. Also discuss what behaviors are absolutely off-limits, and how you will determine who is in charge and who is submissive.

If you have never experimented with BDSM before, you might not be sure where to start. Here are some ideas:

if she wants to be dominated Show your submission by following him obediently to the bedroom. Let him undress you and pin you to the bed, handcuffing you or tying you to the bedpost with his tie. He can experiment with bestowing pain and pleasure simultaneously by biting, spanking, or penetrating you intensely. Men, enhance her arousal by alternating aggression with soft, sensual stroking, bringing her to the edge of an orgasmic explosion and then pulling back. Women, as he has his way with you, moan to express pleasure, or respond with sexy submission by cooing "yes, sir" to every command.

if she wants to dominate Tell him (don't ask him!) to lie down on the bed or the floor. Engage his pain response by lightly tapping him with a riding crop or another erotic object. Be gentle at first, then slowly build intensity based on his response. Continue to engage his senses as your demands become more strict and your actions more fierce: Drip hot candle wax down his chest or grind your high heel gently into his back as you command him to give you sexual pleasure. Order him to call you "Mistress" or some other dominatrix term, and then tell him exactly what you want him to do. Throughout the night, tease him by alternating oral and manual pleasure with biting and other sexily painful actions. Finally, climb on top and control the depth and rhythm of penetration, letting him know that you are in charge and that you decide when he gets to reach orgasm.

the reality of BDSM

The number of people who practice BDSM might be greater than you think. According to research from the Kinsey Institute, 55 percent of females and 50 percent of males derive sexual pleasure from pain (such as biting). And, according to the Durex 2005 Global Sex Survey, 20 percent of people report engaging in "kinky play" with their partner, including incorporating blindfolds, bondage, and masks.

Like all fetishes, BDSM becomes dangerous when it moves from being an enjoyable part of your sex life to a required, uncontrollable part of your sexual behavior. All fetish runs the risk of becoming obsessive, and with BDSM this danger could actually lead to physical pain and injury. As with any other fetish, it's best to keep it an occasional pleasure. If it becomes a must-have occurrence, then it might be time to seek help (for more on this, see page 217).

discovering *tantric sex*

Truly explorative sex is about more than just traditional physical pleasure. Simply dwelling in the private space of intimacy that lovemaking brings is sacred and bonding. However, it can sometimes be difficult to slow down and feel this intimacy, especially since most of us have a hard time living in the present. Tantra is one of the best ways to explore and appreciate this soulful side of sex.

defining tantra Tantra has been practiced in Eastern cultures for thousands of years, and it's all about unity, enlightenment, and slowing down long enough to enjoy and understand the amazing depth of sensory experience that the human body is capable of feeling. You might say that the mission of Tantric sex is to weave together your souls, your minds, and, of course, your bodies. It can help you and your partner refocus and reconnect in a spiritual and a sexual way, bringing you great pleasure and intimacy.

As powerful as Tantric sex can be, it is sometimes intimidating for couples who are new to it due to its "New Age" reputation. In truth, Tantric sex is not some far-fetched New Age philosophy, but a wonderful approach to sex that emphasizes connecting with your partner in a deep and lasting way. Tantric couples generate positive and pleasurable energy that lasts long after they finish having sex.

practicing tantra One of the most well-known Tantric techniques involves delaying ejaculation to intensify and prolong intercourse. This has its roots in Tantric philosophy, which states that the man is fire and the woman is water. If a man becomes overexcited or too quickly aroused, the woman douses out his fire, ending the sexual experience much too quickly. If you instead keep the fire going and let your partner fan the flames, sex becomes more satisfying.

While you shouldn't feel pressure to have sex for hours, think of this as an opportunity to slow down and enjoy sex without limits or goals in mind. Part of the beauty of Tantra is that there is no rush to reach orgasm. This lack of pressure and expectation can create a relaxed atmosphere where you are both primed for pleasure.

Build an environment that enhances your peaceful state of mind by lighting candles and playing relaxing music. As you undress, focus on connecting physically, perhaps incorporating sensual massage (for massage techniques, see page 90). Notice small things: how warm and soft your partner's skin feels beneath yours, how each touch causes a different response, how your partner's breathing rises and falls.

As you slow down and dwell in the sensory moment, you can delay orgasm by focusing on controlling your Kegel muscles (for how to do this, see page 36). In order to keep your Tantric experience relaxed, try to never climb above a "5" on the pleasure scale, to avoid becoming overexcited or frustrated.

a tantric exercise A good Tantric technique for beginners to try is called "soul-gazing." This exercise focuses on intense connection, and it can be done on its own or in preparation for lovemaking. To begin, sit cross-legged on the bed, facing your partner. Arrange your bodies so that your stance and posture mirror each other, with your right hands crossing to touch each other's hearts. You can entwine your other hands or simply place them in your laps.

Next, gaze intently into each other's eyes. Breathe deeply, and notice the way your body feels each time you exhale and inhale. Clear your mind by focusing only on your partner's eyes and on your own breathing. Hold this pose for a few minutes, until your breathing is synchronized and you feel completely present in your body and with your partner. Then, close your eyes and take several deep, cleansing breaths, in which you exhale the stress and emotional toxins of your life. To enhance this exercise, try it without clothing.

do this when . . . you're on vacation

Going away together sets the perfect scene for spiritual sex. On vacation, you are both more likely to relax and feel comfortable enjoying each other's bodies without limits. For a true Tantric retreat, choose a place that is quiet and remote, where you will have space to reconnect with yourself and your partner, and truly dwell in the present without any distractions. In this relaxed atmosphere, Tantra will feel more natural, and you will return home with a deeper understanding of your partner's pleasure and your own.

Tantra is as much about intimate connection as it is about physical pleasure. Take time to relax and be restored simply by your partner's presence.

lotus position

In this position, she adopts the classic "lotus pose," with her legs crossed and her feet tucked over her hips. She then lies back and he leans over to penetrate. Because neither of you can move very much in this position, it's ideal for slow, focused, meditative sex.

yab yum

Sit on the floor in front of your partner. Wrap your arms and legs around each other, with the woman's legs and arms on top of the man's. He supports her in his lap, while she lifts her hips onto him. As he penetrates her slowly and deeply, she embraces him for support and leverage, moving her breasts up and down against his chest. This position will probably not lead to explosive orgasm for either of you, but it will bring deep intimacy and connection.

spiritual sex

If you don't want to practice Tantra, you can still add another level to your sexual experience by focusing on spiritual sex. Spirituality is at the core of Tantra, but Tantric techniques are not the only way to enhance the spirituality of your sex life. Spiritual sex is sex that is about more than just orgasm or physical pleasure.

Regardless of your religion or life philosophy, any time you slow down and worship your partner's body with meaning and intention, you are having spiritual sex. The best way to do this is to set aside time when you're completely alone and have no pressures or restrictions on your physical connection. In these moments, you can focus purely on each other.

nibble her supple,
sensuous breast

willing bondage
The act of bondage is incredibly arousing for both men and women. With your lover tied up in utter submission, let your desire run rampant: kiss his stomach, rub your genitals against his, and put on a tantalizing show with your half-clothed, just out-of-reach body. Watch his arousal grow to unbearable levels—the sex will be all the sweeter for it.

play the provocative,
powerful dominatrix

sex with *multiple partners*

Have you ever fantasized about bringing someone else into the bedroom? Threesomes are one of the most common fantasies among couples, and many men and women confess that they have considered a ménage à trois. Whether this is your own fantasy or something that your partner has admitted considering, the threesome—in theory, if not in practice—can have a place in the bedroom.

the threesome appeal Threesomes are sexy for many reasons. For one thing, they fly in the face of conventional coupling and typical social rules. Doing something this taboo has the potential to make us feel like daring sexual gods or goddesses. For another thing, threesomes have erotic math on their side: three mouths, three sets of hands, three tongues, and three bodies to give and receive pleasure.

Although threesomes are more commonly a male fantasy, they appeal to men and women for largely the same reasons. Men love the thought of having two sets of breasts and bodies to satisfy them, and may also enjoy the same-sex side of threesomes. It is not uncommon for a man to fantasize about being with another man, or about witnessing his partner being ravished by another man. Watching another touch and penetrate your partner reinforces how desirable she is, and can be incredibly arousing.

For women, a threesome lets her choose between two different men to penetrate her and satisfy every desire. Threesomes also appeal to women because they allow the exploration of same-sex fantasies: She can engage in sexual play with another woman, or stimulate as a team by showing the new woman exactly how to touch and please her partner.

threesomes in practice When you dissect the threesome, it's no wonder so many couples find this idea arousing. The truth, however, is that any couple must be very careful with this sensitive sexual scenario. Adding an extra person to your bed brings with it a whole host of problems, primarily jealousy and insecurity. No matter how secure you are in your relationship, it can be very difficult to sit back and watch your partner receive pleasure from another person. You might find yourself wondering if she prefers his touch to yours, or if he finds her body sexier. These are common and understandable fears—and they mean that what may begin as a harmless sexual experiment can soon become a relationship-dissolving mix of anger and hurt feelings that lingers long after the fantasy has played out.

The good news, however, is that you can safely incorporate some of the excitement and arousal that accompanies a threesome without actually adding a new person to your lovemaking. As we've discussed, threesomes are sexy partly because they feel taboo and risqué, and because they have the power to make you feel uninhibited and wild. These are all feelings that you can generate without risking the potential hurt of a threesome. Instead, simply engage in a different daring sex act with your partner. Depending on your individual desires, you might have sex in a public place (see page 206 for more ideas) or experiment with a new sex act, such as anal sex (see page 228). Anything that takes you out of your comfort zone can help to generate adrenaline inside the bedroom.

You can get even closer to the threesome fantasy by self-stimulating or having your partner stimulate you as you verbalize what it would feel like to be part of a threesome. Whisper what you would do if another person were present, or ask what your partner would do to pleasure someone else. Talking about these desires can feel just as naughty as practicing them, increasing your arousal dramatically while still keeping your relationship safe.

threesomes and *erotica*

You can also emulate the threesome effect by bringing erotica into your bedroom. One of the reasons men tend to fantasize about threesomes is because the thought of seeing two beautiful women naked seems to be an easy way to double their pleasure. Create the sense that there is more than one sexy woman in your bedroom with an erotic movie. Turn the volume up, so that you can hear the panting and moaning of the other couple, and join in on the vocal pleasure.

It may seem silly, but it works: making love in front of a mirror is another way to mimic the threesome effect—your reflection works as a third person to give and enjoy touch.

enjoying *anal play*

Anal play is an activity that many men and women enjoy immensely, but it is also something that is rarely discussed. As with other experimental sex practices, it is only just becoming acceptable to admit to enjoying anal play. Fortunately, earlier inhibitions are being reversed, because anal sex is equal parts intimacy and passion—a desirable bedroom combination if ever there was one.

the statistics In recent years, anal play has become increasingly common in bedrooms across America. Statistics show that, by the age of 24, one in three women in America has had anal sex, and that 40 percent of men ages 25-44 have had anal sex. This is a large increase from studies performed in the 1990s, in which only 20 percent of men aged 20 to 39 admitted to having recently engaged in anal sex.

What accounts for this change? For one thing, it is likely that a more widespread use of erotica, where depictions of anal sex are becoming increasingly common, has caused many couples to become more experimental in the bedroom (and to feel more comfortable admitting to anal sex activity). In addition, couples may have simply realized how much pleasure anal sex can bring. Thanks to the perineal sponge and the prostate gland, which are both very sensitive, anal sex can lead to deep and powerful orgasms (for an anatomy refresher, see pages 26–31). There is also something submissively sensual in giving yourself up to your partner for anal sex, and its still-taboo nature can cause both of you to feel naughty and aroused.

practicing anal For all of these reasons, anal sex has become a new sexual frontier with expansive opportunities for pleasure. If you and your partner have considered anal sex but have not yet made it a part of your lovemaking routine, the following tips will help you get maximum enjoyment out of this sexy act.

lubrication is a must Lubrication helps prevent tearing in the anus, and will make sex more comfortable and enjoyable for both of you. Make sure to choose a lube that is compatible with the condoms you are using, such as a silicone- or water-based formula. (Remember that oil-based lubricants should never be used with condoms.) Silicone-based lubricants are thinner than water-based lubricants, but they also last longer, so if you want the best of both worlds, try mixing the two together. Never rely on household items like lotion or Vaseline, as these can irritate the genitals and damage condoms.

never switch from anal sex to vaginal sex without washing thoroughly first. If you don't take this precaution, bacteria from the anus can be transferred to the vagina, which can lead to infection. If you want to have vaginal sex and anal sex in the same encounter, start with vaginal sex, and switch to a new condom before you move onto anal sex. If you are using your fingers, make sure to wash your hands thoroughly in between sex sessions—or better yet, take a steamy shower together before moving on to round two.

relax This is the most important part of anal sex. If you aren't relaxed, you won't enjoy yourself, and your partner might not be able to penetrate you. Anal sex requires trust, which is part of the reason why it works so well in a long-term relationship. You must feel confident that your partner will be sensitive to your needs, and will listen to your cues about depth and intensity of penetration. For women, it helps to be near orgasm before beginning anal sex, and to continue giving yourself clitoral stimulation as your partner penetrates you.

anal for beginners

If you aren't ready to jump right into anal sex, build your way up to this type of pleasure by enjoying anal play. Have your partner manually penetrate your anus with a finger or two as he gives you oral pleasure, or while he is penetrating you vaginally. Test your comfort level by adding more fingers, or perhaps even a small dildo or sex toy. Once you are ready to try the real thing, start slowly and, as with any type of sex, always let your partner know if you feel you don't want to continue for any reason.

Men can become more comfortable with this new experience by having their partner insert a finger into the anus while she gives oral pleasure, or as he penetrates her from a man-on-top position. It's okay to feel a little awkward at first—this is normal in any new sexual experience—but remember that craving anal play is completely healthy and normal. To take things a step further, try one of many (highly erotic) sex toys that have been created for women who want to penetrate their partners in this way.

Remember, anal play can be a sexy way to push your boundaries and try something new in the bedroom, but it isn't for everyone. If you feel scared or uncomfortable even after light experimentation, switch to a different sex act (after you swap out condoms and wash your hands). For all its merits, anal sex isn't something to be rushed. Don't let yourself feel discouraged if it takes a few tries to feel comfortable with this sexual act. As you increase your level of comfort and sensation, this erogenous zone will likely become more and more appealing.

keeping *safe*

Anal sex is on the rise, but sadly, so are anal cancers. This is why it is crucial that you practice safer sex during anal play. HPV, a sexually transmitted disease that is spread through the shedding of skin cells, is thought to be one of the primary causes of anal cancer (as well as cervical and even throat cancer). In the last 30 years, anal cancer has increased 160 percent in men and 78 percent in women. This does not mean that anal sex can't be a safe and healthy way to explore your sexuality, but it does serve as a cautionary reminder always to use protection, as you would during traditional penetrative or oral sex.

the *many colors* of sexuality

Sexuality is a fluid and ever-changing experience. For many of us, alternative sexual experiences help enrich and fulfill different parts of our sexual needs and desires. Whether you identify as gay or straight, or you move along the sexual spectrum and explore bisexuality, there are many ways you can enhance your connection and your sexual experience.

understanding your partner Homosexual couples have the benefit of already knowing and understanding the anatomy of their partner's body, being blessed with similar parts. However, that doesn't mean that sex is straightforward. Sexuality begins in the mind, which means that you must learn about your partner's desires and fantasies before you can become a great lover.

gay sex Like all sex, sex in a gay relationship is complicated and multifaceted. As with all couples, sexual connection and excitement can diminish over time unless you work to keep that intimacy intact. Consider the following ways to keep your sexual sparks flying:
• **Add excitement with sex toys** There are numerous ways to use and enjoy sex toys as a couple. Consider using a prostate stimulator on your partner while performing 69 (some can be heated or cooled for extra sensory pleasure). Dildos and vibrating butt plugs can also

As in any relationship, it's important that lesbian couples communicate in the bedroom in order to maintain a healthy, fulfilling sex life.

be incredibly erotic, as can a wide range of masturbating sleeves. Use these sleeves together to enjoy mutual masturbation as a couple, or use them to keep your arousal levels high when one partner is away. (Phone or webcam sex is much more fulfilling if you have a sleeve to help recreate the feel and touch of your partner's mouth.) For extra experimental pleasure, slip a vibrating cock ring around the shaft of your penis as you penetrate your partner.

• **Make use of erotica** There is a wide range of erotica that gay couples can use to enhance and improve their sexual experiences. For written erotica, consider collections of erotic stories or novels written by popular authors such as Amanda Young and K. A. Mitchell (see Resources, page 282, for more information). Read the stories aloud to each other to add some spice to date night, or act out a particularly sexy scene when you are in the mood for roleplay.

• **Experiment with positions** Certain positions are almost guaranteed to bring pleasure. Kneel or lie flat on the bed to try one of many classic rear-entry positions (for more on rear-entry positions and techniques, see page 152). Or, for something gentler, try lying side-by-side, facing in the same direction, which allows for easy entry from behind (for more on side-by-side positions, see page 136).

lesbian sex Lesbian sex is full of erotic possibility. Whether you prefer to be dominant, submissive, or enjoy a varied power play, there are many orgasmic options. To get started, consider the following:

• **Combine sex toys with roleplay** Try using a strap-on dildo equipped with a harness to penetrate your partner (many of these come with a vibrating insert, so that you can both receive pleasure simultaneously). There are also double dildos, which will permit you to both be penetrated at the same time, along with a whole host of vibrating toys that stimulate everything from your G-spot to your perineum. You can also roleplay with "cock socks," which emulate the look and feel of a man's penis when worn inside your panties, or you can use a handheld dildo, which allows you to lengthen and intensify your manual stimulation, while feeling the warmth and contractions of your partner's body as you pleasure her. If you prefer manual or oral stimulation, there are plenty of ways you can enjoy these activities as a couple without ever missing penetration (for more on technique, see pages 88 and 112–117).

preserving *passion*

Lesbian couples can be threatened by a unique quandary, which some therapists refer to as "lesbian bed death." This term is used to describe the lack of sex that can occur in lesbian relationships. Sadly, this is fairly common among long-term lesbian couples, possibly because, without the testosterone-driven sexual needs of a male partner, women can become blasé about sexual activity. The fact that most women receive their deepest relationship satisfaction from emotional connection instead of sex may also be a contributing factor.

As in any relationship, however, the less you prioritize sex, the less you will want it, and the more disconnected you and your partner will likely become. Because of this, it's important to stay connected sexually, even if one or both of you have willingly let your sexual connection dissipate. Prioritizing sex may not feel natural at first, but the more physically intimate you become, the more bonded and emotionally satisfied you will feel.

sexuality stats

There are over eight million gay, lesbian, and bisexual individuals in the United States, and this number is expected to grow as people begin to feel more comfortable admitting their orientation. A recent study performed by the National Center for Health Statistics found that close to 3 percent of women aged 18–44 identify as bisexual, while close to 2 percent of men aged 18–44 identify as such. In addition, Dr. Alfred Kinsey's groundbreaking research revealed that 46 percent of the men he studied had in some way enjoyed or responded to same-sex stimuli, suggesting that bisexual tendencies might be more prevalent than mainstream society would have us believe.

• **Seduce your partner's mind** When it comes to erotica, there is no shortage of film and written material to add another level of excitement and yearning to foreplay. Experiment with multiple types, from the gay-oriented Crash Pad series of films, to story collections like *The Best Lesbian Erotica* series. If it's BDSM you are after, consider popular fetish films from Maria Beatty, such as *Black Glove* and *Elegant Spanking* (for more information, see Resources, page 282).

• **Play with new positions** There are many positions to explore during oral sex and intercourse. While using a strap-on, you can enter your partner from any angle, including side-by-side, woman-from-behind, and standing positions (for more on these positions, see pages 136, 152, and 168, respectively). Oral sex can also be intensely pleasurable for both of you through positions such as 69.

bisexual sex

If you are bisexual but in a committed relationship, you might crave certain experiences that your partner simply can't give you. This is true whether you are in a same-sex or heterosexual relationship—however, if you choose to explore these desires, you may very well run into potential difficulties in your relationship. Even if your partner appears to be comfortable and secure with the idea of these bisexual desires, the physical act of you making love with another person can still create feelings of jealousy and insecurity. It is important for you to check in regularly with each other and make sure that you still agree on sexual boundaries, and also to ensure that any new partners are respectful of your mate.

A less threatening approach may be to enjoy and explore your bisexual desires without leaving the relationship or being unfaithful to your partner. Here's how you might do this:

for women If your partner is a man, but you find yourself fantasizing about same-sex experiences, rest assured that this is completely normal and healthy, whether you have acted on these fantasies or not. You can embrace your desires by watching or reading bisexual or lesbian erotica. Sometimes mental exploration can be enough to satisfy your desires and provide fodder for fantasies during sex. You can also talk to your partner about your desires and perhaps even roleplay how you would act during a bisexual encounter. For example, you might describe to him all the things you would like a woman to do to you, or all the things you would like to do to a woman. Include him, either as a participant or an erotic observer, and touch yourselves as you explore these fantasies.

If your partner is a woman and you fantasize about opposite-sex experiences, you might find that not everyone in the lesbian community embraces your feelings. While heterosexual women are more often expected to have same-sex desires, many lesbians are looked down upon or judged if they express desires to engage with the opposite sex. Some women are told these feelings mean that they aren't gay, or that they are confused about their sexual identity. This can be very hurtful, not to mention misguided. Most of us move up and down the sexual spectrum throughout our lives, experiencing our sexuality in different ways. It's rare for a woman (or a man, for that matter) to identify exclusively as gay or straight throughout her sexual life.

However, this doesn't mean that your partner will be open to exploring your heterosexual fantasy. Just as you aren't excited by all of her fantasies, she won't necessarily enjoy all of yours. Yet this doesn't mean that you have to eliminate these desires from your fantasy life: You can explore them on your own through fantasy and self-stimulation.

for men It is becoming increasingly common for women to confess to same-sex desires; however, men often feel more hesitant when it comes to making similar admissions. We can see this everyday reality mirrored in Hollywood: Sexy starlets admit to playing around with both sexes fairly frequently, but leading men would be hard-pressed to disclose that they have considered the same thing. The truth, however, is that sexuality doesn't fit into the narrow boxes that society sometimes constructs. A man can be turned on by the thought of another man, even if he is happily married or committed to a woman. By the same token, a man who identifies himself as homosexual might still fantasize about being with a woman on occasion. All of these desires are normal and healthy, but it is up to you and your partner to determine how or if these desires will play out in your sex life.

Talk to your partner about the idea of exploring these desires within the fidelity of your relationship. If you are in a heterosexual relationship, are there specific fantasies that come to mind when you think about other men? Do you like the thought of breaking the status quo? Do you crave being dominated and perhaps even penetrated? These are all fantasies that you can bring to life with your partner. She can dominate you during roleplay, and perhaps even penetrate you while wearing a strap-on harness or using a dildo. You can also explore your bisexual desires by enjoying gay erotica, much of which features a straight man who can't resist exploring his same-sex desires (for recommendations, see Resources, page 282).

bisexual male *fantasies*

For many gay men, the idea of being with a woman isn't enjoyable. Those who do enjoy the idea might meet some strong opposition, similar to the kind of challenges lesbian women face if they admit to being attracted to a man. Bisexual desires, unfortunately, still hold a stigma in the gay community.

If you find the idea of being with a woman arousing, but your partner is not interested in exploring these desires, there are a few possibilities. Your partner may be willing to explore them in a fantasy setting in order to satisfy you. If he doesn't feel comfortable with this, your best option is to keep them in the realm of self-stimulation and fantasy.

loving sex is...
safe

There is simply no substitute for the security that sex with a trusted partner can bring. Sexual intimacy unites you with your lover in unrivaled closeness—but it also requires absolute confidence and intimate knowledge of this person who is sharing your body. In today's world, talking about sexual histories, staying aware of the latest STI news, and deciding on a plan for birth control are all critical to a happy, healthy sex life.

emotional and physical safety

The best sex is uninhibited, wild, and no-holds-barred. However, in order to reach that state of freedom and openness, you must first trust your partner wholly and completely. To do this, it's essential that you prioritize your own emotional and physical safety in every sexual relationship.

building emotional closeness Feeling secure with your partner is important not only for your sexual spark, but also for your own physical and emotional health. Whether you have been married for years or are newly dating, knowing that your partner will protect and treasure your body is a crucial part of feeling comfortable during lovemaking. It is this feeling of closeness and comfort that naturally generates intimacy and mutual respect.

The best way to develop this intimacy and respect is to create an atmosphere in which you both feel loved and nurtured. This means making sure that feelings and needs are never mocked or derided, and that—particularly in the bedroom—you never use a personal feeling or fantasy against your partner. Your bedroom is the one place where you should both feel completely safe and protected from the outside world, a place where love and respect abide, and where all feelings and thoughts are safe to express. Whether you are sharing a naughty fantasy for the first time or reliving a painful childhood memory, the bedroom should be a safe place where you never have to second-guess yourself or feel embarrassed or stifled.

You should also endeavor to keep the bedroom a peaceful retreat. While it's certainly okay to disagree with each other, try to keep the bedroom a neutral zone in which you can both seek sanctuary at the end of a long day. Keep this area free of any negative actions or words, and focus instead on creating positive energy. If you do this often enough, you will find that simply walking into your bedroom gets you thinking in a new way. Make this a space where you breathe deeper, speak slower, and listen more. While no relationship is ever perfect, you have the power to make your bedroom a place without resentment or insecurities.

physical timing When dating someone new, you inevitably face the question, "How soon is too soon?" You may have a strong chemistry, you might both be dying to get each other into the bedroom—but is there a set time period you should wait before taking your relationship from just dating to having sex?

The answer really depends on you and your partner, but there are a few important things you should always consider before getting into bed with someone new. First, it's crucial to talk about safer sex practices and sexual health histories (for more on how to do this, see page 238).

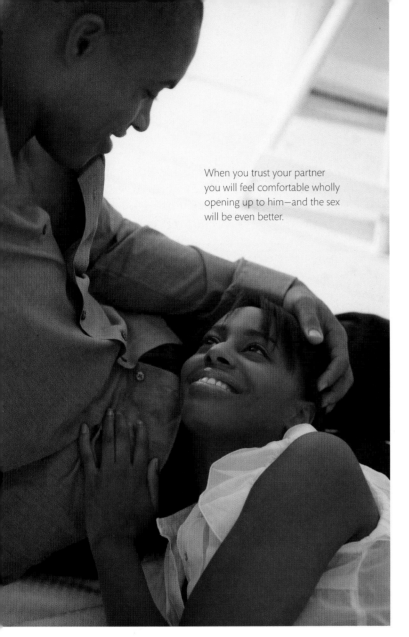

When you trust your partner you will feel comfortable wholly opening up to him—and the sex will be even better.

establishing *your limits*

Physical trust is also important in relationships. No matter how long you have been with your partner, a feeling of trust and safety when it comes to sexual acts is crucial, especially if you are dabbling in new activities like BDSM, anal play, or any other act that feels a little out of your comfort zone. Always remember that it is your right and your responsibility to say "no" or "stop" if you feel like it. It's important that each of you remain aware of the other's limits, and that you listen immediately if your partner says he or she is uncomfortable. This will help keep your relationship intimate and free of pressure.

It's also important to talk about your expectations of how sex will affect your relationship. For example, will your relationship be monogamous, or will you be permitted to see other people?

If you are looking for a serious relationship, I recommend that you don't have sex with a new partner until you are both ready to be monogamous. Not everyone assumes sex equals exclusivity, so having this conversation will help protect both your heart and your body. Once you have talked about your sexual histories and your expectations, you will be much more likely to feel safe with each other in the bedroom, and sex will be more pleasurable for both of you.

practicing *safer sex*

Recently, the term "safe sex" has fallen out of use due to the fact that sex can never be 100 percent safe. No contraceptive method is completely foolproof, and it is possible to contract an STI or become pregnant even if you take every precaution to protect yourselves. The term "safer sex," however, is more accurate. Safer sex is any sexual experience in which a couple takes precautions to protect themselves, physically and emotionally.

talking about sex I truly believe that sex requires protection because of its inherent intimacy. Not only is your body on the line, but so is your heart. You are giving someone the most private and sacred parts of yourself, which naturally involves some risk. Of course, most of us agree that this risk is worth the potential gain, but it's still necessary to take steps to make sex as physically and emotionally safe as possible.

Safer sex should always include a discussion of your emotional expectations. Ask your partner: "What will having sex mean to our relationship? Does this mean that we are committed to one another?" Discussing these issues before you sleep together will help to keep sex mutually pleasurable and enjoyable, with no unhappy surprises.

It's best to choose a neutral time before you have sex to initiate this conversation. Try bringing up the matter in a flirtatious manner. You might say something like, "I love spending time with you, and I can't wait to take things to the next level in the bedroom, but before we do, I think we should talk a little bit about safer sex." Letting your partner know that you can't wait to get more physical will be exciting, and broaching this topic in a relaxed way will help you feel more comfortable.

Consider the following questions you should ask your partner before you have sex:
• When is the last time you were tested for STIs?
• Have you ever had an STI, past or present?
• Have you ever shared needles or injected intravenous drugs?
• Would you be willing to get an STI test with me?
• Have you had unprotected sex since your last STI check?
• Are we going to be exclusive and monogamous?
• What are our expectations/special desires during sex?
• (If your partner has an STI): What steps are we going to take to make sure that we both stay protected during sex?
• (If you have an STI): Now that you are aware of my STI, what questions do you have about maintaining your sexual health?

physical protection When it comes to physical protection, it's essential that you become knowledgeable about different STIs, their symptoms, and methods of prevention (for more on this, see page 240). This is the first step toward establishing the form of protection that will work best for you and your partner. If you are newly dating, condoms are nonnegotiable unless you have both had a complete STI panel 3-6 months after your last sexual experience. The three- to six-month waiting period is critical because it allows enough time for herpes and HIV antibodies to show up in a blood test.

Depending on a person's level of exposure, it's important to remember that some STIs might not show up right away—so even if your partner currently has a clean bill of health, that status could change over time. This is why condoms are so important when you are dating someone new. It's easy for desire to give you a false sense of security when it comes to safer sex, but hooking up without considering the potential effects is a very risky and foolish choice to make. While it may not seem as romantic as moving fearlessly forward into a moment of passion, the truth is that you can't fully relax and enjoy sex if you secretly wonder whether your partner is STI-free. The best sex comes with no worries attached, so do yourself a favor and practice safer sex from the start. You will save yourself a lot of sleepless nights and unnecessary anxiety.

If one of you currently does have an STI, then you should discuss how it is being treated and managed, and how you can protect your partner from contracting it. Informed consent is crucial, even if telling your partner about your STI status can be daunting (see left for tips on how to have this conversation).

condoms Condoms are around 85 to 98 percent successful at preventing pregnancy if used correctly, and they are also a safe, noninvasive way to prevent the spread of STIs. However, even condoms cannot protect you completely. Some diseases, for example HPV, can be transmitted through shedding skin cells rather than transmission of bodily fluids. And, of course, you will be exposed to potential infection if your condom breaks.

Even knowing these risks, it is essential to use condoms during intercourse and during oral sex. Protecting yourself during oral sex is a precaution you can't ignore, particularly if you have just met your partner. Remember that you can contract an STI just as easily through oral sex as you can through penetrative sex. For fellatio, use a condom as a barrier. For cunnilingus, use a dental dam—a small device that acts as a barrier between the mouth and a woman's vulva. In a pinch, you can use plastic wrap, but be careful that it doesn't rip.

experimenting with condoms

Condoms have become much more fun over the past 10 years. Today, using a condom doesn't have to decrease your sexual pleasure. In fact, many of the condoms on the market serve to enhance pleasure. Some are made with polyurethane, so are thinner and less obtrusive than their latex counterparts. Others contain numbing agents to help increase his stamina, allowing him to last longer and receive more pleasure, or come equipped with strategically placed "pleasure dots" to stimulate her. Flavored condoms can also be a great way to add spice during oral sex.

increasing awareness about STIs

Sexually transmitted infections are much more common than you might think. In fact, one in five adults in the United States has an STI. Despite these alarming statistics, less than half of sexually active adults ages 18–44 have been tested for anything beyond HIV/AIDS. Read on to learn about the most common STIs, along with their prevention and treatment plans.

HPV

HPV (otherwise known as human papillomavirus) is the most common STI, across all ages, races, and sexual histories . More than five million men and women become infected with HPV each year, and almost half of all sexually active individuals will contract HPV at some point in their lives.

There are two types of HPV. High-risk strains endure for many years and can lead to cervical cancer, so it's very important that your doctor monitor your symptoms closely with regular Pap smears. Low-risk strains of HPV are not as long-lasting. They sometimes lead to genital warts or warts around the mouth, but there are often no symptoms. In fact, many people aren't even aware they have the infection.

HPV is spread through shedding skin cells, which come into contact with the genitals, anus, or mouth of another person, and even condoms cannot prevent infection. Fortunately, vaccinations are currently in place for women under the age of 30, and a trio of shots can help prevent certain strains of HPV, including two of the high-risk strains. However, the vaccine doesn't protect against all forms of HPV, and if you are already infected, you cannot receive the vaccination.

Although some strains of HPV are asymptomatic and not life-threatening, it's important not to treat this disease casually. In recent years, rates of cervical, anal, and oral cancers have skyrocketed, and some doctors believe this is linked to the increased rates of HPV. (In men and women, anal cancer alone has increased 160 percent and 78 percent, respectively—and this just in the last three decades.)

chlamydia

Chlamydia is one of the most common STIs in America , surpassed only by HPV. Known as the "silent STI," chlamydia is spread through oral sex, intercourse, and anal sex, and can also be passed from mother to baby during childbirth. Chlamydia is often asymptomatic. When symptoms do occur, they include burning during urination, abnormal discharge from the vagina or penis, pain during sex (for women), pain in the testicles, and burning and itching around the opening of the penis (for men). Women also tend to suffer from lower back pain, nausea, fever, and non-menstrual bleeding.

Thankfully, chlamydia can be diagnosed with a simple urine test or swab test, and it is then easily treated with a course of antibiotics. However, it is key to catch chlamydia early on before it develops into PID (pelvic inflammatory disease), which can potentially cause irreversible damage to the reproductive system. In women, chlamydia can damage the uterus and fallopian tubes, and can cause pneumonia and eye infections in newborns if passed from mother to child. In men, chlamydia can harm the epididymis and lead to sterility, although this is very rare. It can also lead to infertility issues in men, and swelling of the prostate and scarring of the urethra. Abstinence is the only way to truly prevent chlamydia, but you can protect yourself from this disease by using condoms and undergoing regular STI testing.

gonorrhea   Over 1 million people in the United States have gonorrhea. The group most at risk for this disease are sexually active teenagers and women, who are twice as likely as men to contract gonorrhea. Symptoms of gonorrhea are similar to those of chlamydia, and the two are often confused: even a doctor generally needs to perform an STI test in order to decipher the nature of your infection. For women, these symptoms include pain during urination, discharge

women and teens: at greater risk of STIs

Across the board when it comes to STI stats, women are more at risk for developing STIs than men are. This is because the female genitals are more susceptible to infection and bacteria. The penis is protected by a small membrane opening that can help to ward off bacterial entry, but women aren't so lucky. As for teenagers, they are less likely to use protection regularly and correctly as their older counterparts, which puts them in the high-risk group, too—and reinforces our need to educate about STIs and contraception.

Being open about your sexual history, including any exposure to STIs, is crucial to establishing trust in a new relationship.

herpes outbreaks:
what to expect

The first herpes outbreak usually occurs within a few weeks of infection, generally repeating a few times in the course of a year, particularly during times of stress.

This first outbreak is generally the worst. It begins a couple of weeks after infection, and lasts for 1-3 weeks. Recurrent infections are generally shorter and not as widespread and painful, although this varies from person to person. As with many other STIs, it's important to remember that even if you aren't having an outbreak, you can still pass herpes on to a partner.

from the vagina (which is often puslike or bloody), pain during sex, and excessive menstrual bleeding or bleeding that is non-menstrual. For men, symptoms include burning during urination, pain inside the penis, discharge from the penis, and swollen testicles. As with chlamydia, untreated gonorrhea can lead to PID. It can also cause eye infections for babies who are born to mothers with gonorrhea, as well as a host of other internal issues, including a condition known as Disseminated Gonococcal Infection (DGI) that causes joint pain and infection of the heart. It can also lead to meningitis and arthritis.

Gonorrhea is easily diagnosed and treated with antibiotics, so long as you begin treatment before the infection can cause permanent and irreversible damage to your reproductive organs. To protect against this disease, use condoms each and every time you have sex, whether you are having vaginal, anal, or oral intercourse.

herpes Studies suggest 90 percent of those who have herpes don't even know it . It's more common in women than in men (in the US, about one in five women aged between 14 and 49 have genital herpes).

There are two types of herpes, HSV-1 (oral herpes) and HSV-2 (genital herpes). Oral herpes is more commonly called a cold sore, and although it is possible for HSV-1 to spread to the genitals through oral sex, HSV-2 is generally spread during sexual contact. Symptoms are similar in both types, however, and include blisterlike sores around the genitals or mouth, which are often painful and uncomfortable. Both types of herpes can also be accompanied by flulike symptoms, including fever, joint pain, and nausea, as well as burning in the genitals.

Medication can help treat herpes and diminish symptoms, but there is currently no cure for this disease. There is also no foolproof way to protect against herpes, although using condoms during all types of intercourse, including oral and anal, can help. (Remember to use a dental dam for cunnilingus.)

syphilis Syphilis affects over 100,000 Americans. This disease begins with nothing more than a single sore, called a chancre, which is located at the spot of infection (common areas of infection are the anus, the penis, the vagina, or the mouth). This sore is not very painful and soon goes away even without treatment.

However, the longer you wait to treat syphilis, the worse it will be for your body and your health. Once the sore heals, the second stage of syphilis begins, which causes flulike symptoms and rashes. If still left untreated, it then moves onto the latent stage, in which your body seemingly returns to normal. However, for some people, syphilis then moves onto the late stage, in which everything from blindness to paralysis, dementia, and damage to the liver, bones, eyes, and heart can occur. Severe syphilis infections can even result in death.

While these symptoms are scary, the good news is that if you get tested and treated, syphilis can be easily cured. Condoms can help protect you from contracting syphilis, as can other safer sex practices, such as receiving regular STI testing from your doctor.

trichomoniasis Otherwise known as "the trich," this STI affects 3 million Americans. Symptoms include a yellow discharge from the vagina (for women), itching or burning in the genitals, and pain during sex or urination. Even if you don't show any symptoms, you can still spread trichomoniasis, which also damages your immune system and puts you at greater risk of contracting other STIs, such as HIV.

Trichomoniasis can be spread to the genitals or anus, but not the oral area. It is curable through a course of antibiotics that can be prescribed by a doctor. As with other STIs, practicing safer sex can help protect you from contracting this infection.

HIV/AIDS In the United States, more than one million men and women live with HIV (human immunodeficiency virus), and it is estimated that there are between 40,000–50,000 new cases each year. HIV occurs when the body begins to attack its own blood cells, specifically the CD4+ T cells, which are needed to stave off infections. When these cells are compromised, the body is unprotected against potential infections. Symptoms of HIV include rashes and flulike symptoms, such as fever and swollen lymph nodes. While there is no cure for HIV, treatment can help to promote better health and stave off AIDS.

If left untreated, HIV is likely to develop into AIDS (acquired immunodeficiency syndrome) within 10 years of infection. A person moves from HIV into AIDS status when their T-cell count drops to below 200 per cubic millimeter, and symptoms of this advanced disease include severe infection, weight loss, fatigue, rashes/lesions, tuberculosis, Kaposi's Sarcoma, pneumonia, lymphoma, and cervical cancer. While there is likewise no cure for AIDS, treatment can help decrease symptoms and promote improved health.

Although not 100 percent effective, condoms are the best way to guard against HIV/AIDS. You should also never share needles or handle anyone else's blood. Although there is no cure for AIDS yet, medical advances are helping patients live longer, healthier lives.

when to *get tested*

I cannot overstate the importance of being tested for STIs, nor should you wait until you experience symptoms before you go for testing. Many STIs are asymptomatic or take months or even years to surface. In fact, 90 percent of people who have herpes don't know it. This means that both you and any potential partners could be at risk if you aren't fully aware of your sexual history.

your contraception choices

Protecting yourself against unwanted pregnancy is an important part of a healthy sex life. There are a number of contraceptive methods available, and they all come with their own pros and cons. It's an important decision that you should discuss with your partner and your doctor—likely more than once, as your contraceptive needs will change as you grow within your relationship.

the oral contraceptive pill The pill is a simple and unobtrusive way to protect against unwanted pregnancy. It consists of estrogen and progesterone, which work together to prevent fertilization. The average birth control pill has an efficacy rate of more than 99 percent, but there is also plenty of room for human error. It's important to take the pill at the same time every day for maximum protection. It's also a good idea to speak to your doctor about other medication that you are taking, to ensure that it won't interfere with the pill's effectiveness (ampicillin and some diabetes medications can do this, as can some herbal supplements). Because the pill doesn't protect against STIs, you must take additional precautions to protect yourself, such as using a condom. (For more on condoms, see page 239).

Disadvantages of this method of contraception include weight gain, headaches, mood swings, blood clots, and a decreased libido. You can decrease these side effects by taking a pill that has a lower hormonal dose. In addition, you should make sure that you do not smoke while you are on the pill, as this can lead to increased risk of blood clots.

Two alternative hormonal options are not administered orally. The birth control injection is given by your doctor and is effective for up to three months. The birth control implant is a small rod that is inserted into the arm, and is effective for up to three years. (Most women cannot see the implant once it is in place.)

vaginal contraceptive rings Contraceptive rings are small, transparent rings that are inserted into the vagina once a month, and then removed during your period. Like the pill, the ring releases a small dose of hormones throughout the month, although it is thought that the hormones are absorbed directly to reproductive organs, rather than throughout the body, so users of the ring may suffer fewer side effects than those on other forms of hormonal birth control. You can leave the ring in during sex: Most men report that they can't feel it, or that it feels similar to the cervix and isn't disruptive in any way.

Like the pill, the ring's efficacy rate is 99 percent if used correctly. Side effects are also similar (weight gain, blood clots), although some women also experience yeast infections or vaginal discomfort as a result of using the ring. If you are too busy or too forgetful to take the pill at the same time every day, then the ring might be useful—just remember that, like the pill, the ring does not protect against STIs.

diaphragms, sponges, and spermicide The diaphragm and the sponge are referred to as "barrier methods" because they prevent the sperm from reaching the egg, as opposed to hormonally changing a woman's body to prevent sperm from becoming implanted. The sponge is a small, donut-shaped barrier that is inserted into the vagina before sex. If used correctly, it has an 87 percent efficacy rate; however, human error can decrease this percentage.

The diaphragm is a latex cup, which you insert into your vagina before sex. Like the sponge, it prevents the sperm from reaching the egg, and is around 85 percent effective when used correctly. The diaphragm and the sponge can be used with spermicide, a liquid, gel, or foam which breaks down sperm before they reach the egg.

the IUD IUDs (short for intrauterine devices) have been around for decades; however, problems with this form of birth control in the 1970s have made many women hesitant to consider it. The early IUD was linked to increased risk of pelvic inflammatory diseases (PID), and sadly, some cases even led to death. Fortunately, these issues have been fixed, and IUDs are now a safe and viable contraceptive option.

The IUD is a small, T-shaped device implanted into your uterus by your gynecologist. It prevents pregnancy by damaging or killing sperm before they reach the egg, and, once implanted, is effective for anywhere from 5 to 10 years, depending on the type of IUD selected.

There are two forms of IUD: hormonal and non-hormonal. Non-hormonal IUDs are made of copper, which is fatal for sperm and hence prevents pregnancy. This is a great option for women who wish to avoid hormones. Hormonal IUDs are made of plastic, and contain a small dose of progestin. This hormonal option can help decrease the risk of pelvic inflammatory disease, and may also minimize pre-menstrual (PMS) symptoms. While you won't be able to feel either form of IUD during sex, some women report increased cramps and lower-back pain, along with headaches, increased bleeding, and acne.

One additional caveat for this method of contraception: the IUD is only recommended for women who are in a monogamous relationship. If you contract an STI while you are using an IUD, the device could cause the STI to move into the uterus and potentially cause PID. So this form of protection is only advised for women who are not exposed to risk of infection through sex with multiple partners.

the IUD and *fertility*

The IUD   an effective   own the road   enience, this mig   who are cons   ve short term, since the device is effective for five years or longer, and since implantation requires a medical procedure, which can be expensive if not covered by insurance.

One other caveat: For women who have not yet given birth, the process of inserting the IUD might be more painful, as the cervix isn't as open before childbirth.

sex struggles for men

Almost 30 percent of men suffer from premature ejaculation, or early ejaculation, as I prefer to call it. Premature ejaculation sounds judgmental and can cause feelings of embarrassment and shame. However, the truth is that early ejaculation is nothing to be ashamed of. Millions of men struggle with these issues at some point or another, and thankfully, there are several simple techniques that can help keep both you and your partner satisfied in the bedroom.

causes Early ejaculation occurs when a man reaches orgasm before he wishes. The average sex session lasts around seven and a half minutes, and anything less can be considered early, with some men lasting only a few seconds after penetration. Men who suffer from early ejaculation often feel as though they have no control over their sexual response, which can cause feelings of frustration and anxiety. In certain cases, this frustration is so intense that a man avoids sexual activity altogether, sidestepping sexual or even romantic contact in order to prevent the potential shame of sexual failure.

There are many causes for early ejaculation. These causes range from the physical (including hormonal changes and the side effects of certain medications) to the emotional (including depression, performance anxiety, and stress). In addition, the shame that men often feel as a result of this difficulty adds to the emotional causes of early ejaculation. The more a man worries about reaching ejaculation too soon, the more anxious he will feel and the less control he will have over his sexual response. As with many sexual struggles, it can become a vicious cycle.

treatment Thankfully, treatment for early ejaculation is available. The first step is to speak with your doctor. It's natural to feel embarrassed or awkward during this conversation, but the truth is that your doctor has discussed this same issue with many other patients, so you can be reassured that your symptoms and your concerns are nothing new or unusual. Make sure that you see a doctor who has a specialty in this area, such as a urologist who specializes in sexual medicine. You can also ask your general practitioner for recommendations, or see page 282 for more suggestions of how to find a specialist in your area.

Talking to a doctor can help you learn whether medication might be interfering with your sexual response. In fact, depending on your age, your doctor may even perform a hormone panel to find out whether you are reaching the early stages of andropause (for more on andropause, see page 252). Once you have eliminated any possible medical causes for early ejaculation, you can then move onto the emotional and behavioral side of your sexual experience.

First of all, it's important to examine when and where the early ejaculation began. Has the timing of your sexual response always been an issue, or is it a relatively new concern? Many men find that this sexual difficulty began happening around the time they lost a job,

If your partner struggles with early ejaculation, your support and love are especially crucial to his self-esteem in the bedroom.

or as they entered a difficult stage of their relationship. Life crises such as these can have a huge impact on sexual response and enjoyment, and they can help to explain many early ejaculation issues.

Once you have established and worked through any emotional causes of early ejaculation, you can move on to technique-based, behavioral treatments that addresses your concerns in the bedroom. There are many treatments beyond talk therapy that can address both the emotional and the physical barriers of early ejaculation, many of which we've covered earlier in this book. These might include the stop-and-start technique (for more on this, see page 98) or the slower, less climax-focused techniques used in Tantric sex (for more on Tantra, see page 220). Even condoms can help to slow your arousal down, especially given all the options available. For example, benzocaine condoms can help decrease sexual sensation and bring your sexual response down to a more manageable level. You can even use them during self-stimulation to prolong and control your excitement, and help you train for intimacy with a partner.

Talking with your partner about any struggles in the bedroom is an important part of treatment.

erectile dysfunction Erectile Dysfunction (ED) is another common sexual difficulty that men encounter, characterized as an inability to reach or maintain an erection. Around 18 million men in the US suffer from ED, and again, there is a wide range of potential causes. Along with deciphering any emotional or relational causes, it's important to tackle the physical side of this issue. Impotence is often related to other physical difficulties and can be a sign of compromised blood flow in the body, whether that stems from a lack of exercise, a mechanical issue with blood flow to the penis, or a medical condition such as diabetes. It can also be one of the earliest signs of heart disease.

Living a healthy lifestyle can go a long way toward treating or preventing ED. A nutritious diet, plenty of exercise and sleep, minimal alcohol, and refraining from smoking can help keep you in optimum sexual health. In addition, behavioral techniques such as the ones outlined above can help train your body to relax and stay focused.

Medical options such as Viagra and Cialis can also help to get you back on track, with one caveat: Men who use nitrates should not take this medication. Many men consider this to be the least invasive option. It works by increasing blood flow throughout the body, including to the genitals. There might also be a bit of a placebo effect in the boost of confidence and assurance that comes with knowing that you are addressing your sexual needs.

There are also devices available to assist you in creating and sustaining an erection. A penis pump is a simple tube attached to a hand-powered pump that creates suction. The man inserts his penis into the tube and operates the pump, which draws blood to the penis to encourage an erection. Alternatively, in extreme cases, inflatable implants can be surgically inserted into the penis tissue. These can be expanded on demand to create an erection.

You might also consider penile injection therapy, in which you inject yourself with chemicals such as phentolamine, papaverine hydrochloride, and prostaglandin E-1. The injection causes an erection to occur shortly thereafter and, in clinical trials, almost 80 percent of men achieved satisfying erections. There are some risks involved in this method, including priapism (a painful erection that will not subside), so, as with any treatment, it is important to talk with your doctor.

Remember, nearly every man suffers from erectile difficulties at some point in his life. As you work through these issues, talk with your partner about any worries you might have, and keep your sex life satisfying by finding other ways to enjoy sex, such as through VENIS, self-stimulating together, using sex toys, or performing erotic massage.

seeking *therapy*

If early ejaculation has been an issue throughout your adult life, it's a good idea to seek the assistance of a sex therapist. A sex therapist is trained in all issues of sexual dysfunction, and can help you discover what may be causing these feelings of stress and powerlessness in the bedroom. In some cases, early ejaculation stems from inadvertent training to rush through masturbation for fear of getting caught. In other cases, it may be related to a sense of sexual shame or performance anxiety, or to emotional troubles with your partner.

Childhood sexual abuse can also be a factor that contributes to early ejaculation: a scary and little publicized fact is that one in six boys will receive unwanted sexual contact by the age of 16. Healing from this trauma is particularly difficult for men because our society still often upholds the "boys don't cry" myth, which means that sexually abused boys often have no outlet for recovering from this pain. Again, a therapist can be an invaluable resource to you as you work through these issues, either alone or with a partner.

finding a *balance*

Sexual response varies for everyone, and, as we've discussed, it is often very different for men and women. While you might be aroused by nothing more than the sight of your partner in a lacy black bra, she might need more mental stimulation to get her sexual arousal to heat up. However, lining up your mismatched libidos doesn't have to be difficult. In fact, it can become a natural, even erotic part of your foreplay.

knowing her stimuli We all respond differently to sexual stimuli. Men often respond quickly to visual cues (such as the classic black lace bra), while women respond to more subtle stimuli, such as the sound of her partner's voice in her ear or the romantic email he sends her in the middle of the day. Because female turn-ons are often more involved, discovering what type she prefers will help you set the mood—and can even keep her in a state of arousal virtually all the time. Of course, I don't mean keeping her at an orgasmic 10 every minute—I mean creating a slow burn of sexual energy that constantly flows between you (for more on this, see page 62).

One way to do this is spend time discovering your partner's needs and then keep that stimulus ever-present. For example, if you know that she needs to feel feminine to be in the mood, offer to watch the kids, so that she has time to take a bubble bath. Or, if you know that she responds to spontaneity, sweep her off her feet with a sensual kiss before she leaves for work, or surprise her with a bottle of wine and her favorite meal when she comes home from work. These little gestures will help build a slow and steady system of arousal that will more easily match with your quick-fire sexual awakening.

thinking like him Have you ever wondered why men always seem ready to go when it comes to sex, but women tend to have a million other things on their mind? This phenomenon is not your imagination. Women are notorious multitaskers who can have a hard time letting go of their to-do list and enjoying sex (for more on this, see page 72). But sometimes this can mean you and your partner miss out on chances for intimacy and relaxation. So the next time your partner makes an advance and you are tempted to run off and unload the dishwasher, stop. For a moment, try to think like a man. Simply put: Sex feels good and makes people happy—so just do it! It's okay if you aren't immediately in the mood and need a bit of foreplay to get warmed up. Just give it a few minutes. Before you know it, your body will start responding and your mind will forget all about the dishes.

It's also important that you sometimes take the reins and initiate sex, instead of just waiting for him to do the work. Not only will it make him feel incredibly desired and attractive, but it will also help you feel empowered and sexy. It's good to be sexually receptive, but you should also work to be sexually proactive. Your sex life will thrive as a result.

setting boundaries Boundary issues are one of the main concerns among couples with mismatched libidos. For example, if a man (or a woman—it's not always men who have higher levels of desire) is always asking for sex and being turned down, resentment will build. As a result, he might pressure her into having sex, or make jokes about their sexual relationship. Although hurtful, this type of response likely covers the sadness that he feels due to being rejected. To avoid this kind of pain, it's important to set boundaries that will be helpful for both of you. Discuss how much sex you each want, and reassure your partner that a lower libido isn't a reflection of your attraction to him.

Take the initiative to ask for sex every once in a while—it can do wonders for both your own libido and your partner's.

maintaining *privacy*

It's also a good idea to set boundaries regarding what details, if any, you will share with your friends. I strongly recommend that you don't tell anyone personal details of your sex life, as it can compromise your intimacy and sense of trust. Even if your friends confide intimate facts about their sexual relationships, keep your own bedroom matters where they belong—in the bedroom. This is an infinitely valuable way to nurture trust and respect in your relationship.

menopause and andropause

Aging is a fact of life, and sadly, while we grow older and wiser, our bodies often just grow older. Changing hormones and the "change of life" impact everything from our metabolism to our sexual response. The changes women go through during menopause are commonly known and openly talked about, but for men, this change—called andropause—is often less familiar. Menopause and andropause can sometimes wreak havoc on our bodies and our minds, but there are simple treatments and techniques to get you through these challenges with your relationship (and your sex life) intact.

perimenopause The first signs of menopause occur during a stage called perimenopause, which some women experience as early as age 35, although for most, it does not begin until age 40 or later. During perimenopause, a woman's estrogen and testosterone levels are lowering. As a result, menopausal symptoms such as sleep disturbances, mood swings, hot flashes, vaginal dryness, and decreased libido can begin to occur. As time passes and you continue to move into the menopausal stage of life, these symptoms will intensify.

The perimenopausal stage can last anywhere from two to 10 years, although it can be difficult to determine when a woman first enters perimenopause. One sign that these hormonal changes may have begun is a shortened menstrual cycle, which will continue to slow as the woman progresses into menopause.

symptoms of menopause During menopause, women may also experience night sweats, weight gain, and a lowered libido, along with emotional symptoms, including feelings of insecurity. You might feel like less of a woman once you stop menstruating, or weight gain may make you feel unattractive. Grappling with these self-esteem issues is all part of the menopause process, but there are things you can do to feel better. For one thing, exercise can help to inspire energy and confidence. Even better, many people find that they actually become more comfortable and secure with themselves as they age. If you do find yourself struggling and unable to cope with these feelings, then a therapist might be useful in helping you to adjust to these new life changes (for tips on finding a therapist, see Resources, page 282).

It's not uncommon to experience feelings of guilt or confusion during this time. Because women like to please others, we often feel guilty about hormonal mood swings or about our lowered libido. If you fall into this category, remember that all of these new emotions are stemming from hormonal changes, and the best thing you can do to minimize the effect is to get the physical and emotional support you need with a doctor who understands hormones and a therapist who can help put your emotional symptoms in perspective (see Resources, page 282, for how to find a therapist in your area) Also, remember that this stage of life is temporary. After surviving menopause, many women say that they feel stronger, more confident, and more like themselves than at any other period in their life.

treating menopause Most menopausal symptoms can be treated with a wide array of medical and behavioral options. Hormone replacement therapy (also known as HRT) can help adjust hormone levels and decrease symptoms—however, a recent study from the World Health Organization linked HRT to increased risk of cancer, so it's important to talk to your doctor about this and any other hormonal treatment, to make sure that it is a viable option for you.

Another hormonal option is bioidentical hormone therapy (BHRT). Bioidentical hormones are derived from a variety of sources, including plants and animals, and mimic the hormones that are naturally produced in the body. Your doctor can customize each dose to your unique hormonal needs, which also allows you to take the smallest dose possible. However, some risk is still involved. It's crucial to find a good pharmacy to compound the hormone cocktail to get maximum benefit with minimum side effects, and it's important to note that these hormones aren't regulated by the FDA. Additionally, there haven't been any studies into the long-term effects of BHRT, so there could be potential risks down the road that the medical community is not yet aware of. As with any other treatment, it's important to do your own research and talk to your doctor about potential benefits and risks

low libido during menopause

Low libido can impact a woman's self-esteem and self-worth, particularly if it is accompanied by other menopausal symptoms. Worst of all, it can make her feel as though she is no longer a sexual being. These feelings are normal, yet it's important to work through them and make sure they don't derail your sexual enjoyment and relationship happiness.

To work through these libido changes, you need to find time for intimacy. Keep in mind that most of us don't have as much energy at night during this time—so it's important to talk to your partner and find compromises that work for both of you. (Do you have more energy and desire in the morning? Or can you meet for lunch?)

You will also feel more energized and sensual if you find activities that reconnect you to your feminine power. Make it a point to spend time with girlfriends; engage in empowering exercise, like dance; and find other strong women role models to emulate. You'll feel more like yourself in no time.

Spending time alone with your partner can help you restore your sense of self during the changes of menopause and andropause.

a dip in *testosterone*

Testosterone levels can vary among men at any stage of life, but this is especially true during andropause. Experts at The Mayo Clinic state that older men generally have less testosterone than younger men, and it is thought that men lose about one percent of their testosterone each year after they turn 30. This means that, by the time most men turn 70, they may have lost 40–50 percent of their testosterone. Hormone treatments and natural supplements can help boost testosterone levels, and regular exercise and good nutrition can help you feel more youthful and energized.

involved, in order to determine if it is a good option for you. If menopausal symptoms are greatly interfering with your life, then BHRT might be worth investigating, but otherwise you might opt to forgo this path in favor of something less invasive.

Many women also swear by herbal remedies like black cohosh and damiana leaf, herbal supplements that are believed to help treat the symptoms of menopause. However, these have not been approved by the FDA and there are no clinical studies that reinforce these statements at this time.

Perhaps the most important thing to minimize any uncomfortable symptoms of menopause is to practice a healthy lifestyle. Following a healthy diet and exercising regularly can help keep weight gain at bay, and sex aids like lubrication, erotica, and sex toys can help to increase your arousal and keep your sexual desire functioning at a higher level. Communicating with your partner is also important, as is getting enough sleep and minimizing stress as much as possible.

andropause Andropause generally begins in men around age 35. It is caused by a decrease in testosterone, and an increase in levels of oxytocin and the hormone SHBG (sex hormone-binding globulin). As a man moves into his 40s and 50s, these hormonal shifts intensify, as do any symptoms. Symptoms of andropause may include low libido, weight gain (particularly around the midsection), insomnia, lack of energy, and depression.

There are many potential treatments for andropause, including testosterone replacement therapy (also known as TRT). TRT can be administered through injections, creams, or pills, and any of these can help replace testosterone and decrease symptoms. As with HRT, it has been suggested that TRT is not a good option for everyone, especially those who are known to be at risk for prostate cancer. However, a growing body of research indicates that testosterone treatments may not be linked to prostate cancer. Because of this, many prescribing doctors are starting to explore this option more readily with andropausal patients. If you are interested in this treatment, speak to your doctor about your compatibility.

You can also decrease the impact of andropause by eating healthily, and getting plenty of rest and exercise. It's important to limit your intake of fatty foods and dairy during this time, as the hormones in dairy products can exacerbate your hormonal balance further. Zinc supplements have been shown in some preliminary studies to be potentially beneficial in increasing testosterone, but remember to talk to your doctor before beginning any new supplement regimen. Also, remember that scheduling regular prostate exams becomes increasingly important as you grow older.

   If you suffer from sexual side effects such as erectile dysfunction, make sure to discuss this with your doctor (to learn more about this, see page 246). Just as many women struggle to repair their feminine identity once they stop menstruating, men often feel as though they have lost part of their "maleness" if their sexual needs or level of desire change. Identifying any of these emotional struggles, and speaking to your doctor or even a therapist about how to treat any symptoms, can help you navigate these changes.

   Finally, it's very important to communicate with your partner and make sure that you are both on the same page with all the changes that are taking place. Aging is a fact of life that long-term couples can confront together, and if you stay bonded and open about your journey, there is no reason why menopause or andropause should sap your desire for each other or your zest for life.

Couples in the midst of menopause and andropause may struggle with lowered libidos. Cuddling, massage, and other sensual activities can keep your connection strong, bonded, and intimate.

dealing with *loss of desire*

Loss of desire can happen to any person at any age. Sometimes the reasons behind low libido are physical, while other times they are emotional or stress-related. Deciphering where and when your loss of desire began will help you to treat the issue effectively before it can impact your relationship.

why desire changes Loss of desire is not only harmful to your relationship—it also harms your self-esteem and sense of identity. For each of us, sex is an important part of a happy and healthy life, and denying that side of yourself can be devastating. However, many of us feel as though this is our only option, especially as we age.

Fortunately, the truth is that there is no expiration date on sexuality. Loss of desire does not have to mean that you should give up on sex or assume that your sexual experiences are over. Thanks to modern medicine and many other advances, there is virtually no roadblock in the bedroom that can't be overcome with medical or psychological assistance, or even with good communication.

Loss of desire can occur for many reasons, including menopause or andropause, stress, fatigue, depression, anxiety, medical issues (including as a side effect of certain medication), or relationship or sexual concerns, such as early ejaculation or erectile dysfunction. That's a long list of possible causes, and, in truth, there are even more individual factors that minimize our libidos, whether it's recent weight gain or an overwhelming work schedule that causes sex to be the last thing on your mind.

treating low desire Finding your own personal culprit(s) will require a bit of investigative work, which should include speaking to your doctor. This is a very important step, not only because a medical professional can help determine if a particular medication or hormonal imbalance is part of the problem, but also because loss of desire can sometimes be one of the first signs of a more serious health concern (such as decreased circulation). Explaining your symptoms to your doctor is the only way to uncover what your body is trying to tell you.

After identifying any medical concerns, you can then tackle emotional or relationship issues, if these exist. To do this, it's important to talk to your partner about what's happening inside of you. If your partner doesn't know why you are always turning down sex, or why you have become distracted and disconnected, then you are going to hit some major relationship issues. In love as in most other parts of life, knowledge is key—and your partner won't know what's wrong unless you speak up.

If talking about the emotional issues you are facing seems overwhelming, you can enlist the help of a sex therapist. This unbiased source can help you to work on any troubling issues both individually and as a couple.

Sensual massage is a good way to treat low desire—it allows you to enjoy intimate touch without any performance pressure.

Whether it is you or your partner who is struggling, a therapist can help encourage openness, healing, and renewed intimacy in your relationship. Even if your partner refuses to see a therapist, it's a good idea to seek therapy on your own. This is all part of taking care of your mental and sexual health. As a bonus, your subsequent change of attitude and increase in energy can help your partner see the positive effects of therapy and want those changes, too. (One side note: If you believe that depression or anxiety might be contributing to a loss of libido for either of you, turn to page 56 for more on how to tackle these struggles.)

choosing *sex*

A simple truth is that the more you have sex, the more you crave sex. (The opposite is often true: The less you think about sex, the less important sex becomes to you.) One way to treat low desire is to consider sex even when you don't feel in the mood—so long as there aren't serious physical or emotional issues preventing you. Choosing to have sex can help boost your libido and deepen your connection with your partner.

If you feel unable to enjoy the actual act of intercourse, you can find other ways to keep that part of yourself alive, perhaps through fantasy, self-stimulation, or erotica. As you go through this self-treatment, it may help to remember that desire is a passionate, powerful force that helps define our very identities. Without it, we lose an intimate piece of the person our partners fell in love with—which is why it's important to keep your sexual side thriving.

loving sex is...

beautiful

Nothing is more beautiful than the knowledge that you are loved and cherished by another person. One of the most rewarding parts of being in a committed relationship is watching this love grow over time. Sex acts as a source of nourishment for your love, keeping it fruitful over the years, and strengthening the root of your connection. Through change and challenges, a healthy sex life will keep you close, commited, and intimately connected.

sharing intimacy after lovemaking

Nothing is more intimate than the quietness and warmth that follows lovemaking. In this sensual space, feel-good chemicals like endorphins and oxytocin help you bond on a deep, almost spiritual level. Dwelling fully in these moments reminds us of the beauty and romance of sex, and is one of the most restorative things you can do for your relationship.

post-coital bonding The problem is that we don't always take advantage of these bonding moments. If you immediately go your separate ways after sex—or worse, switch on the television or your laptop—you miss the opportunity to enjoy this intimacy and to appreciate your partner fully. This is especially important for women. The more romantic and connected she feels during sex, the more satisfied she will be. Fully revelling in this time after sex prolongs the intimacy of the experience and can also help increase your libido levels for next time. (For more on the sex/intimacy cycle, see page 42.)

Fortunately, there are many ways to cherish this time together and build intimacy that will last for weeks to come. Instead of rolling over and going to sleep, lie in each other's arms as your heart rate comes down. Because you are already relaxed and satisfied, this is a good time simply to talk about the day—you will find yourself sharing more openly after the intimacy of sex. Conversations like this will help stoke the slow burn between you and keep your connection strong.

Alternatively, take a hot bath together and wash each other. Pile the tub with bubbles and enjoy the soft, slippery sensation of your partner's wet skin. You might even find that this inspires a second round of sex! (For more on this, see page 192.)

sensual snacking If you aren't in the mood for a bath, follow your appetites to the kitchen. After lovemaking, our energy levels go down and we often crave a snack to help regulate blood sugar. Because of this, it can be both sexy and energy-renewing to eat together after sex, especially if you choose snacks that are sensual in nature.

Prep for your post-coital meal by cutting up some fruits ahead of time. Eat with your fingers and feed each other. Be present in the activity and notice how juicy and sweet the fruit tastes, and how the texture of the fruit feels in your hands as you hold it. You can also share a bowl of ice cream or a piece of dark chocolate, or enjoy a popsicle together. As you eat, keep your conversation light, sexy—and maybe even a little bit dirty. Because sharing a meal is something we do often with our partners, speaking flirtatiously will help separate this time from more prosaic daily meals. Pillow talk should never be stressful or focused on real-world problems. Instead, tell your partner what you enjoyed about your last session, or whisper to him all the things you want to do to him on your next time around.

Enjoying your partner's company after lovemaking makes sex that much more satisfying. Playful touch and laughter can strengthen your bond and remind you both that the bedroom is a place for fun.

creating an intimate atmosphere You can also set the atmosphere in the bedroom ahead of time. Not only will this create a sensual mood for sex, but it will also help sustain that peaceful, sexy mood after you and your partner have finished lovemaking. Set a few candles around the bed and, instead of rushing to throw your clothes back on afterward, keep a robe or blanket nearby to cover up and stay warm after the act. Cuddling nude under the blankets or wearing a soft, slinky robe will be much sexier than throwing your clothes back on, and it will be one more element that will help keep you present and in a sensual frame of mind.

And ladies, if you tend to rush to the bathroom to use the facilities after sex, keep some lingerie on a hook inside the door. This way, when you return to the bedroom you will keep the mood alive if you and your partner want to go at it another time. In fact, all of these post-coital routines can be funneled into foreplay for another session, whether that is your plan or it happens organically. Making this effort to enjoy the warmth of your connection and prolong the lovemaking experience can create an abundance of intimacy and pleasure in your relationship—and will make sex all the sweeter.

slide closer
for a whisper-soft kiss

fight dirty *for sexual favors*

bedroom banter The best sex reminds us that we are both lovers and friends. Remember the teasing techniques you learned in grade school? As adults, playful flirtation is still one of the most powerful forms of seduction. Have a pillow fight nearly nude; wrestle on the bed; tickle, tease, and taste. By the time you get to sex, you'll be more deeply in love then ever.

rip off clothing as you wrestle

difficult relationships

Every relationship experiences challenging moments, whether it is a passing disagreement or a more prolonged misunderstanding. These types of conflict are inevitable, and are not, in themselves, bad for your relationship. As long as you know how to express what you are feeling in a positive way, you will be able to move toward a happy, relationship-strengthening resolution.

fighting effectively Although all couples fight, some are more vocal and passionate than others. If you are the argumentative type, let me reassure you: This doesn't mean that you and your partner aren't meant to be. Some couples simply fight more than others, and this isn't always a negative quality. Instead, it can signal that you are both strong people who believe in expressing your individual emotions and needs. Still, it's important that you express these emotions in the correct way—and that you learn how to listen to one another.

In order to fight effectively, you must master a few communication techniques. First, it's important always to phrase your needs in a way that is not accusatory, and that can be easily understood. For example, if you want to effect change in your relationship, you need to give your partner clear-cut guidelines and expectations. Simply articulating the emotion you are feeling (sad, angry, scared, etc.) and the thoughts that are inspiring those emotions (that you don't love me, that you aren't attracted to me anymore, etc.) will help you communicate your feelings in a positive, helpful way. So, instead of saying, "I am so sick of the way you treat me in front of your friends!" you might say, "I love spending time together, but sometimes I feel embarrassed or awkward when you make fun of me in front of your friends. Could we call a moratorium on jokes about my fashion sense?" Explaining that you feel embarrassed helps your partner understand why you are upset, and giving clear guidelines for what you want to happen in the future helps you both see clearly how to improve the situation. Not only will this type of communication prevent regular blowouts, but it will also be more likely to generate positive results.

You can follow this same approach when you want to solve a problem in your relationship. For example, if your sex life becomes a concern, you might say: "We haven't had sex in a month and it makes me feel sad and unattractive. Can we talk about this and come up with a strategy to improve our sex life?" This will be heard and reacted to very differently than an angry response, such as: "What's wrong with you? We haven't had sex in ages and I can't take it anymore!"

In the first example, you are taking responsibility for your own thoughts and feelings, and communicating your belief that you are allies who work together. In the second example, you are pointing the finger of blame at your partner, which often leads to emotional dart throwing, and doesn't help to resolve the core issue.

The best part of fighting? Makeup sex. Use the passion that develops during an argument to initiate explosive, intimate lovemaking.

listening An equally key part of communicating as a couple is learning to listen authentically. In fact, this is perhaps the most important and neglected communication skill. You can never know what is happening inside someone's internal world unless you listen.

If, as you listen, you find yourself feeling angry or scared in response to what your partner is saying, focus on a tangible object that you can appreciate. This can be something in your environment (the flowers on the table, the color of the walls), or, even better, something positive about your partner (his beautiful eyes, her sexy figure). When you do this it actually creates a shift in your brain, moving your brain activity from the amgydala, where intense emotions are experienced and processed, to more rational centers like the left prefrontal cortex. This will help you stay calm and receptive rather than defensive or angry.

Once your partner has finished expressing his or her feelings, don't immediately respond. Take a minute to reflect on what you have heard, then repeat it. For instance, if she has said that she hates when you stay at work too long and are subsequently late to pick up the kids, you can say, "You don't like it when I am late to pick up the kids because you believe this shows that I put my job above my family." Responding in this way is called "mirroring." By mirroring your partner's feelings, you can help avoid any miscommunications and start a constructive conversation that leads to resolution.

acting as *allies*

Whenever you feel attacked, defensive, or impatient with your partner, try to remember that you are allies. Remember that you want the best for each other and your relationship—and then ask yourself in that context if it is really important to be right. One good rule to live by is this: It's better to be in love than to be right. Being the "winner" can be a lonely feeling and it won't keep you warm at night. A happy, loving partner and a peaceful relationship are more valuable than the few seconds of satisfaction you will get from berating your partner into admitting his or her fault. Keep this as a central tenet in your relationship, and it will be easier to stay connected and in love.

sex during *pregnancy*

Pregnancy is unarguably one of the most beautiful and awe-inspiring phases of any relationship. However, it does change your sexual connection. People often think that pregnancy signals the end of your sex life for nine months, but the truth is that sex during pregnancy can be quite pleasurable. In fact, many women experience a boost in their libido during pregnancy, particularly during the second trimester.

the pregnant libido During the first trimester, women often struggle with morning sickness, fatigue, and other symptoms that make sex (among other things) difficult. However, as you move into the second trimester and these symptoms dissipate, a woman's libido usually returns. Shifting hormones, such as progesterone and estrogen, will heighten her sensitivity in pleasure spots like the genitals and breasts, and she will experience greater lubrication in the vagina, too. Even better, many women feel more feminine and alive than ever before during this time, as they grow into their new curves and feel a life growing inside them.

All of this means that you can have great sex during pregnancy. In fact, enjoying sex during these nine months is incredibly healthy for both mother and baby. By having sex, you ensure that you stay bonded and intimate as you prepare for your relationship to change dramatically. It may even be that a woman's increased libido during pregnancy is evolution's way of keeping couples bonded, which in turn ensures that the baby will have two healthy adults as caregivers during the precarious years of infancy. Whatever the reason, taking advantage of your increased libido is a good way to make sure that you are both getting your needs met during pregnancy.

Great sex with your partner is so important for your energy, mood, and sense of connection. Even better, the endorphins and oxytocin released during orgasm help to relieve stress—and they feel good to the baby as well. Fathers often worry that they are hurting the baby, or that the baby will know what's happening. I can promise you that none of these fears is true. Sex is a benefit to your relationship and to the emotional and physical health of Mom, Dad, and baby.

pregnancy positions Inevitably, during pregnancy, your sex life undergoes certain changes. Especially in the later stages, part of your sexual experience is about finding the positions that make sex comfortable. Although your growing belly means that some of your favorites might not be possible any more, there are many positions that will give you pleasure and keep your baby safe.

• **Man-on-top** is still possible, but make sure he doesn't place any significant weight on her stomach. Instead, have him kneel while she lies before him. She can put her legs straight up in the air and rest them on his torso as he penetrates. (For more on this, see page 116.)

• **Woman-on-top** is the most pleasurable for many pregnant women, whether she kneels facing him or turns to face his feet. Always erotic because it allows her to direct the pressure and pace of thrusting, it can give both of you peace of mind for her to have this type of control as you adjust to the idea of a tiny person growing inside her body. (For more on woman-on-top positions, see page 126.)

• **Seated positions** are also a good idea, allowing for minimum impact on her tummy. He can sit on a chair while she straddles him. Or, you can use the bed or the couch as a softer seat. (For more ideas for seated positions, see page 140.)

• **Side-by-side positions** work well, too, especially if you lie facing the same way and he penetrates her from behind. Facing each other can be more difficult as her belly might get in the way. (For more techniques for side-by-side positions, see page 134.)

• **Standing positions** are also possible, but as she moves into the later stages of pregnancy, you may find that these are too tiresome and hard on her joints, which are already supporting extra weight from the baby. (For more on standing positions, see page 166.)

concerns during pregnancy
One of the benefits of sex during pregnancy is that you don't have to grapple with contraception concerns. However, there are a few things to remember. First, while oral sex is still safe, it's important that he never blows air into the vaginal cavity, as this can potentially cause an embolism to occur within the womb. It's also important to make sure that you don't adopt positions that put any weight on your belly. A good rule of thumb is that if you are comfortable, your baby likely is as well, so let your body be a barometer for what type of positions you pursue.

It's also important to check with your doctor about whether it's okay to be sexual. While sexual activity is generally safe, your doctor may want you to abstain if your pregnancy is considered high risk or if you are targeted for early delivery. Women who can't have intercourse can still enjoy intimacy through VENIS or mutual self-stimulation (for more on these pursuits of pleasure, see pages 90 and 100).

Pillows can greatly increase your pleasure during sex, as can other aids such as lubrication and even toys (see page 180 for more on sex aids). However, it's always best to get your doctor's approval before using toys during pregnancy—and external toys are usually safest.

intimate *caressing*

Although it is common for women to desire sex during pregnancy, this is not the case for everyone. If you aren't in the mood, it's still important to connect through touch. Both partners are vulnerable during this period of change, and touching one another is a normal and reassuring way to ease any fears and strengthen your bond. Try sleeping in the nude together, allowing your hands to explore your partner's body fully. Kissing and massage can also keep you close.

sex and the family

While pregnancy changes your sex life, the real transformation sets in once the baby arrives. There is no denying that a baby will have a huge impact on your relationship with your partner, especially your sex life. However, these changes don't have to be negative. Many people find that having a child brings them closer together, making intimacy more natural and constant, and sex perhaps rarer, but also more beautiful.

protecting your connection With a child in the picture, you are no longer just lovers and best friends, you are parents and caregivers, a true family unit that exists with one goal: to love and support one another unconditionally. All of this can add up to greater intimacy and togetherness, but any time change occurs outside the bedroom, it impacts what happens inside the bedroom, too. This is why it's important to check in with one another regularly and make sure that you both feel your relationship is still fresh and exciting.

The most important skill to master as parents is the ability to multitask and balance your numerous responsibilities. You might think that the best way to do this successfully is always to put your child first, but this is not so. Never ignore your own needs to focus exclusively on your child. Instead, make your relationship and your own happiness a priority. When you do so, you will ensure that your marriage stays strong—and that you are the best parent you can possibly be. It's tempting to put your child ahead of everything, not only out of love, but also out of guilt. Society today creates the expectation that we must give our children all we have, including all of our time. However, my personal belief is that a happy, healthy connection between parents—and a model of what a loving relationship looks like—is the absolute best gift you can give to your child.

the balancing act So what does this look like? First and foremost, lighten your load. This means proactively choosing to spend time with your mate alone on a daily basis, even when you could be spending time with the kids. It means going on a date night once a week even when your child is screaming and holding on to your leg. (When this happens, remind your child that parents who love each other need special time alone.) Set date nights in stone and don't get into the habit of canceling or rescheduling them at the last minute. If you train yourself always to think of one night of the week as "date night only," it will become part of your schedule that you automatically work to keep, as you would with any other commitment that is important to you. Remember, you love your kids, but you are in love with your spouse, which means that if you want to maintain a healthy relationship, you need to set aside time for sex, romance, and intimacy each and every week. If time together is an afterthought, you will simply never get around to it.

the *schedule* solution

If you and your partner never seem to have time for yourselves, it might be a good idea to scale back on your child's after-school activities. Try to limit these to one or two a season. Overscheduling your kids is hard on you and your relationship because it is so time-consuming. For this same reason, it's also hard on your children. In today's society, we seem to think that kids should be mini-adults, learning new languages, mastering new skills, and getting into all the best clubs and sports teams, but this just puts undue stress on them—and it takes away from the pure fun of being a kid.

Children will change your relationship, but they will also bring you closer and make you more bonded.

You can also put your partner before your kids by prioritizing what is truly important. This means stepping back and realistically assessing your commitments. It can be dangerous to funnel all your energy into certain passing activities, like planning a huge blowout for your child's third birthday party. He won't remember much beyond the cake and ice cream, so there is no reason to give yourself premature gray hair as you try to color-coordinate the invitations with the napkins. Instead, focus on what really matters—your family and your relationship.

sex for *special populations*

Everyone has roadblocks to overcome in the bedroom, whether these are emotional, physical, or a combination of both. Great sex simply doesn't happen overnight, and this is especially true if you are living with a disability. However, sex and disability are not mutually exclusive. It is entirely possible to have a rich and fulfilling sex life regardless of your challenges. It just requires an open mind and a little creativity.

making sex work There aren't many models in the media for the sexual satisfaction that can go hand in hand with a disability, but people with disabilities can and do enjoy healthy sex lives. Even if you do not have sensation below your chest or waist, or if penetration is not possible, don't assume that your sex life is over. You are still a sexual person able to have rich, meaningful, intimate experiences.

Most people find that it is still possible for them to enjoy sex regardless of any ailment, provided they make a few adjustments to positioning, incorporate necessary props, communicate with their partner, and commit to making sex a priority. Consider the following:

talk to your doctor First, talk to your doctor and get the green light for sexual activity. It's important to make sure that you are able to have sex in a way that is beneficial, not harmful, to your physical and emotional well-being. So, ask your doctor if there are things you should be aware of regarding your condition. For example, some medications interfere with birth control efficacy, while others could negatively impact your performance or enjoyment. Your doctor should be able to give you information about these and other concerns.

talk to your partner Often, lovers of people with disabilities are afraid of hurting their partner so they leave certain questions unasked. Unfortunately, this passivity can be read as a lack of interest. Let your partner know that, with a few tweaks, it is still possible for you to enjoy an active sex life. Once you are both aware of the other's desire and excitement, you'll feel more secure in your sexual connection. It may also be a good idea to bring your partner along to the doctor, so he or she can bring up any concerns or questions.

use sex aids If you live with a physical disability, it may be that your sexual response will take a little longer than it did before the injury. More stimulation and time might be required to spur arousal. If this is the case, sexual aids can be invaluable. If you have decreased genital sensation due to your disability, for example, a sex aid such as a strong clitoral vibrator or prostate stimulator can help create intense stimulation and enjoyment. Many toys also come with long handles that make it easier to reach the genitals. And, for men, tools such as Viagra and penile implants might be an option.

Specialized bedroom furniture, including specialty pillows and beds, can also make sex more comfortable. And, you might consider a swing, which can allow you to support a more vulnerable area, while giving a thrilling, weightless feeling. Swings are hung from the ceiling, and have special openings that allow for penetration.

don't give up If the mind is willing, the body can do just about anything—and this is especially true when it comes to sex and disability. In fact, it is typical that in the absence of one sense, sensation in other areas grows stronger. (This sensory phenomenon also works in sex between able-bodied partners: When blindfolded, we all feel physical sensation more intensely.) This means that people with disabilities can still experience deep pleasure and orgasm. For example, I have met individuals with spinal-cord injuries who have taught themselves to climax from having their ears kissed.

It's an amazing fact that sexual attraction and arousal begin in the brain, and it means that sexual enjoyment can begin there, too. Focusing on the possibilities in the bedroom and working to reach new levels of pleasure will keep your sex life fresh and exciting.

A disability does not have to end your sex life: Trying new positions, adjusting pillows to support injured areas like the back, and communicating with your partner will help to keep sex pleasurable.

sex in later life

There is no expiration date on sexuality. No matter how old you are, sex can and should always be a spectacular part of life. Aging might decrease or dampen your libido in some instances, but it in no way signals the end of your sexual pleasure.

healthy sex A recent study from the University of Chicago found that many people enjoy sex well into their 70s, 80s, and beyond. According to the findings, more than half of people aged 57-85 are sexually active, and some of them even have sex on a weekly basis.

This study also found that general health and sexual health were closely linked: The healthier an individual was, the more likely he or she was to maintain sexual activity on a regular basis. This fits in with a number of theories about the physical benefits of good sex. Sex releases endorphins, which help to combat stress, and it might also help to promote better sleep and physical fitness, as it gets the blood flowing and keeps couples active. It also generates feelings of intimacy and happiness, which keep you bonded with your partner.

As you can see, sex is a crucial part of our general health and well-being. When we approach sex in an unhealthy way (or not at all), it can have a ripple effect on our relationships, our bodies, and our sense of self. In contrast, when we recognize sex as an integral part of our humanity, we are more likely to stay healthy, happy, and emotionally close with our partners.

physical changes in later life Of course, this doesn't mean that sexual activity carries on into the golden years without any change. As your body changes, your needs change, but fortunately there are plenty of bedroom tools to accommodate these new needs. For example, if you are struggling with joint pain or the mobility issues that often come with aging, it is helpful to experiment with different positions and use the support of pillows or wedges (for more on this, see page 270). Many older people also experience vaginal dryness, low libido, and difficulty maintaining an erection. Luckily, all of these difficulties are generally treatable once diagnosed, so they shouldn't permanently impact your sex life (see pages 246–257 for more information on diagnosis and treatment).

If you have any particular concerns that need assistance, whether you struggle with an inability to maintain an erection or a dip in libido, it's important to speak to your doctor. Most doctors now realize that sexuality is a significant—even a defining—part of a person's life, regardless of age. A good doctor will help you maintain a healthy sexuality, and will listen to your concerns. If your doctor doesn't do this, it's time to find someone new.

emotional difficulties Just as important as negotiating physical difficulties, we must also address the potential emotional difficulties of sex in later life. One of the main troubles for older people is the antiquated notion that making love is only for youngsters. This is not true! In fact, many people find that the older they get, the more they are able to let loose in the bedroom and release their inhibitions. Maturity brings with it many benefits, including an ability to truly tap into your inner sexual desires. In addition, once you've gone through menopause, you don't have to worry about birth control, which can bring a new sense of freedom to the bedroom.

Although older people are often ahead of younger couples when it comes to being in touch with their bodies and desires, they don't necessarily take the precautions that they should when it comes to safer sex. Researchers were recently surprised to discover that people who are middle-aged and older are increasingly becoming infected with STIs, with rates doubling for those over the age of 45 in the last 10 years. It was also found that men who take Viagra and other erectile enhancement medications were at a higher risk of STIs, presumably because they are having sex at higher rates and not using protection.

Practicing safer sex (such as by using condoms and dental dams) might seem foreign to you, especially if you are new on the dating scene and it's not something you did in your youth. However, it is incredibly important. In addition to other STIs, older people are being diagnosed with HIV at higher rates. AIDS occurs more often in people over the age of 40 than in younger people and 10 percent of all AIDS cases in the United States occur in people over the age of 50.

HIV/AIDS can be life-threatening at any age, but the older you get, the harder it will be for your body to fight it. Because of this and many other concerns, it's crucial to practice safer sex each and every time you have sex, and to schedule regular STI testing (a step that many older lovers tend to forgo). Sadly, many doctors tend to skip this step as well, either because they wrongly assume it isn't necessary or because they don't know if their patient is sexually active. So, speak up and be an advocate for your own health. Request STI testing and ask the same of all your sex partners. Remember, you can enjoy sex throughout your life, but first you must take precautions to safeguard your health. Safer sex is sex at its most pleasurable and beautiful. (For more on safer sex, see page 238.)

inhibitions and age

One of the best things about sex in later life is that our inhibitions tend to melt away. As we age, those things that seem intimidating or embarrassing earlier in life seem less scary. This is probably because, as you go through life experiences, your ideas of what things are—and are not—okay sexually expand and grow. This is true whether you are with a long-term partner or whether your relationship has changed and you are with someone new—and it means that some of our best sexual experiences can come years after what is traditionally considered to be our sexual prime. Long live sexual pleasure!

recovering from *infidelity*

Fidelity is the cornerstone of a healthy, monogamous relationship. Anyone who has ever encountered infidelity knows that being betrayed can be one of the most painful experiences you can go through. Despite this, cheating is still a fairly common occurrence. Sadly, research states that around half of all married couples will cheat at some point in their relationship.

setting relationship boundaries Before you let this statistic scare you into giving up on the concept of monogamy, remember that your relationship is as strong and secure as you make it. If you communicate with your partner regularly and put each other's needs first, there is no cause for you to fear infidelity. One of the main reasons that people cheat is because they are looking for the attention and excitement that they aren't finding at home. This doesn't give them a right to cheat, of course, but it is a good reminder that we all have needs to be met, and that these needs don't go away simply because they are ignored.

It's also important to remember that we are all human. No matter how much you love your partner, it would be silly to presume that you will always be immune to the advances of an attractive stranger. A good way to prevent this temptation from taking hold is to set guidelines that you each commit to following. Most importantly, you need to define what constitutes cheating in your relationship. While it seems like this definition should be simple, there are many potential layers to infidelity, especially given continuing advances in technology. Ask your partner: Is talking to an old flame online considered cheating? Or is only physical interaction considered cheating? Is it deceitful to dress seductively when you know you are going to run into a sexy friend? Is it okay to flirt with the cute waiter?

You can set guidelines for what you each believe to be cheating, but ultimately, the true answer to these questions is found within your own heart. If you feel guilty after spending time with a friend that you find attractive, then you might have crossed a line emotionally, even if you didn't physically. If you see your partner talking intimately to his coworker and feel nauseated, then your body is signaling that you are not okay with their relationship. If you listen to your heart, it will be easy to decipher whether your relationship is entering rough waters.

the recovery program If one or both of you have already crossed the line into infidelity, the first thing you must do is immediately cut off all contact with the affair. This means no phone calls, no texts, no emails, and certainly no in-person meetings. If you truly want to save your relationship, that person must be gone from your life. Otherwise, your partner will never be able to let go of the past, and neither will you. I also advise that you seek the help of a therapist who is well-versed in helping couples repair their relationship after infidelity.

Honest communication is one of the best ways to recover from infidelity—but there is no reason to share every detail about an affair.

Another strategy for recovery is the "15 minute rule." Each day, for 15 minutes only, the betrayed partner can vent, scream, and otherwise let out any inner turmoil toward the cheating partner. Then, once those 15 minutes are up, you must both let go and move on. This process helps couples avoid replaying the same fight over and over, and also prevents their conversation from being entirely dominated by the affair. During this time, it's important to tell the whole truth and answer any questions your partner might have, but it's also best not to share every last little detail. You can be honest about what happened without sharing hurtful facts, such as how many times you had sex in one night or how well-endowed he was. Information like this is not helpful in the healing process.

Repairing your relationship after an affair won't be easy, and forgiving such a betrayal requires maturity and emotional strength. The cheating partner will need to earn trust by being accountable for every action. It can take months, sometimes years, to get that trust back and truly heal, but this healing is essential. In the end, even if you decide to break off the relationship, you must learn how to forgive your partner if you truly want to move on and be happy in the future.

sharing information

As we've discussed, although it's important to be honest with your partner, there's no need to share every bit of information about your affair. Gory details can't easily be erased from memory. Once your partner hears about your lover's sexual prowess or affinity for oral sex, she will never be able to forget that. Certain sexual activities might always be tainted as a result.

If your partner asks you for details, you can give him or her the bare facts, "We had sex on five different occasions." If asked about positions or other intimate details, simply say, "I don't want to tell you all the explicit details—it will be painful for both of us." Talk it through in therapy and be patient. It takes time to heal, and to stop wondering, about this hurtful act.

seductive romance
It's common knowledge that romance and sex are inseparable. To be a great lover, you must also be a romantic. This is why it's so important to seduce your partner. Dress up for date night, indulge in slow, sensual kisses—perhaps even twirl around a dance floor. The sex that follows will be magnificent.

tease her with
the promise of a kiss

slip your hands
underneath her dress

keep steamy eye contact
as you grasp her waist

conclusion: *finding passion*

It has been said that the greatest thing you will ever learn in life is to love and be loved in return. And learning to give and receive sexual love is at the core of a passionate and fulfilling love life. Sex is more than just a few minutes of pleasure. Our sexuality is an indelible and enduring part of who we are, and sexual pleasure and connection is the cornerstone of a happy relationship. By making this pleasure a priority, you can ensure that you and your partner will stay bonded and intimate throughout your lives.

As a sex therapist, I have seen firsthand how powerfully sex can impact and enhance our connection to our own selves, and the depth of love we can share with someone else. I have seen sex bring couples together in times of crisis, build bridges during times of emotional distress, and reignite flames of passion and love that have long since burned out. I truly believe that if the will is there, you and your partner can traverse any chasm and rediscover each other again and again, sexually and in all other parts of your life.

There are many ideas in this book that can help you take your intimate life to new heights or embark on an entirely new sexual journey. Sex can and should be a part of your daily life. This doesn't mean that you'll ooze sexual desire every minute of every day—but you can honor and enjoy your sexual side throughout your week, instead of reserving all that energy for date night. Sex is not meant to be saved just for special occasions!

Making your sexuality a daily part of your relationship is all about creating that "slow burn" I've discussed throughout this book. The idea is to make sure that your sexual flame never goes out, since it can be very difficult to reignite once it is extinguished. Instead, keep your desire set to a constant simmer, then simply turn up the heat when you hit the bedroom. To do this, you can use the tips suggested in this book—read erotica, wear sexy lingerie, turn your bedroom into a sensual haven, send your partner naughty emails—or you can come up with your own unique ideas for spicing up your connection.

It may come as a surprise to hear that the most passionate relationships require time apart. Loving sex is not just about keeping the sensual energy alive, but about respecting your partner's independence. Ideally, you and your partner should be open books to one another, but you should also have enough trust to allow for individual space. This will help keep mystery alive in your relationship, and will ensure you remain the interesting, engaging, and well-rounded person that your partner fell in love with. Building this level of trust will be one of the most fulfilling and enriching experiences you will ever enjoy, and it will transform you into a more open, happy individual.

Along with this foundational trust, the best lovers always maintain the highest level of respect for one another. Sometimes we find ourselves giving our best to the outside world, being kind and patient to coworkers or friends, only to come home and be short-tempered with the most important person of all. Luckily, you can stop a bad mood in its tracks by taking time to identify the real cause of your sadness or anger, and giving both yourself and your partner time to unwind at the end of a long day.

And remember, your sexual journey isn't always built for two. There might be work that you need to do your own, whether that's addressing past trauma or breaking through your own sexual inhibitions. Although your partner can support you along the way, much of your happiness and sexual satisfaction needs to come from within, and it needs to stem from a loving acceptance of your own body and spirit. Although this might take time and soul-searching, it can help you become a more confident, authentic person, sexually and otherwise.

All of this means that a sexy, passionate, and exciting life is yours for the taking, regardless of your age or the amount of time you and your partner have been together. So long as you communicate openly, trust one another, remain interested in the world around you, and respect each other's individual needs and interests, you can reach sexual and emotional heights you might never have imagined.

Enjoy!

Laura Berman

bibliography

Each of the works below was referenced in this book, and is a good source for more information on our sexual nature as humans, and how to achieve a passionate, loving relationship and sex life.

loving sex is ... *physical*

Ann, Dr. Chua Chee. *Journal of British Association for Sex and Marital Therapy*, vol. 12, no. 4 (November 1997).

Elton, Catherine. "Learning to lust." *Psychology Today*, March 1, 2010. http://www.psychologytoday.com/articles/201005/learning-lust.

Gupta, Neha. "Close couples can smell partner's emotions—study." *The Med Guru*, June, 3, 2010. http://www.themedguru.com/ 20100603/newsfeature/close-couples-can-smell -partners-emotions-study-86136151.html.

The Kinsey Institute for Research in Sex, Gender, and Reproduction. "Frequently Asked Sexuality Questions to The Kinsey Institute: Frequency of sex," fact sheet. December 2010. http://www.iub.edu/~kinsey/resources/FAQ.html.

Miller, S., & Manner, J. "Scent of a woman: Men's testosterone responses to olfactory ovulation cues." *Psychological Science* (February 2010).

loving sex is ... *emotional*

Fisher, Helen. *The Sex Contract: The Evolution of Human Desire*. New York: William Morrow & Company, 1983.

Fisher, Helen. *Why We Love: The Nature and Chemistry of Romantic Love*. New York: Henry Holt & Company, 2004.

Money, John. *Lovemaps: Clinical Concepts of Sexual/Erotic Health and Pathology, Paraphilia, and Gender Transposition in Childhood, Adolescence, and Maturity*. New York: Irvington Publishers, 1993.

loving sex is ... *seductive*

"How hugs can aid women's hearts." *BBC News*, August 8, 2005, http://news.bbc.co.uk/2/hi/4131508.stm.

Kastner, Stephen. "The scent of arousal—licorice, lavender, and love." *Sexologie*, October 24, 2009. http://sexologie.us/2009/10/the-scent-of-arousal-licorice-lavender-and-love/.

Landau, Elizabeth. "Pucker up: Scientists study kissing." *CNN Health*, February 13, 2009. http://articles.cnn.com/2009-02-13/health/kissing.science_1_first-kiss-hormone-levels-oxytocin-levels?_s=PM:HEALTH.

Rubin, Gretchen. "September's challenge: Be more affectionate." *WomansDay*, August 31, 2010. http://www.womansday.com/Articles/Lifestyle/September-s-Challenge-Be-More-Affectionate.html.

Zimmerman, Mike. "15 facts you didn't know about your penis." *Men's Health*, July 2010. http://www.menshealth.com/mhlists/penis_facts/index.php.

loving sex is ... *ecstatic*

Freeman, Shana. "What happens in the brain during an orgasm?" *Discovery Health*. http://health.howstuffworks.com/sexual-health/sexuality/brain-during-orgasm.htm/printable.

Henderson, Mark. "Women fall into 'trance' during orgasm." *The Sunday Times Online*, June 20, 2005. http://www.timesonline.co.uk/tol/life_and_style/health/article535521.ece.

Nixon, Robin. "Do animals enjoy sex?" *LiveScience*, March 25, 2009. http://www.livescience.com/9631-animals-enjoy-sex.html.

Orazem, Katherine. "In defense of romance: proving the stereotypes wrong." *The Yale Herald*, February 12, 2010. http://yaleherald.com/arts/in-defense-of-romance-proving-the-stereotypes-wrong/.

loving sex is ... *passionate*

Berkowitz, Bob and Susan. "10 surprising facts about men who have lost interest in sex." *ThirdAge.com*, August 20, 2008. http://www.thirdage.com/sex/10-surprising-facts-about-men-who-have-lost-interest-in-sex-0.

loving sex is ... *insatiable*

Babeland "Babeland statistics," press kit. http://www.babeland.com/about/presskit/about/stats.

loving sex is ... *adventurous*

Chynoweth, Carly. "10 best places to have sex at work." *The Best Article Everyday*, November 2007. http://www.bspcn.com/2007/11/13/10-places-to-have-sex-at-work/.

Gammon, Katharine Stoel. "She's gotta have it—in her dreams." *ABC News/Health*, June 14, 2007. http://abcnews.go.com/Health/WomensHealth/story?id=3276142&page=1.

loving sex is ... *experimental*

"Changing sexual behavior may explain rise of anal cancer." *ScienceBlog*, July 6, 2004. http://scienceblog.com/3205/changing-sexual-behavior-may-explain-rise-of-anal-cancer/.

Durex 2005 Global Sex Survey. http://data360.org/pdf/20070416064139. Global%20Sex%20Survey.pdf.

The Kinsey Institute for Research in Sex, Gender, and Reproduction, "Frequently Asked Sexuality Questions to The Kinsey Institute: BDSM," fact sheet. December 2010. http://www.iub.edu/~kinsey/resources/FAQ.html.

Mirdad, Michael. *Sacred Sexuality: A Manual for Living Bliss*. Maryland: Grail Press, 2004.

National Cancer Institute, "Human papillomaviruses and cancer," fact sheet. December 2010. http://www.cancer.gov/cancertopics/factsheet/Risk/HPV.

Saletan, William. "Ass backwards: The media's silence about rampant anal sex." *Slate*, September 20, 2005. http://www.slate.com/id/2126643/.

loving sex is ... *safe*

"Anal cancer on the increase." *Aphrodite Women's Health*, July 12, 2004. http://www.aphroditewomenshealth.com/news/20040612005751_health_news.shtml

Bierma, Paige. "Ills and Conditions, Trichomoniasis." *CVS Health Resources*, March 26, 2009. http://www.cvshealthresources.com/topic/trich.\

Bryner, Jeanna. "The pill makes women pick bad mates." *MSNBC.com*, August 13, 2008. http://www.msnbc.msn.com/id/26180187/ns/health-womens_health/

Centers for Disease Control and Prevention, "Chlamydia—CDC fact sheet," fact sheet. April 28, 2010. http://www.cdc.gov/std/chlamydia/stdfact-chlamydia.htm.

Centers for Disease Control and Prevention, "Chlamydia and Gonorrhea — Two Most Commonly Reported Notifiable Infectious Diseases in the United States." April 28, 2010. http://www.cdc.gov/Features/dsSTDData/

Centers for Disease Control and Prevention, "Estimates of new HIV infections in the United States," fact sheet. August 2008. http://www.cdc.gov/hiv/topics/surveillance/resources/factsheets/incidence.htm.

Centers for Disease Control and Prevention. "Genital HPV is common in men and women," fact sheet. June 3, 2010. http://www.cdc.gov/std/hpv/common-downloads.htm.

Centers for Disease Control and Prevention, "Syphilis—CDC fact sheet," fact sheet. September 16, 2010. http://www.cdc.gov/std/syphilis/STDFact-Syphilis.htm.

Chisholm, Ken. "STD facts and statistics." *Livestrong.com*, July 16, 2009. http://www.livestrong.com/article/13924-std-information/.

Cleveland Clinic. "Treatments and procedures: Testosterone replacement therapy," fact sheet. August 3, 2009. http://my.clevelandclinic.org/services/testosterone_replacement_therapy/hic_testosterone_replacement_therapy.aspx.

The Complete Herpes Information Center. "Herpes Statistics," fact sheet. http://www.globalherbalsupplies.com/herpes/stats.html.

"Frequently asked questions about genital herpes." *WebMD*, March 26, 2010. http://www.webmd.com/genital-herpes/guide/genital-herpes-faq.

Minnesota Men's Health Center. "Facts about erectile dysfunction," fact sheet. http://www.mmhc-online.com/articles/impotency.html.

Parkin, DM. "The global health burden of infection-associated cancers in the year 2002." *International Journal of Cancer* 2006; 118(12): 3030–3044.

World Health Organization. "WHO Drug Information," vol. 18, no. 1, 2004. http://apps.who.int/medicinedocs/en/d/Js5407e/3.2.html.

loving sex is ... *beautiful*

Behen, Madonna. "Drugs like Viagra linked to higher rates of STDs." *KLTV.com*, July 5, 2010. http://www.kltv.com/global/story.asp?s=12759347.

Center for AIDS Prevention Studies, "What are HIV prevention needs of adults over 50?" fact sheet. September 1997. http://www.caps.ucsf.edu/pubs/FS/over50.php.

Donnely, Jerre and Williams, Edith. "Older Americans and AIDS: Some guidelines for protection." *Social Work* (April 2002).

"The female orgasm." *Pregnancyinfo.net*. http://www.pregnancy-info.net/sex_orgasm.html.

Jayson, Sharon. "Seniors still have sex, study finds." *USAToday*, August 23, 2007. http://www.usatoday.com/news/health/2007-08-22-senior-study_N.htm

Sharples, Tiffany. "More midlife (and older) STDs." *Time*, July 2, 2008. http://www.time.com/time/health/article/0,8599,1819633,00.html.

resources

Sometimes loving sex calls for inspiration. The resources on this page will help you become smarter, sexier, and safer lovers, whether you want to spice up your relationship with some steamy erotica, need new position ideas, are shopping for sex toys, or are looking for support and advice during a challenging time in your relationship.

books and publications

health and relationships

Enabling Romance: A Guide to Love, Sex and Relationships for People with Disabilities (and the People who Care About Them)
by Ken Kroll
(No Limits Communications, 2001)

A Tired Woman's Guide to Passionate Sex: Reclaim Your Desire and Reignite Your Relationship
by Laurie Mintz, Ph.D
(Adams Media, 2009)

The Ultimate Guide to Sex and Disability: For All of Us Who Live with Disabilities, Chronic Pain, and Illness
by Miriam Kaufman, Cory Silverberg, and Fran Odette
(Cleis Press, 2007)

erotica

The Best Lesbian Erotica of 2010
edited by Kathleen Warnock
(Cleis Press, 2009)

The Darker Side of Pleasure
by Eden Bradley
(Bantam, 2007)

Gay Love
by Elizabeth Coldwell, et al
(Xcite Books, 2010)

Girls On Top: Explicit Erotica For Women
by Violet Blue
(Cleis Press, 2009)

My Secret Garden: Women's Sexual Fantasies
by Nancy Friday
(Pocket Books, 1998)

Sexiest Soles: Erotic Stories About Feet and Shoes
by Rachel Kramer Bussel and Christopher Pierce
(Alyson Books, 2006)

Wild Side Sex: The Book of Kink: Educational, Sensual, and Entertaining Essays
by Midori
(Daedalus Publishing, 2005)

Women on Top
by Nancy Friday
(Pocket Books, 1993)

websites

American Association of Sex Educators Counselors and Therapists
http://aasect.org/
Online listings to help you find a sex therapist near you.

Bend Over Your Boyfriend
www.bendoveryourboyfriend.com
Advice on sex positions and techniques, including anal play.

Sex Health Matters
www.sexhealthmatters.org
Up-to-the-minute news on how health impacts sex, including recent study results, breaking news headlines, a list of local experts in sexual health, and a video library for interactive instruction.

World Health Net
www.worldhealth.net
An in-depth, international resource on anti-aging medicines and preventative health, with an extensive library of articles on various conditions, and educational videos.

films

American Fetish
directed by Michael Simmons
(American Fetish Film, 2009)

The Black Glove
directed by Maria Beatty
(Bleu Productions, 1997)

The Crash Pad
directed by Shine Louise Houston
(Pink & White Productions, 2006)

The Elegant Spanking
directed by Maria Beatty
(Bleu Productions, 1995)

Femme Productions
www.candidaroyalle.com

Going Under
directed by Eric Werthman
(Argot Pictures, 2006)

Secretary
directed by Steven Shainberg
(Slough Pond, 2002)

toys and games

Adam and Eve
www.adamandevetoys.com
A vast array of sex toys for everyone from the novice user to the ultimate collector. Color images and user reviews help you find your perfect toy.

Amazon.com
www.amazon.com
A surprisingly good selection of sex toys and costumes from one of the largest online retailers, with discreet packaging.

California Exotics
www.calexotics.com
Vibrators, dildos, masturbating sleeves, cock rings, and just about any other sex toy you could possibly desire, all designed to fulfill your deepest fantasies.

Drugstore.com
www.drugstore.com
Toys and tools to improve your time in the bedroom, including a great selection of lubricants and contraceptive options.

Make Your Own Dildo
www.makeyourowndildo.com
A step-by-step guide to creating an exact rubber replica of your partner's privates.

bedroom songs

Glory Box
by Portishead
(Go! Discs, 1994)

Ignition
by R. Kelly
(Jive, 2003)

I Couldn't Love You More
by Sade
(Sony, 2000)

Kiss All Over Your Body
by Angie Stone
(Universal Music, 2010)

Love All Over Me
by Monica
(J Records, 2010)

Never as Good as the First Time
by Sade
(Sony, 2000)

One In A Million
by Aaliyah
(Atlantic Records, 1996)

Pretty Wings
by Maxwell
(Columbia Records, 2009)

Twenty Fourplay
by Janet Jackson
(A&M Records, 1996)

Your Body's Calling
by R. Kelly
(Zomba Recording, 1993)

index

DK

London, New York, Melbourne, Munich, and Delhi

Author's dedication: For all those individuals and couples who love sex and have shared their stories with me, as well as all those who want to love it more. This one is for you!

Project Editor Daniel Mills
US Editor Shannon Beatty
Senior Art Editor Nicola Rodway
Jacket Design Lisa Lanzarini
Managing Editor Penny Warren
Managing Art Editors Glenda Fisher and Marianne Markham
Production Editor Tony Phipps
Production Controller Seyhan Esen
Creative Technical Support Sonia Charbonnier
Art Directors Lisa Lanzarini and Peter Luff
Publisher Peggy Vance

Produced for DK by:
Editor Nichole Morford
Designer Jo Grey
Photographer Jilly Wells (jillywells.com)
Art Director for Photography Kat Mead
Illlustrator Adam Brackenbury

First American Edition, 2011
Published in the United States by
DK Publishing, 375 Hudson Street, New York, NY 10014

11 12 13 14 15   10 9 8 7 6 5 4 3 2 1
001–179002–Aug/2011

Published in Great Britain by Dorling Kindersley Limited.
A catalog record for this book is available from the Library of Congress.

ISBN 978-0-7566-7147-1

DK books are available at special discounts when purchased in bulk for sales promotions, premiums, fund-raising, or educational use. For details, contact: DK Publishing Special Markets, 375 Hudson Street, New York, New York 10014 or SpecialSales@dk.com.

Printed and bound in Singapore by Tien Wah Press

Discover more at **www.dk.com**

DK encourages safe and responsible sex
- Use condoms to reduce the risk of contracting or transmitting sexually transmitted diseases (STIs).
- Ensure that you and your new partner have been tested for STIs before engaging in any unprotected sexual activity.
- Speak to your doctor if you have any concerns about your sexual health.

author's acknowledgments

Thank you to Dorling Kindersley, especially Peggy Vance, who always so gently tells me what she really thinks; Nichole Morford, who is a fabulous editor (and often my memory); and Daniel Mills, who's always there behind the scene with details, creative input, and the sweetest way of breaking any bad news. A big appreciation goes to my amazing agents, Binky Urban and Nick Kahn at ICM Talent. I can always count on you to have my back, give me your honest opinions, and act as my strong arm when I need it! Thank you also to my managers at ROAR, especially Greg Suess, for believing in me and always staying the course with your creative juices flowing. And special, special thanks to Bridget Sharkey, who's so quiet on the outside and so full of ideas on the inside. Were it not for you nothing would make it to paper! A big thank you also goes to Empower Public Relations, as well as Sonia Koo at OWN and Bridget Maney at Harpo, for working so hard and well at getting the word out there. I would be preaching into a vacuum were it not for you!

I feel such gratitude to Oprah Winfrey, Harpo, and OWN for giving me the amazing platform to do what I love most. You have provided me with a home and a space for connecting with people and ideas that I likely never would have accessed otherwise. From working with you, I've gained new confidence in myself, and a willingness to always trust my gut. I am so thankful for the wisdom, support, lightness, and tirelessness of the devoted executives, producers, and crews I've had the pleasure of working with, including Larissa Matsson, Jon Sinclair, and Claire Vandepolder at Harpo; Lisa Erspamer, Jill Dickerson, and Renata Lombardo at OWN; and Corny Koehl, Alicia Haywood, Katie Baker, and Courtney Cebula at Oprah Radio.

This book would not have been possible if not for all of my teachers. And by teachers, I don't just mean the professors who taught me about the physiology and mechanics of sexuality, and the clinical aspects of the mind/body connection and of healthy relationships. I have learned so much from the thousands of men and women who have reached out to me over the years, sharing their tips, their stories, and their struggles. Many of the ideas in this book come from you!

My parents, Irwin and Linda Berman, are the ones who taught me from the beginning about the gift of sexuality, and that it is a natural and normal part of a loving relationship. My husband, Sam Chapman, has taught me how to let go of fear, and has shown me how deep love can go and how much joy comes with complete trust and with making your relationship the priority. My children, Ethan, Sammy, and Jackson, have inspired me to experience what selfless love feels like, and have shown me the aliveness that can be gleaned from living in the moment and letting go of inhibitions.

dk acknowledgments

DK would like to thank: Isabel de Cordova and Charlotte Johnson for illustration research; Romaine Werblow, picture librarian; David Fentiman and Kate Meeker for editorial assistance; Kat Mead for producing and styling photography; Peter Mallory for assisting photography; Steve Crozier for retouching images; Margaret Parrish for proofreading; and Marie Lorimer for indexing.

The publisher would like to thank the following for their kind permission to reproduce their photographs:
(Key: a-above; b-below/bottom; c-center; f-far; l-left; r-right; t-top)
21 Getty Images: Blend Images / Gabriela Medina (bl). **56-57 Corbis:** Beau Lark. **70 Corbis:** Kevin Dodge. **211 Alamy Images:** Holger Scheibe / Corbis Cusp. **230 Corbis:** Nicky Niederstrasser. **233 Corbis:** Image Source. **248 Getty Images:** Tetra Images. **253 Corbis:** Paul Burns. **267 Mother & Baby Picture Library:** James Thomson. **269 Mother & Baby Picture Library:** Ian Hooton. **273 Getty Images:** Ghislain & Marie David de Lossy / The Image Bank.
All other images © Dorling Kindersley
For further information see: www.dkimages.com